Ultimate AWS Data Engineering

Design, Implement, and Optimize Scalable Data Solutions on AWS with Practical Workflows and Visual Aids for Unmatched Impact

Rathish Mohan
Shekhar Agrawal
Srinivasa Sunil Chippada

www.orangeava.com

First Published: January 2025

Published By: Orange Education Pvt Ltd, AVA®

Address: 9, Daryaganj, Delhi, 110002, India

275 New North Road Islington Suite 1314 London,
N1 7AA, United Kingdom

ISBN (PBK): 978-93-48107-94-7
ISBN (E-BOOK): 978-93-48107-29-9

Scan the QR code to explore our entire catalogue

www.orangeava.com

Dedicated To

My Beloved Parents:

Shri Shashi Prasad

Late Smt. Madhurima Prasad

and

My Wife Avantika Bhandari

- Rathish Mohan

My Beloved Parents:

Shri Shyam Sundar Agrawal

Smt. Pushpa Agrawal

and

My Wife Sujata Agarwal, and Daughters Eva and Elvi

- Shekhar Agrawal

My Beloved Parents:

Sri Venkata Ramana Chippada

Smt. Amaravathi Chippada

and

My Wife Sravanthi, My Kids Ria and Reyansh, and My Brother Srinivas

- Srinivasa Sunil Chippada

About the Authors

Rathish Mohan is a distinguished applied scientist and AI/ML leader with over a decade of experience in machine learning, natural language processing (NLP), and computer vision. Currently, he is a Senior Applied ML Scientist at Lore | Contagious Health, where he leads cross-disciplinary teams to develop advanced AI systems. Rathish specializes in real-time conversational AI and personalization, leveraging cutting-edge technologies like prefix tuning, LLMs, and RAG pipelines to improve user health and well-being. In previous senior roles at Twitch, OfferUp, and Bold, he led initiatives in personalization, content moderation, and recommendation systems. Rathish holds a master's degree in Electrical Engineering from the University of Cincinnati, where his thesis focused on optimizing sensor placement for fault detection using advanced machine learning techniques. Passionate about real-world AI applications, he advances solutions in health, e-commerce, and user personalization.

Shekhar Agrawal is a seasoned AI and data engineering expert with over 14 years of experience in leading large-scale AI, ML, and NLP initiatives across globally recognized organizations. Currently a Senior Director of Data Science at Oracle Corporation, Shekhar spearheads the development of cutting-edge Generative AI platforms and enterprise-scale machine learning systems that serve thousands of customers worldwide. Known for building scalable AI governance frameworks and integrating technologies such as Kubernetes and Spark, Shekhar has held impactful roles at IQVIA, Comcast, and AOL. With advanced degrees in Electrical and Computer Science from the University of Cincinnati and a BE from BIT, he combines technical expertise with strategic vision to drive AI innovation.

Srinivasa Sunil Chippada is a Data Science Engineering expert with 18 years of experience. He offers valuable technical insights to help organizations maximize data value through Feature Stores, Data Marts, Data Pipelines, and Data Integration techniques. His expertise empowers organizations to build efficient and scalable data systems that leverage the full potential of data to drive innovation and business growth. Srinivasa is passionate about building scalable data capabilities and helping organizations to maximize the value of their data. He holds a double master's degree (MIS and MBA), is a certified Project Management Professional, and has earned several technical certifications.

About the Technical Reviewer

Shivam Shukla is an experienced technology leader with nearly 10 years of expertise in designing and delivering advanced Data, Machine Learning, and Generative AI solutions. As a Lead Software Engineer (Senior Manager) at Prudential plc, he leads the development of comprehensive data products tailored for insurance, finance, and marketing industries.

Shivam holds an MBA in Data Science and a B.Tech in Information Technology. His skillset encompasses cloud computing (Azure, GCP), data engineering (Databricks), and DevOps practices. Key accomplishments include creating and deploying GitOps frameworks for seamless data pipeline onboarding, forecasting, and bug detection.

Passionate about innovation and leadership, Shivam drives impactful data-driven transformations that deliver measurable business value.

Acknowledgements

Writing this book has been a deeply rewarding journey. I am sincerely grateful to everyone who supported me along the way, especially my co-authors, whose collaboration, dedication, and expertise were instrumental in shaping this work.

I also want to thank my family and friends for their unwavering encouragement, patience, and understanding during the long hours of research and writing. Without their constant support, completing this book would not have been possible.

Lastly, a special note of appreciation goes to the broader AWS and data engineering community, whose innovations and shared knowledge inspired much of the content in this book.

- Rathish Mohan

Writing this book has been both challenging and fulfilling, and I am deeply grateful to my co-authors. Their enthusiasm, technical expertise, and commitment to excellence have been truly inspiring, elevating this work to new heights.

I am immensely thankful to my mentors and colleagues who provided valuable insights and guidance during the development of this book. Their encouragement and feedback were pivotal in refining the concepts and structure of the content.

I also wish to acknowledge the incredible support system provided by my family and friends, who stood by me throughout this endeavor.

- Shekhar Agrawal

This book reflects months of effort, made possible by the support of remarkable individuals. I am deeply grateful to my co-authors for their collaboration, shared vision, and tireless contributions, which have enriched every chapter.

I extend my heartfelt thanks to the thought leaders, colleagues, and mentors who have shaped my understanding of data engineering and AWS technologies over the years. Their shared wisdom and encouragement have been instrumental in making this book a reality.

Finally, I am deeply grateful to my loved ones for their patience, understanding, and unwavering support, which gave me the strength and energy to complete this project.

- Srinivasa Sunil Chippada

Preface

Data engineering is the backbone of modern digital transformation, enabling organizations to collect, process, and analyze vast volumes of data to derive actionable insights. "*Ultimate* AWS *Data Engineering*" is a comprehensive guide designed for professionals and enthusiasts aiming to master the art and science of data engineering using AWS services. This book takes you on a journey through the core concepts, tools, and best practices required to design and implement efficient, scalable, and secure data engineering solutions on AWS. Whether you are a novice entering the field or an experienced professional looking to refine your skills, this book offers valuable knowledge and practical insights.

Chapter 1. Unveiling the Secrets of Data Engineering: This chapter introduces the fundamental concepts of data engineering, tracing its evolution and its critical role in the digital era. It explores why AWS is the preferred platform, highlighting its scalability, flexibility, cost-efficiency, and innovation. Readers gain a holistic view of the data landscape, preparing them for the chapters ahead.

Chapter 2. Architecting for Scalability: Data Replication Techniques: This chapter delves into data replication techniques crucial for high availability and fault tolerance. It discusses synchronous and asynchronous replication, strong and weak consistency models, and practical implementation strategies on AWS using services such as Amazon RDS.

Chapter 3. Partitioning and Sharding: Optimizing Data Management: This chapter introduces readers to the distinctions and benefits of partitioning and sharding in distributed databases. Practical insights into AWS services such as DynamoDB for partitioning and sharding strategies help ensure efficient data management and scalability.

Chapter 4. Ensuring Consistency: Consensus Mechanisms and Models: This chapter tackles consistency models and consensus algorithms such as Paxos and Raft. Readers will explore AWS services, such as Aurora, to balance consistency and availability while navigating challenges such as latency and trade-offs.

Chapter 5. Balancing the Load: Achieving Performance and Efficiency: This chapter uncovers load balancing strategies and scalability approaches. The chapter covers AWS Elastic Load Balancing (ELB), Auto Scaling Groups, and tips for optimizing resource usage and cost-efficiency.

Chapter 6. Building Fault-Tolerant Architectures: This chapter emphasizes designing resilient systems, covering fault detection, redundancy, failover, and self-healing systems. It also highlights AWS tools such as Elastic Beanstalk for creating reliable, distributed architectures.

Chapter 7. Exploring the Realm of AWS Data Storage Services: This chapter provides an overview of AWS storage options, including Amazon S3, DynamoDB, Redshift, and RDS. This chapter showcases how each service excels in storing and managing different types of data.

Chapter 8. Orchestrating Data Flow: This chapter explains how to design and manage data pipelines, covering tools such as AWS Glue, Kinesis, and Lambda. It provides practical examples of integrating diverse data sources into cohesive, real-time analytics pipelines.

Chapter 9. Advanced Data Pipelines and Transformation: This chapter explores the advanced concepts in pipeline orchestration, monitoring, and transformation. It includes techniques for anomaly detection, feature engineering, and managing large-scale data transformations on AWS.

Chapter 10. Data Warehousing Demystified: This chapter explains the concepts of data warehouses and lakes, focusing on Redshift for building efficient, scalable data warehouses. It also covers advanced analytics and cost optimization techniques.

Chapter 11. Visualizing the Unseen: This chapter focuses on the power of data visualization, exploring tools such as Tableau and Power BI. The chapter highlights effective visualization techniques and connecting BI tools to AWS data sources for interactive dashboards.

Chapter 12. AWS Machine Learning: Classic AI to Generative AI: This chapter explores machine learning and generative AI capabilities on AWS. From SageMaker to Bedrock, readers learn to build, train, and deploy models efficiently while managing costs and security.

Chapter 13. Advanced Data Engineering with AWS: This chapter examines cutting-edge data engineering concepts, including serverless architectures, real-time analytics, and data governance. It wraps up with insights into building secure, scalable, and future-ready data systems.

Get a Free eBook

We hope you are enjoying your recently purchased book! Your feedback is incredibly valuable to us, and to all other readers looking for great books.

If you found this book helpful or enjoyable, we would truly appreciate it, if you could take a moment to leave a short review with a 5 star rating on Amazon. It helps us grow, and lets other readers discover our books.

As a thank you, we would love to send you a free digital copy of this book, and a **30%** discount code on your next cart value on our official websites:

www.orangeava.com

www.orangeava.in (For Indian Subcontinent)

☑ **Here's how:**

Leave a review for the book on Amazon.

Take a screenshot of your review, and send an email to **info@orangeava.com** (it can be just the confirmation screen).

Once, we receive your screenshot, we will send you the digital file, within 24 hours.

Thank you so much for your support – it means a lot to us!

Downloading the code bundles and colored images

Please follow the links or scan the QR codes to download the **Code Bundles and Images** of the book:

https://github.com/ava-orange-education/Ultimate-AWS-Data-Engineering

The code bundles and images of the book are also hosted on ***https://rebrand.ly/40ed26***

In case there's an update to the code, it will be updated on the existing GitHub repository.

Errata

We take immense pride in our work at **Orange Education Pvt Ltd,** and follow best practices to ensure the accuracy of our content to provide an indulging reading experience to our subscribers. Our readers are our mirrors, and we use their inputs to reflect and improve upon human errors, if any, that may have occurred during the publishing processes involved. To let us maintain the quality and help us reach out to any readers who might be having difficulties due to any unforeseen errors, please write to us at :

errata@orangeava.com

Your support, suggestions, and feedback are highly appreciated.

DID YOU KNOW

Did you know that Orange Education Pvt Ltd offers eBook versions of every book published, with PDF and ePub files available? You can upgrade to the eBook version at **www.orangeava.com** and as a print book customer, you are entitled to a discount on the eBook copy. Get in touch with us at: **info@orangeava.com** for more details.

At **www.orangeava.com**, you can also read a collection of free technical articles, sign up for a range of free newsletters, and receive exclusive discounts and offers on AVA® Books and eBooks.

PIRACY

If you come across any illegal copies of our works in any form on the internet, we would be grateful if you would provide us with the location address or website name. Please contact us at **info@orangeava.com** with a link to the material.

ARE YOU INTERESTED IN AUTHORING WITH US?

If there is a topic that you have expertise in, and you are interested in either writing or contributing to a book, please write to us at **business@orangeava.com**. We are on a journey to help developers and tech professionals to gain insights on the present technological advancements and innovations happening across the globe and build a community that believes Knowledge is best acquired by sharing and learning with others. Please reach out to us to learn what our audience demands and how you can be part of this educational reform. We also welcome ideas from tech experts and help them build learning and development content for their domains.

REVIEWS

Please leave a review. Once you have read and used this book, why not leave a review on the site that you purchased it from? Potential readers can then see and use your unbiased opinion to make purchase decisions. We at Orange Education would love to know what you think about our products, and our authors can learn from your feedback. Thank you!

For more information about Orange Education, please visit **www.orangeava.com**.

Table of Contents

CHAPTER 1
Unveiling the Secrets of Data Engineering

Introduction

In the information age, data has become the lifeblood of modern society. Like an unrefined diamond, raw data holds immense value, but only when it is unlocked and harnessed can its true potential be realized. Enter the world of Data Engineering, where skilled professionals act as architects of information, constructing pipelines that guide data through its lifecycle. From ingestion and storage to processing and analysis, they orchestrate the transformation of raw bytes into valuable knowledge. This chapter serves as your launchpad, guiding you through the captivating world of Data Engineering. Together, we will unveil the secrets of data pipelines, explore the diverse ecosystem of AWS services, and equip you with the foundational knowledge necessary for your data journey. Prepare to unlock the power of data, one byte at a time, as we embark on this exciting adventure!

Let the data speak for itself, and together, we will discover the secrets that lie within and the pervasive role data plays in our current world. This chapter emphasizes the need to harness the power of data effectively and introduces the concept of data engineering as the key to unlocking its potential.

Structure

In this chapter, we will cover the following topics:

- Defining Data Engineering
- The Data Landscape: Past, Present, and Future
  - A Journey through Time: Tracing the Evolution of Data
  - A Glimpse into the Future: Anticipating the Next Frontier
- Demystifying the Role of AWS in Data Engineering
  - A Comprehensive Ecosystem for Data-Driven Success

- Scalability and Flexibility
- Reliability and Security
- Cost-Effectiveness: Unleashing Efficiency and Value
- Breadth of Services
- Continuous Innovation
- Global Community and Support

Defining Data Engineering

Data engineering is the practice of building, maintaining, and automating the infrastructure and processes used to collect, store, process, analyze, and interpret data.

It involves designing and implementing data pipelines, which are the workflows that move data through various stages of the data lifecycle.

Data engineers are responsible for a variety of tasks, including:

- **Data Ingestion:** Acquiring data from various sources, such as databases, APIs, and sensors.
- **Data Storage:** Choosing and managing storage solutions for different data types and needs.
- **Data Processing:** Cleaning, transforming, and enriching data to prepare it for analysis.
- **Data Analysis:** Using tools and techniques to extract insights and patterns from data.
- **Data Reporting:** Creating and maintaining reports, dashboards, and visualizations for stakeholders.
- **Data Pipelines**: Designing, building, and automating workflows to move data through various stages.
- **Data Governance:** Establishing policies and procedures to ensure data quality, security, and compliance.

By effectively managing the data lifecycle, data engineers play a critical role in enabling data-driven decision-making. They provide valuable insights that can inform strategic business decisions, optimize operations, and drive innovation across various industries.

Examples:

- A data engineer working for a retail company might build a pipeline to ingest customer purchase data, transform it for analysis, and then create reports that help the company understand customer behavior and improve marketing campaigns.

- A data engineer working for a healthcare organization might build a pipeline to collect and analyze patient data to identify trends in disease outbreaks and develop more effective treatments.

The Data Landscape: Past, Present, and Future

Let us look at the history of data and how it has evolved over time.

A Journey through Time: Tracing the Evolution of Data

The history of data engineering is a fascinating tale of human ingenuity and technological advancement. It is a journey that began with rudimentary data collection methods, evolved through the era of mainframes and specialized databases, and finally culminated in the present day, where data is ubiquitous and cloud-based solutions reign supreme.

Early Beginnings:

- **Pre-Computers:** Data was primarily collected and stored in physical forms such as handwritten records, punch cards, and magnetic tapes.
- **Mainframe Era**: The advent of mainframes in the 1950s marked a significant shift. They provided centralized data storage and processing capabilities, enabling early forms of data analysis.
- **Rise of Relational Databases**: In the 1970s, relational databases emerged, offering structured data organization and efficient querying capabilities. This revolutionized data management, paving the way for more complex analyses.

The Dawn of Modern Data Engineering:

- **Personal Computing**: The rise of personal computers in the 1980s triggered a further democratization of data access and analysis. Spreadsheets and desktop databases became accessible tools for individuals and small businesses.
- **Big Data Explosion:** The turn of the 21st century ushered in the era of big data. The exponential growth in data volume and variety necessitated new approaches to data management and analysis.
- **Cloud Computing**: Cloud-based solutions emerged as a game-changer, offering scalable and cost-effective platforms for data storage, processing, and analysis.

The Present Landscape:

- **Data-driven Decision-Making**: Today, data is at the heart of decision-making across industries. Organizations rely on data insights to optimize operations, understand customer behavior, and drive innovation.
- **Advanced Data Analytics:** Powerful data analytics tools and techniques, such as machine learning and artificial intelligence, are enabling deeper and more complex data analysis, unlocking new frontiers in discovery and prediction.
- **Democratization of Data**: Cloud-based solutions and open-source tools are making data and data analysis more accessible than ever before, empowering individuals and organizations to leverage the power of data.

A Glimpse into the Future: Anticipating the Next Frontier

The future of data engineering shimmers with excitement. Technology's relentless march unlocks uncharted territories with each innovation, presenting both thrilling possibilities and invigorating challenges.

- **Real-Time Data Processing**: Imagine a world where data analysis happens at the speed of thought. Streaming technologies and distributed computing will make this a reality, delivering instant insights and fueling lightning-fast decision-making.
- **Greater Automation**: Get ready for a revolution in efficiency! Automation will streamline data pipelines, reducing manual intervention to a mere memory. This frees up data engineers to focus on the truly strategic tasks, allowing them to unlock the full potential of their expertise.
- **Continuous Learning**: Data pipelines will become self-aware. Machine learning models will continuously learn and adapt, optimizing themselves over time to become smarter and more efficient. This constant evolution will push the boundaries of data engineering and propel us into a new era of data-driven innovation.
- **Data Security and Privacy**: As data becomes the lifeblood of our world, safeguarding it becomes paramount. Robust security and privacy solutions will be crucial, ensuring the ethical use of data and protecting sensitive information from harm. This is a challenge we must embrace, for it holds the key to building a responsible and trustworthy future where data empowers everyone.

The future of data engineering is a horizon brimming with promise and possibility. It is a future where data flows freely, analyzed with lightning speed, and used ethically to improve our lives in countless ways. Are you ready to embark on this exciting journey?

As data engineers, we are at the forefront of this revolution, equipped with the knowledge and skills to unlock the potential of data and shape the world around us.

Demystifying the Role of AWS in Data Engineering

In today's data-driven world, choosing the right platform for your data engineering needs is crucial. With its unparalleled scalability, comprehensive suite of services, and robust security features, AWS stands out as the ideal platform for building and managing modern data pipelines.

Let us delve into the compelling reasons why AWS should be your go-to platform for data engineering:

A Comprehensive Ecosystem for Data-Driven Success

In the vast landscape of data engineering, Amazon Web Services (AWS) has emerged as a leader, offering a comprehensive ecosystem of tools and services specifically designed to address every stage of the data lifecycle.

Data Acquisition and Integration:

- **Amazon Kinesis**: Real-time data ingestion service for streaming data from various sources.
- **Amazon S3**: Object storage service for storing massive amounts of unstructured data.
- **Amazon DynamoDB**: NoSQL database for storing and managing high-velocity data.
- **AWS Glue**: Crawls and extracts data from various sources, creating a unified data catalog.
- **AWS Data Pipeline**: Orchestrates complex data workflows with data movement and transformations.

Data Processing and Transformation:

- **Amazon EMR**: Cloud-based Hadoop platform for running large-scale data processing jobs.
- **Amazon Athena**: Serverless interactive query service for analyzing data stored in S3.
- **Amazon Lambda**: Serverless compute service for running code without managing servers.

- **Amazon SageMaker**: Machine learning platform for building, training, and deploying machine learning models.
- **AWS Step Functions**: Workflow management service for coordinating and automating complex data processing tasks.

Data Storage and Management:

- **Amazon S3**: Object storage service for storing structured and unstructured data.
- **Amazon S3 Glacier**: Archive storage service for storing data that is accessed less frequently.
- **Amazon DynamoDB**: NoSQL database for storing and managing fast-changing data.
- **Amazon Redshift**: Data warehouse for storing and analyzing large datasets.
- **Amazon EBS**: Block storage service for attaching storage to EC2 instances.

Data Analysis and Visualization:

- **Amazon QuickSight**: Cloud-based BI service for building dashboards and visualizing data.
- **Amazon Athena**: Serverless interactive query service for analyzing data stored in S3.
- **Amazon Redshift Spectrum**: Analyzes data stored in S3 directly from Redshift.
- **Amazon Managed Grafana**: Managed service for creating and sharing dashboards and visualizations.
- **Amazon SageMaker Studio**: Integrated development environment for building, training, and deploying machine learning models.

Data Governance and Security:

- **AWS IAM:** Identity and access management service for controlling access to AWS resources.
- **AWS CloudTrail**: Auditing service for tracking API calls and user activity.
- **AWS KMS**: Key management service for encrypting data at rest and in transit.
- **AWS Lake Formation**: Provides data governance and security for data lakes.
- **AWS CloudHSM**: Hardware security module for protecting sensitive data.

But why choose AWS for your data engineering endeavors? Let us delve into the compelling reasons that make it the ideal platform for data-driven success.

Scalability and Flexibility

AWS provides unparalleled scalability, allowing you to easily adapt your data infrastructure to meet your ever-changing needs. Whether you are dealing with small datasets or petabytes of data, AWS has the resources to handle any workload.

This flexibility empowers you to start small and scale up seamlessly as your data needs grow. You can scale individual services independently, ensuring cost-efficiency and optimal resource utilization.

Here are some ways AWS ensures scalability and flexibility:

- **Horizontal Scaling**: You can add more instances or resources to an existing service to increase its capacity. This is particularly useful for services such as Amazon EMR, Amazon Redshift, and Amazon ElastiCache.
- **Vertical Scaling**: You can increase the resources (CPU, memory, and so on) of an existing instance to improve its performance. This can be done with services like Amazon EC2 and Amazon RDS.
- **Serverless Computing**: Services such as AWS Lambda and Amazon Fargate eliminate the need to manage servers, allowing you to scale your applications automatically based on demand.
- **Auto-Scaling**: You can configure services to automatically scale up or down based on predefined metrics, such as CPU utilization or network traffic.
- **Open-Source Tools**: AWS supports a wide range of open-source tools and technologies, such as Apache Hadoop, Spark, and Cassandra. This gives you the flexibility to use the tools that are best suited for your needs.

Reliability and Security

AWS is an ideal platform for mission-critical data engineering workloads because of its dedication to reliability and security. Here is a deeper dive into these aspects:

Reliability

- **Global Infrastructure**: AWS operates a vast network of data centers around the world, ensuring redundancy and failover capabilities. This geographically distributed infrastructure minimizes downtime and ensures data availability even in the event of regional outages.
- **Service Level Agreements (SLAs):** AWS offers SLAs for many of its services, guaranteeing uptime and availability. This provides peace of mind and ensures consistent performance for your data engineering workloads.
- **High Availability (HA) Features:** Most AWS services offer HA features built-in, such as multi-AZ deployments and auto-scaling, which automatically adjusts resources to maintain performance during peak loads or unexpected events.
- **Resilient Architecture**: AWS infrastructure is designed with resilience in mind, including redundant power supplies, cooling systems, and network

connections. This minimizes the impact of hardware failures and ensures continued data access.

Security:

- **Comprehensive Security Features**: AWS offers a wide range of security features, including encryption at rest and in transit, access control mechanisms, identity and access management (IAM), intrusion detection and prevention systems (IDS/IPS), and data loss prevention (DLP).
- **Compliance Certifications**: AWS is compliant with various industry-specific and global security standards, including HIPAA, PCI DSS, and SOC 2. This guarantees data protection and regulatory compliance for sensitive data.
- **Security Best Practices**: AWS provides extensive documentation and resources on security best practices, helping data engineers build secure and compliant data pipelines.
- **Dedicated Security Team**: AWS employs a dedicated team of security experts who are constantly monitoring the infrastructure and identifying and mitigating potential threats.

Benefits of AWS reliability and security for data engineering:

- **Reduced Risk of Downtime**: Data is available and accessible, minimizing disruptions to your data pipelines and ensuring business continuity.
- **Enhanced Data Protection**: Security measures safeguard sensitive data from unauthorized access, loss, or misuse.
- **Improved Compliance**: Meeting regulatory requirements becomes easier with AWS's compliance certifications and security best practices.
- **Peace of mind:** Data engineers can focus on building and maintaining their data pipelines without worrying about infrastructure reliability and security.

Examples of how AWS reliability and security are used in data engineering:

- A financial institution stores sensitive customer data in Amazon S3 and utilizes encryption and access controls to ensure data security.
- A healthcare organization leverages AWS Kinesis to process real-time healthcare data and relies on AWS's HIPAA compliance for data privacy.
- A government agency utilizes AWS Redshift for data analysis and relies on AWS's high availability and security features to ensure data integrity and availability for critical decision-making.

Cost-Effectiveness: Unleashing Efficiency and Value

Cost-effectiveness is a crucial factor in choosing a data engineering platform, and AWS excels in this aspect with its pay-as-you-go model and diverse pricing options:

Pay-as-you-go Model:

- **Eliminate Upfront Costs**: No need for large upfront investments in hardware or software.
- **Pay Only for What You Use**: Scale your resources up or down based on your dynamic data needs, avoiding overprovisioning and reducing unnecessary expenses.
- **Optimize Spending**: Gain granular control over your data engineering costs, enabling efficient resource allocation and maximizing ROI.

Pricing Options:

- **Reserved Instances**: Lock in discounted rates for specific resources for a defined period, ideal for predictable workloads.
- **Discounts for Sustained Usage**: Utilize services such as AWS Spot Instances and Savings Plans to unlock significant cost reductions for sustained data processing jobs or storage needs.
- **Free Tier**: Experiment and explore various AWS services with a free tier, allowing you to learn and test before committing to paid plans.

Benefits of AWS cost-effectiveness for data engineering:

- **Improved Resource Utilization:** Optimize resource allocation based on actual usage patterns, reducing idle resources and unnecessary costs.
- **Increased Cost Predictability**: Leverage transparent pricing models and forecasting tools to plan and manage your data engineering budget effectively.
- **Reduced financial risk**: Minimize upfront investments and experiment with new technologies without incurring significant costs.
- **Greater Agility and Scalability**: Adapt your data infrastructure quickly and cost-effectively to meet changing business needs.

Examples of how AWS cost-effectiveness benefits data engineering:

- A startup leverages AWS Lambda serverless functions for event-driven data processing, minimizing costs by only paying for the milliseconds of execution time used.
- A research institution utilizes AWS Spot Instances for computationally intensive data analysis jobs, maximizing resource utilization and achieving cost savings.
- A large enterprise employs AWS S3 storage classes such as Glacier for long-term data archiving, benefitting from significantly lower costs compared to traditional storage solutions.

Breadth of Services

AWS offers an extensive range of services specifically designed for data engineering, from storage solutions such as S3 and EFS to processing engines such as Redshift and EMR.

This comprehensive suite eliminates the need to rely on multiple vendors and provides a seamless experience for managing your entire data pipeline within the AWS ecosystem.

Integration with other services: AWS services are designed to work together seamlessly, allowing you to build complex data pipelines that integrate with other parts of your infrastructure.

Examples of how the AWS breadth of services benefits data engineering:

- A startup uses Amazon Kinesis to ingest real-time sensor data, AWS Lambda for processing, and Amazon QuickSight for visualization, enabling real-time monitoring and decision-making.
- A research institution leverages Amazon EMR for large-scale genomic data analysis, Amazon Redshift for storing the results, and Amazon SageMaker for building machine learning models to accelerate scientific discovery.
- A large enterprise utilizes AWS Glue to extract data from various sources, AWS Data Pipeline to orchestrate data transformation, and Amazon Redshift for analyzing customer data to personalize marketing campaigns and improve customer experience.

Continuous Innovation

AWS is constantly innovating and introducing new data engineering services and features. This allows you to stay ahead of the curve and leverage the latest technologies to improve your data operations. AWS actively invests in research and development, ensuring that its services are always optimized for performance, scalability, and security.

Global Community and Support

AWS boasts a vast community of users and developers, readily available to offer support and share best practices.

AWS offers comprehensive documentation and tutorials, along with dedicated support channels to ensure you have the resources necessary to succeed.

Your Journey Begins Now: Embarking on the Path to Data Mastery

Congratulations on taking a significant step towards becoming a data engineer! You have grasped the fundamentals of the field, its dynamic nature, and the advantages of choosing AWS as your platform. Now, it is time to transform yourself into a data engineering master.

- **Continuous Learning**: Embrace a learning mindset. Explore new technologies, techniques, and best practices. View challenges as learning opportunities. Remember, knowledge is endless, and great data engineers are lifelong learners.
- **Mastering the Fundamentals**: A strong foundation is crucial. Understand data modeling, relational databases, SQL queries, data warehousing, and data pipeline stages. These core skills will provide the base for your expertise.
- **Experimentation and Practice**: Learn by doing. Experiment with AWS services and tools. Build small projects to apply your knowledge. Practice regularly and seek opportunities to implement your skills. The more you practice, the more confident you become.
- **Leveraging the Community**: The data engineering community is vibrant. Join online forums, attend events, and connect with fellow engineers. Share experiences, ask questions, and learn from others. This community is a valuable resource for knowledge and inspiration, and connecting with them can accelerate your learning and career growth.
- **Mentorship and Guidance**: Find a mentor or advisor. Their personalized guidance, answers, and insights can help you navigate challenges, avoid pitfalls, and accelerate your progress towards your goals.
- **Continuous Exploration**: Don't limit yourself to popular tools and techniques. Explore niche areas, delve into emerging technologies, and stay on the forefront of the field. The more you explore, the more opportunities you discover to apply your skills uniquely and impactfully.

Start your journey today and unlock endless possibilities!

Conclusion

By choosing AWS for your data engineering endeavors, you gain access to a comprehensive platform that delivers unmatched scalability, reliability, cost-effectiveness, and breadth of services. With its commitment to innovation, global community, and reliable support, AWS empowers data engineers to focus on what matters most–extracting valuable insights from data and driving positive outcomes.

Start your data engineering journey with confidence and explore the boundless potential of data with AWS as your trusted partner.

In our forthcoming chapter, we will delve into the intricacies of data storage, guiding you through essential considerations when navigating the diverse range of AWS offerings within this domain. Consider this chapter your roadmap to unlocking the full potential of AWS data storage solutions.

CHAPTER 2

Architecting for Scalability: Data Replication Techniques

Introduction

In the realm of distributed systems, data replication is a critical force that breathes life into resilience and availability, ensuring that information remains accessible and consistent even in the face of failures. Replication is the silent guardian of data integrity, enabling systems to withstand disruptions and maintain service continuity across vast networks and diverse regions. This chapter embarks on a journey through the intricate world of data replication, where redundancy, synchronization, and availability converge to safeguard data against the unpredictable challenges of distributed environments.

As we delve into the principles and practices of replication, we will uncover the varied strategies, from synchronous to asynchronous approaches, that offer unique balances of consistency, performance, and reliability. AWS provides a robust ecosystem to facilitate these replication strategies, enabling organizations to deploy resilient architectures at scale. This chapter will serve as your guide to mastering replication techniques that enhance system stability, minimize downtime, and ensure that data is always within reach. Join us as we explore the fundamental pillar of fault tolerance in distributed systems–replication–and learn how to build systems that remain steadfast, even in the most dynamic and demanding landscapes.

Structure

In this chapter, we will cover the following topics:

- Introduction to Data Replication
- Types of Data Replications

  - Replication Strategies in AWS
  - Consistency and Availability Trade-offs in Replication
  - Monitoring and Managing Data Replication
- Synchronous versus Asynchronous Replication
  - Synchronous Replication: Strong Consistency at a Cost
  - Asynchronous Replication: Enhancing Availability and Performance
  - Use Cases and Trade-offs
  - Hybrid Replication Models
  - Monitoring Replication Performance in AWS
- Implementing Replication in Distributed Systems on AWS
  - Key AWS Services for Replication
  - Configuring Multi-AZ replication with Amazon RDS
  - Setting up DynamoDB Global tables for Cross Region Replication
  - Using S3 Cross-Region Replication (CRR) for Backup and Compliance
  - Best Practices for Managing Replication on AWS
  - Case Study: Implementing a Multi-Region Replication Strategy for a Global SaaS Platform
- Replication Best Practices and Use Cases
  - Best Practices for Data Replication
  - Use Cases for Replication in Distributed Systems
  - Monitoring and Optimizing Replication in AWS

Introduction to Data Replication

Data replication is a fundamental technique in distributed systems, ensuring data availability and reliability by creating copies of data across multiple nodes or locations. In distributed environments, replication helps mitigate the risk of data loss from node failures, network outages, or other disruptions. The primary goals of data replication are to:

- **Enhance Fault Tolerance:** If one replica fails, other replicas can continue serving requests, preventing downtime.
- **Increase Availability:** Replicated data can be accessed even during failures, enabling continuous operation.
- **Improve Read Performance:** Replication allows read operations to be distributed across replicas, reducing load on a single node and improving response times.

In cloud environments such as AWS, replication is essential for maintaining high availability and fault tolerance across geographically distributed regions.

Types of Data Replication

Data replication is generally classified into two main types, each with its unique trade-offs in consistency, availability, and performance:

- **Synchronous Replication:** Data is updated on all replicas simultaneously. This approach ensures that all replicas maintain identical data states, providing strong consistency. However, synchronous replication may introduce higher latency, as the system waits for acknowledgments from all replicas before proceeding.

  Example: In a financial application, synchronous replication is used for transaction records to maintain strict consistency and avoid discrepancies.

- **Asynchronous Replication:** Data is updated on the primary node first and then propagated to replicas after a short delay. Asynchronous replication improves system availability and reduces latency, but replicas may experience temporary inconsistencies.

  Example: In a social media application, asynchronous replication is used for posts and comments, where temporary inconsistencies are acceptable, and availability is prioritized.

Replication Strategies in AWS

AWS provides various options for implementing data replication, supporting both synchronous and asynchronous replication depending on the application's requirements:

- **Amazon RDS Multi-AZ Deployments:** Supports synchronous replication across multiple Availability Zones within a region. This setup ensures high availability and fault tolerance for critical databases. In the event of an AZ failure, automatic failover enables continued access to the database.
- **Amazon DynamoDB Global Tables:** Offers cross-region asynchronous replication, enabling data distribution across multiple AWS regions. This approach is ideal for applications requiring low-latency access to data globally, as each region has a local copy of the data.

  Example: In a retail application with global customers, DynamoDB Global Tables replicate inventory and user data across regions, providing quick access to data regardless of user location and maintaining availability during regional outages.

Consistency and Availability Trade-offs in Replication

Consistency and **availability** are two critical factors affected by replication strategies. These trade-offs are illustrated by the **CAP theorem**, which states that a distributed system can guarantee only two of the following three properties:

- **Consistency:** Ensures all replicas reflect the same data at any given time.
- **Availability:** Guarantees that each request receives a response, regardless of node failures.
- **Partition Tolerance:** Ensures the system continues to operate even with network partitions.

The choice between synchronous and asynchronous replication impacts the balance between consistency and availability:

- **Synchronous Replication** provides high consistency but may reduce availability, as nodes must wait for all replicas to update.
- **Asynchronous Replication** prioritizes availability, allowing replicas to serve data even if they are not fully consistent.

  Example: An online banking system may favor synchronous replication to maintain transaction accuracy, while a content delivery network (CDN) uses asynchronous replication to ensure high availability.

Example: Real-World Application of Data Replication in AWS

Scenario: A video streaming service needs high availability to serve users in different regions without latency issues.

- **Asynchronous Replication with DynamoDB Global Tables:** User data, such as watch history and preferences, is replicated across multiple regions. This setup ensures that users have low-latency access to their data, regardless of location.
- **Synchronous Replication for Transactional Data:** Billing and payment information is replicated synchronously in a Multi-AZ RDS deployment, ensuring that each transaction remains consistent across replicas, avoiding data discrepancies.

This approach allows the streaming service to achieve both availability and data consistency for critical transactions, catering to user experience while maintaining data integrity.

Monitoring and Managing Data Replication

Effective replication requires ongoing monitoring to ensure that data remains consistent and available across replicas. AWS provides tools such as:

- **Amazon CloudWatch:** Tracks metrics such as replication latency, request rates, and error counts, allowing administrators to detect issues in replication performance.
- **AWS CloudTrail:** Logs API calls, helping to audit and troubleshoot replication processes, ensuring that data remains accurate and accessible.
- **AWS Database Migration Service (DMS):** Supports ongoing data replication across different AWS databases, useful for migrating or replicating databases with minimal downtime.

Example: In a data warehousing scenario, CloudWatch monitors replication latency between Amazon Redshift clusters, ensuring that analytics queries use up-to-date data.

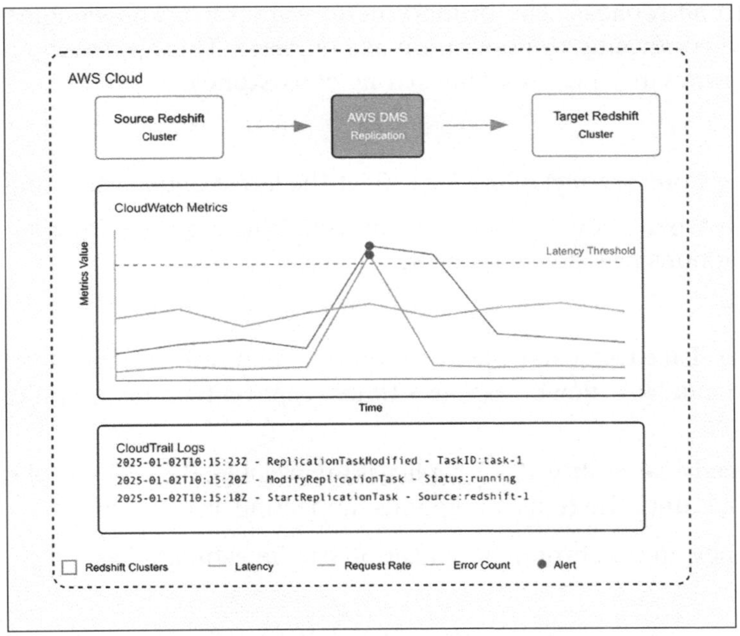

Figure 2.1: *Database Replication Latency - Amazon RDS*

Synchronous versus Asynchronous Replication

In distributed systems, the choice between **synchronous** and **asynchronous** replication is critical for balancing consistency, availability, and performance. Both approaches are designed to create data copies across multiple nodes or locations, but each serves different use cases depending on the requirements for data consistency, response time, and tolerance to network delays.

- **Synchronous Replication:** Ensures that all replicas are updated simultaneously, providing strong consistency across nodes.
- **Asynchronous Replication:** Allows replicas to be updated with a delay, prioritizing availability and performance over immediate consistency.

Each replication type has unique advantages and limitations, which are explored in detail in the following section.

Synchronous Replication: Strong Consistency at a Cost

In synchronous replication, data changes on the primary node are immediately propagated to all replicas. The primary node waits for acknowledgment from each replica before confirming the operation as complete. This approach ensures that all replicas are always in sync, providing **strong consistency**.

Advantages:

- **Strong Consistency:** All nodes reflect the latest data, preventing conflicts.
- **Data Integrity:** Ideal for applications requiring high accuracy, such as financial transactions or medical records.

Disadvantages:

- **Higher Latency:** Each update requires acknowledgments from all replicas, which can slow down response times, especially in geographically dispersed systems.
- **Reduced Availability:** If any replica is unavailable, the entire replication process may halt until the replica responds, impacting availability.

The total latency in synchronous replication can be estimated as:

$$L_s = L_p + \sum_{i=1}^{n} L_{r_i}$$

Here, L_p is the processing time on the primary node and L_{r_i} is the response time for each replica.

Example: In a banking application, synchronous replication is essential for transactions. If a customer withdraws money, this information must be updated across all replicas immediately to avoid potential overdrafts.

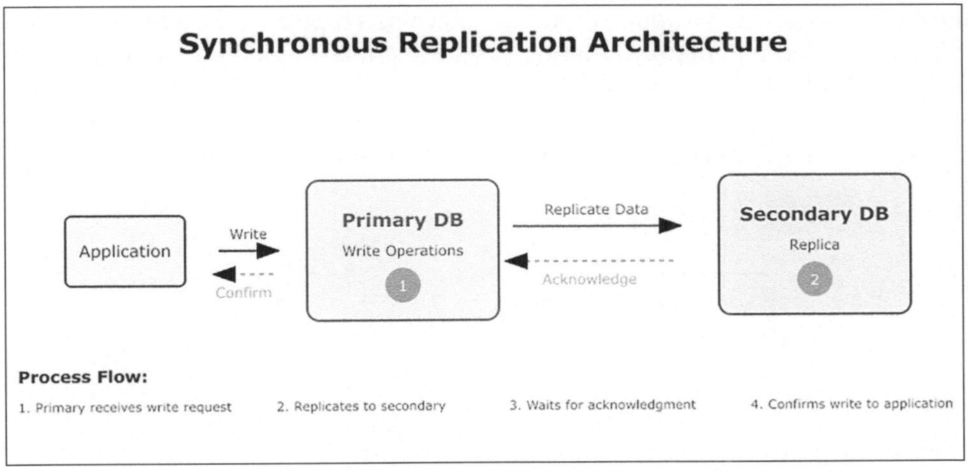

Figure 2.2: *Synchronous Replication Architecture*

Asynchronous Replication: Enhancing Availability and Performance

In asynchronous replication, the primary node updates replicas with a delay. It does not wait for acknowledgments from replicas, allowing operations to complete faster. This approach prioritizes **availability** and **performance** but may result in temporary inconsistencies.

Advantages:

- **Low Latency:** Since the primary node does not wait for all replicas to respond, operations complete faster, reducing response times.
- **High Availability:** The primary node can continue operations even if some replicas are offline, making it resilient to network partitions.

Disadvantages:

- **Eventual Consistency:** Replicas may not always reflect the latest data immediately, leading to potential conflicts.
- **Data Loss Risk:** If the primary node fails before updates are propagated to replicas, some data may be lost.

Asynchronous replication latency L_a is lower, as it only includes the primary node processing time:

$$L_a = L_p$$

Here, L_p is the time taken by the primary node to complete the operation.

Example: In a social media application, asynchronous replication is suitable for actions such as posting comments or updating profiles, where immediate consistency is not essential and performance is prioritized.

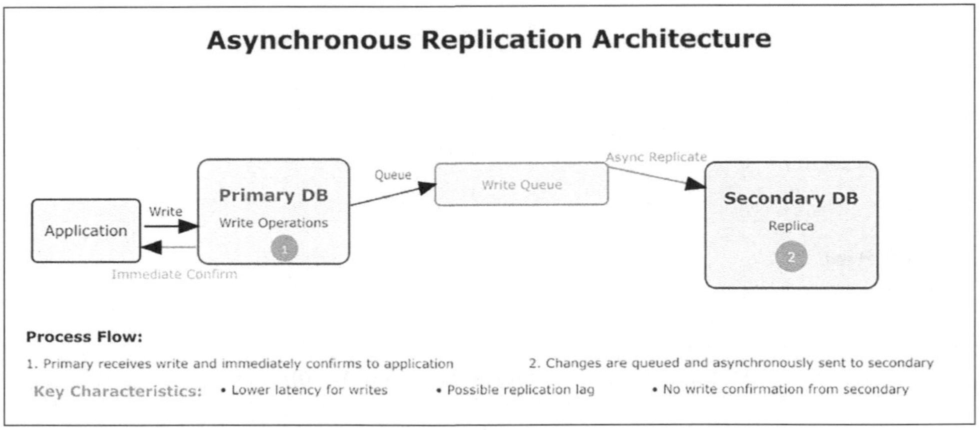

Figure 2.3: *Asynchronous Replication Architecture*

Use Cases and Trade-offs

The choice between synchronous and asynchronous replication depends on application requirements:

- **Synchronous Replication Use Cases:**
  - **Financial Transactions:** Banking systems where data accuracy is critical.
  - **Inventory Management:** Real-time inventory updates across locations to prevent overselling.
  - **Medical Records:** Ensuring patient data is accurate and consistent across systems.
- **Asynchronous Replication Use Cases:**
  - **Content Delivery Networks (CDNs):** Allowing temporary inconsistencies for faster access to content.
  - **E-commerce User Data:** Customer browsing and shopping preferences, where slight delays are tolerable.
  - **IoT Sensor Data:** Aggregating sensor data, where immediate consistency is not necessary, and availability is prioritized.

Hybrid Replication Models

In some distributed systems, hybrid replication models are employed to balance the benefits of both synchronous and asynchronous approaches. For instance:

- **Quasi-Synchronous Replication:** Combines elements of both synchronous and asynchronous replication by ensuring that critical updates are propagated immediately, while less critical data is replicated asynchronously.

  Example: A stock trading platform may replicate buy/sell orders synchronously, while trade history is updated asynchronously to reduce load.

- **Selective Asynchronous Replication:** Allows asynchronous replication for certain data types or during peak times, prioritizing synchronous replication during regular operations.

  Example: In an online marketplace, asynchronous replication can be used for product views and user interactions, while synchronous replication ensures accuracy for purchase transactions.

Example: Synchronous and Asynchronous Replication in AWS

Scenario: A multinational retail company requires data replication for two primary functions: inventory management and customer engagement.

- **Synchronous Replication with Amazon RDS Multi-AZ:** Inventory data is replicated synchronously across Availability Zones. This approach ensures that all regions have accurate stock levels, preventing overselling or stockouts.
- **Asynchronous Replication with DynamoDB Global Tables:** Customer engagement data, such as product views and user preferences, is replicated asynchronously across regions, ensuring high availability without impacting user experience due to slight delays.

This hybrid model allows the company to prioritize accuracy for inventory while optimizing performance and availability for customer data.

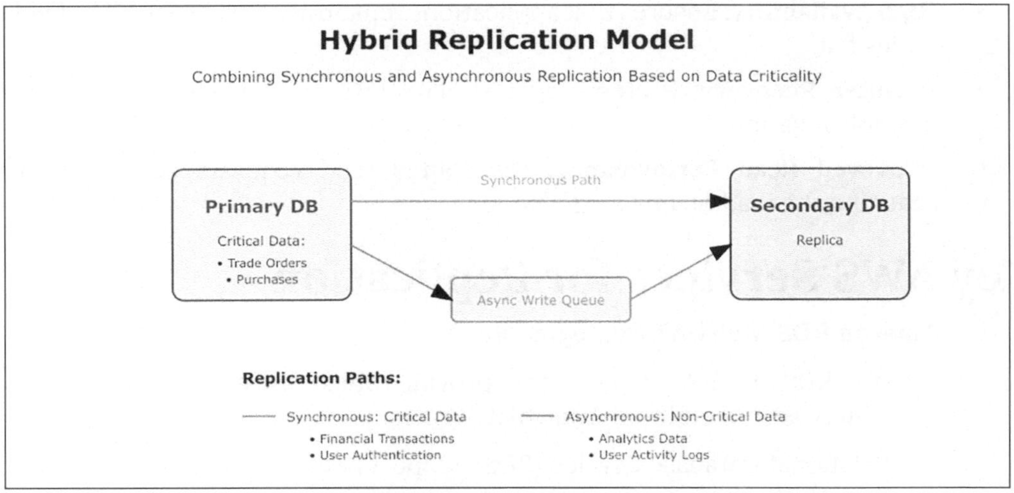

Figure 2.4: *Hybrid Replication Model*

Monitoring Replication Performance in AWS

AWS provides tools to monitor the performance of synchronous and asynchronous replication:

- **Amazon CloudWatch:** Tracks metrics such as replication lag, request latency, and availability, enabling early detection of performance issues.
- **AWS Database Migration Service (DMS):** Enables continuous replication of databases with metrics on data lag, ensuring asynchronous replication is timely.
- **AWS CloudTrail:** Provides audit logs to monitor replication actions, helping verify that replication is functioning correctly.

  Example: In a data analytics system, CloudWatch monitors replication lag for DynamoDB Global Tables, ensuring that asynchronous replication remains within acceptable delays.

Implementing Replication in Distributed Systems on AWS

AWS offers various services and configurations that simplify replication for distributed systems, catering to different application needs. Each service is designed with a specific purpose—some prioritize high availability and fault tolerance within a single region, while others support global replication for geographically dispersed users.

Replication on AWS enables:

- **High Availability:** Ensures that applications remain accessible even if individual nodes fail.
- **Disaster Recovery:** Protects against data loss by duplicating data across multiple locations.
- **Improved Read Performance:** Distributes read requests across replicas, reducing the load on any single node.

Key AWS Services for Replication

- **Amazon RDS Multi-AZ Deployments**

  Amazon RDS Multi-AZ deployments provide robust disaster recovery and high availability across multiple Availability Zones.

  - Relational Database Service (RDS) supports Multi-AZ deployments, where data is synchronously replicated across Availability Zones (AZs) within a region. This setup ensures high availability and automatic failover in case of an AZ outage.

    - Multi-AZ is ideal for transactional applications requiring strong consistency and availability.

  Example: A banking application using Amazon RDS with Multi-AZ ensures that if the primary database instance goes down, a standby instance in another AZ can automatically take over without data loss.

- **Amazon DynamoDB Global Tables**
    - DynamoDB Global Tables provide cross-region replication for low-latency access to data across multiple regions. Asynchronous replication ensures that each region has a local copy of the data, providing eventual consistency.
    - This configuration is optimal for applications needing global availability and low-latency access, such as e-commerce platforms or social media applications.

  Example: An online retailer with customers worldwide can use DynamoDB Global Tables to store product information, ensuring quick access to data regardless of user location.

- **Amazon S3 Cross-Region Replication (CRR)**
    - Amazon S3 supports cross-region replication, which asynchronously copies objects from a bucket in one region to a bucket in another. This setup provides redundancy and improves data access speeds for users in different regions.
    - S3 CRR is commonly used for backup, disaster recovery, and compliance requirements.

  Example: A media streaming service uses S3 CRR to store video files in multiple regions, ensuring availability and reduced latency for users around the globe.

Configuring Multi-AZ Replication with Amazon RDS

In Amazon RDS, Multi-AZ deployments are configured to provide high availability through synchronous replication:

- **Primary Instance and Standby Instance:** In a Multi-AZ setup, the primary instance handles all database requests, while a standby instance in another AZ remains synchronized with the primary through synchronous replication.

- **Automatic Failover:** If the primary instance experiences an outage, RDS automatically promotes the standby instance to primary, minimizing downtime and ensuring data consistency.

Step-by-Step Configuration:

1. **Create an RDS Database**: In the AWS Management Console, select Multi-AZ deployment when creating a new RDS instance.
2. **Specify Regions and Availability Zones**: Choose the primary AZ and a secondary AZ within the same region.
3. **Enable Monitoring**: Use Amazon CloudWatch to track metrics such as latency, replication lag, and instance health.

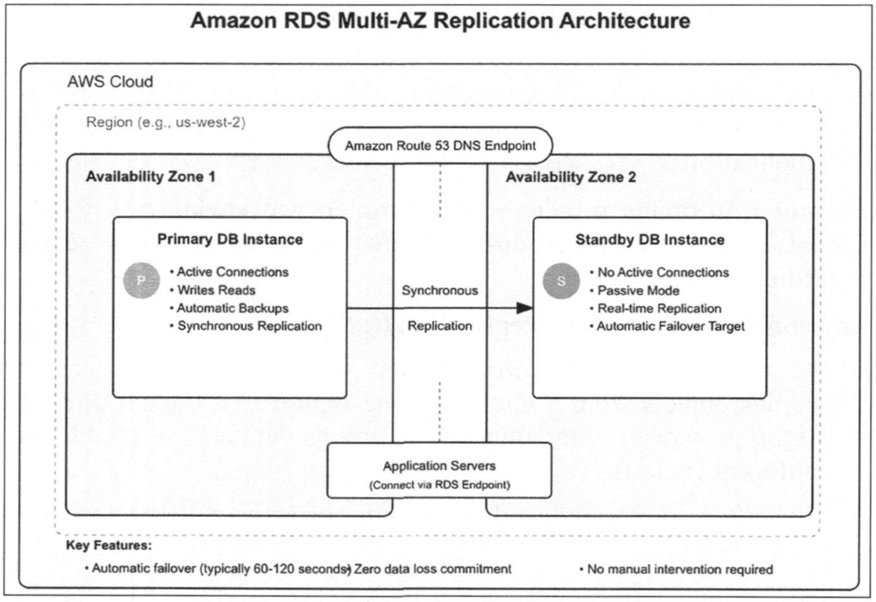

Figure 2.5: *Amazon RDS Multi-AZ Replication Architecture*

Example Use Case: An ERP system with critical financial data benefits from RDS Multi-AZ by maintaining data consistency across AZs and ensuring availability during peak business hours.

Setting Up DynamoDB Global Tables for Cross-Region Replication

Amazon DynamoDB Global Tables offer an easy setup for cross-region replication, supporting asynchronous replication with eventual consistency:

- **Define the Primary Region:** Begin by selecting a primary region for the DynamoDB table.

- **Enable Global Tables:** In the table settings, select the Global Tables option and choose the additional regions for replication.
- **Automatic Replication:** DynamoDB handles the replication automatically, ensuring that changes in one region are asynchronously propagated to other regions.

Example Workflow:

- For a gaming application with players around the world, DynamoDB Global Tables replicate player profiles across regions. This configuration allows players to access their profiles quickly, regardless of location, with the assurance that data will eventually sync across regions.

Monitoring and Managing Replication:

- **Amazon CloudWatch:** Tracks metrics such as replication lag, request throughput, and error rates, allowing for real-time monitoring and troubleshooting.
- **DynamoDB Streams:** Captures item-level changes in DynamoDB tables, enabling custom replication workflows or backup strategies.

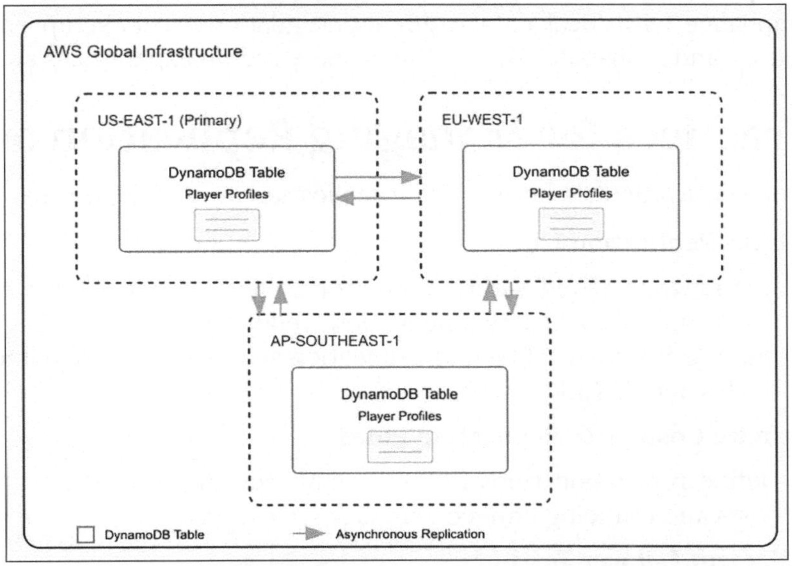

Figure 2.6: *AWS Cloud cross-region replication*

Using Amazon S3 Cross-Region Replication (CRR) for Backup and Compliance

Amazon S3's Cross-Region Replication (CRR) feature supports asynchronous replication of objects between S3 buckets in different regions. This feature is particularly valuable for disaster recovery, regulatory compliance, and improved access speed for distributed users.

- **Configuring S3 CRR:**
  - **Select Source and Destination Buckets:** Identify the source bucket for data and a destination bucket in the target region.
  - **Enable Versioning:** Ensure versioning is enabled on both buckets, as CRR requires versioning to track changes.
  - **Define Replication Rules:** Set up rules to specify which objects to replicate based on prefixes or tags, optimizing costs by only replicating necessary data.
- **Use Cases for S3 CRR:**
  - **Disaster Recovery:** Maintain a backup of essential data in a secondary region, ensuring data availability in case of an outage.
  - **Compliance:** For regulated industries, replicate data to regions that meet local data residency requirements.

  Example: A healthcare provider uses S3 CRR to store patient records in compliance with local data residency regulations. This setup ensures data security and availability, even if the primary region experiences an outage.

Best Practices for Managing Replication on AWS

Here are some best practices for managing replication on AWS platforms:

- **Monitor Replication Lag:**
  - Use **Amazon CloudWatch** to monitor replication latency and ensure data synchronization meets application requirements. This is particularly important for asynchronous replication setups such as DynamoDB Global Tables and S3 CRR.
- **Optimize Costs with Replication Rules:**
  - Define replication rules in S3 to only replicate critical data, optimizing costs and reducing unnecessary storage expenses.
- **Implement Failover Testing:**
  - Regularly test failover capabilities in Multi-AZ setups to ensure the system can seamlessly switch to standby instances without data loss or downtime.
- **Leverage IAM Policies for Access Control:**
  - Use AWS Identity and Access Management (IAM) to restrict access to replicated data, enhancing security and ensuring that only authorized users can access data across regions.

Example: An e-commerce application regularly tests its RDS Multi-AZ failover process to ensure that database replicas can seamlessly take over during a primary instance failure, ensuring minimal downtime during high-traffic periods.

Case Study: Implementing a Multi-Region Replication Strategy for a Global SaaS Platform

Scenario: A Software as a Service (SaaS) provider with customers in North America, Europe, and Asia requires a resilient, low-latency data replication solution for its user data and application settings.

- **Primary Storage with DynamoDB Global Tables:** The SaaS provider uses DynamoDB Global Tables to replicate user data across regions, ensuring low-latency access for customers worldwide. This approach also provides resilience to regional failures.
- **S3 Cross-Region Replication for Backups:** Application logs and backup data are stored in Amazon S3, with cross-region replication enabled for disaster recovery. This setup ensures data integrity and availability across all regions.
- **RDS Multi-AZ for Critical Transactions:** For transaction records and sensitive settings, RDS Multi-AZ provides high availability within each region, ensuring that critical data remains accessible during outages.

Replication Best Practices and Use cases

Effective data replication requires careful planning to balance consistency, availability, performance, and cost. Best practices for replication ensure that data remains available, accurate, and cost-effective, regardless of system demands or failures. These practices are crucial for building a resilient and efficient distributed system that can handle real-world workloads.

Key considerations include:

- **Choosing the Right Replication Type**: Select synchronous or asynchronous replication based on consistency and latency requirements.
- **Minimizing Replication Lag:** Monitor and optimize replication lag to ensure that data remains up-to-date across replicas.
- **Managing Cost Efficiency:** Use selective replication and replication rules to control costs.
- **Implementing Security Controls:** Protect replicated data with strict access controls, encryption, and monitoring.

Best Practices for Data Replication

Some best practices for data replication are mentioned as follows:

- **Optimize for Consistency and Latency Requirements**
    - Synchronous replication is suitable for applications needing strict consistency, such as banking and healthcare systems, while asynchronous replication benefits applications prioritizing availability and performance, such as social media platforms.
    - Hybrid models can combine both approaches, ensuring critical data is synchronously replicated while less critical data uses asynchronous replication.

  Example: A retail platform uses synchronous replication for inventory data to ensure real-time accuracy and asynchronous replication for product reviews, where temporary inconsistencies are acceptable.

- **Monitor and Manage Replication Lag**
    - Use Amazon CloudWatch to monitor replication metrics, especially lag, which can impact data consistency.
    - For asynchronous setups such as DynamoDB Global Tables, monitoring replication lag is critical to ensure that delays are within acceptable limits for user experience.

  Example: A streaming service monitors replication lag on DynamoDB Global Tables to ensure that user preferences and playback data are updated promptly across regions.

- **Implement Selective Replication to Reduce Costs**
    - Define replication rules in Amazon S3 to selectively replicate only the essential data, avoiding unnecessary storage expenses.

  Example: S3 Cross-Region Replication (CRR) rules can specify that only critical files or frequently accessed data be replicated, optimizing both cost and performance.

- **Enable Versioning and Backup Policies**
    - Enable versioning on replicated storage such as S3 to keep track of changes, allowing rollback if issues arise with new updates.
    - Establish backup policies for critical data, even if replication is enabled, ensuring that data can be restored in case of accidental deletion or corruption.

- **Apply Security Controls to Replicated Data**
    - Use AWS Identity and Access Management (IAM) policies to restrict

access to sensitive data replicas, ensuring that only authorized users or applications have access.

- Encrypt data at rest and in transit, especially for sensitive data replicated across regions, to maintain compliance with data protection regulations.

Example: A healthcare application applies strict IAM policies to its replicated S3 buckets containing patient data, ensuring compliance with regulations such as HIPAA.

Use Cases for Replication in Distributed Systems

Let us examine practical examples that demonstrate how these replication concepts are implemented in real-world distributed systems.

- **Disaster Recovery and Business Continuity**
  - Replication enables rapid recovery from data loss due to system failures, network issues, or natural disasters. By replicating data across multiple regions, distributed systems can maintain availability and data integrity during outages.
  - AWS Solution: Amazon S3 Cross-Region Replication (CRR) provides an ideal solution for disaster recovery, allowing organizations to store backup data in geographically separate regions.

  Example: A financial institution replicates transaction logs to a secondary region using S3 CRR to ensure that critical data is available in case of regional failures.

- **Improving Read Performance and Reducing Latency**
  - By distributing read requests across multiple replicas, data replication reduces latency and balances the load. Global applications can benefit from replication across regions, serving users from the nearest available replica.
  - AWS Solution: DynamoDB Global Tables support cross-region replication, enabling low-latency access for globally distributed users.

  Example: A gaming platform uses DynamoDB Global Tables to replicate player profiles across regions, ensuring fast access for players worldwide.

- **Compliance with Data Residency Requirements**
  - Data residency laws require that data be stored within specific geographic locations. Replication can ensure that data is available in compliant regions without restricting user access.

- AWS Solution: With S3 Cross-Region Replication, organizations can maintain separate copies of data in regions that meet local regulatory requirements.

Example: An international e-commerce company uses S3 CRR to store customer data in regions compliant with local data residency laws, such as GDPR in Europe.

- **Scaling Read-Intensive Applications**
    - Replication allows scaling of read-intensive workloads by distributing requests across multiple replicas. For applications that experience high read-to-write ratios, replication can dramatically improve performance and resource efficiency.
    - AWS Solution: RDS Read Replicas create read-only replicas of a database, distributing read traffic across replicas while maintaining consistency with the primary database.

  Example: A news website with high traffic uses RDS Read Replicas to distribute content retrieval across multiple replicas, reducing load on the primary database and improving response times.

- **Enhanced Availability for Critical Applications**
    - Replication ensures that applications can continue to operate even if some nodes fail, enhancing availability. Multi-AZ deployments in AWS provide built-in failover mechanisms for critical applications, reducing the risk of downtime.
    - AWS Solution: Amazon RDS Multi-AZ deployments support synchronous replication across Availability Zones, providing high availability and automatic failover.

  Example: A payroll management system for a multinational corporation uses RDS Multi-AZ to ensure that employee payment data is always accessible, even during infrastructure issues in one AZ.

Case Study: Replication Strategy for a Global E-Commerce Platform

Scenario: A global e-commerce platform requires a replication strategy that ensures data availability and low latency for customers in North America, Europe, and Asia.

- **DynamoDB Global Tables for Product Data**: Product information, such as descriptions, pricing, and stock levels, is replicated across regions with DynamoDB Global Tables. This setup ensures low-latency access to data regardless of customer location, enhancing the shopping experience.

- **Amazon S3 Cross-Region Replication for Images**: Product images and multimedia are stored in S3, with CRR enabled to replicate data to regions close to customers. This setup allows quick image loading, even for users in distant regions.
- **RDS Multi-AZ for Transactions**: Transactional data, such as customer orders and payment details, is stored in an RDS Multi-AZ deployment to ensure strong consistency and availability. This configuration enables the platform to maintain accurate transaction records and reduces downtime risks.

Implementation Workflow:

- Configure DynamoDB Global Tables to automatically replicate product data across primary customer regions.
- Use S3 replication rules to copy multimedia content to selected regions, improving access speed for international customers.
- Deploy RDS in a Multi-AZ setup for handling critical order processing, ensuring transactional integrity across locations.

Monitoring and Optimizing Replication in AWS

To maximize the benefits of replication, ongoing monitoring and optimization are essential. AWS provides several tools for this purpose:

- **Amazon CloudWatch**: Tracks metrics such as replication lag, request rates, and error counts. Custom CloudWatch alarms can alert administrators if replication lag exceeds acceptable limits, allowing prompt corrective actions.
- **AWS X-Ray**: Provides detailed insights into application performance, identifying latency sources and bottlenecks in replication processes.
- **AWS CloudTrail**: Logs all API calls and events, providing an audit trail for replication operations. CloudTrail logs are useful for troubleshooting replication issues and ensuring that replication workflows remain secure and compliant.

  Example: A media streaming company uses CloudWatch to monitor replication lag on DynamoDB Global Tables, ensuring user preferences and recent activity sync quickly across regions.

Conclusion

In this chapter, we explored the essential role of data replication in distributed systems, focusing on strategies to ensure high availability, fault tolerance, and performance. We discussed the two primary replication types—synchronous and asynchronous—

highlighting their unique benefits, trade-offs, and optimal use cases. Through the AWS replication tools such as RDS Multi-AZ, DynamoDB Global Tables, and S3 Cross-Region Replication, we saw how cloud infrastructure can simplify and enhance replication across geographically dispersed regions. By following best practices in managing replication lag, cost efficiency, and security, organizations can implement reliable and resilient distributed systems that meet the demands of modern applications. These insights lay a strong foundation for further exploration of partitioning and sharding in distributed data management in the next chapter.

CHAPTER 3
Partitioning and Sharding: Optimizing Data Management

Introduction

As data continues to grow in volume and complexity, efficient management of that data becomes both an art and a necessity in distributed systems. Partitioning and sharding serve as the keystones of scalability, allowing systems to divide and conquer vast datasets by breaking them into manageable segments that can be stored, processed, and queried independently. This chapter delves into the sophisticated techniques of partitioning and sharding, the powerful strategies that enable distributed systems to expand effortlessly, optimize performance, and prevent bottlenecks.

We will explore various partitioning methods, from range-based and hash-based strategies to composite approaches, each offering unique benefits tailored to different data access patterns and application requirements. Sharding, a specialized form of partitioning, allows data to be distributed across multiple databases, supporting horizontal scalability essential for handling high-traffic, high-volume applications. With practical insights and AWS-specific examples, this chapter will equip you with the tools and understanding needed to design a data architecture that can scale and adapt to the demands of modern applications. Embark with us on this journey to master the art of dividing data for maximum efficiency, agility, and resilience in distributed environments.

Structure

In this chapter, we will cover the following topics:

- Fundamentals of Data Partitioning and Sharding
  - Definitions and Key Concepts

- Partitioning versus Sharding
- Types of Data Partitioning
- Sharding in Distributed Systems
- Challenges in Implementing Partitioning and Sharding
- Partitioning Strategies in Distributed systems
  - Range-Based Partitioning
  - Hash-Based Partitioning
  - List-Based Partitioning
  - Composite Partitioning
  - Choosing the Right Partitioning Strategy
  - Challenges in Managing Partitioning in Distributed Systems
- Implementing Sharding in Cloud-Based Distributed Systems
  - Sharding Strategies
  - Sharding on AWS
  - Challenges in Implementing Sharding
  - Best Practices for Sharing in Cloud-Based Systems
  - Case Study: Implementing Sharding for a Video Streaming Service on AWS
- Challenges and Best Practices for Managing Partitioning and Sharding
  - Best Practices for Partitioning and Sharding in Distributed Systems
  - Applying Best Practices for Sharding in a Global E-Commerce Platform

Fundamentals of Data Partitioning and Sharding

Data partitioning and sharding are techniques used in distributed systems to divide large datasets into manageable segments, improving scalability, performance, and resource utilization. These approaches are essential for applications with high data volumes, enabling efficient data storage and retrieval across distributed nodes.

- **Data Partitioning:** Involves splitting a dataset into distinct segments, or "*partitions*," which are then distributed across different storage nodes. Each partition stores a subset of the data, reducing the load on individual nodes.
- **Data Sharding:** A specific form of partitioning that distributes data across multiple physical databases or storage locations, known as "*shards*." Each shard acts as an independent database, but together they form a cohesive data store.

Partitioning and sharding allow distributed systems to handle large data volumes effectively by distributing storage and processing demands across multiple resources.

Types of Data Partitioning

Partitioning strategies are chosen based on the application's data access patterns, consistency requirements, and scalability needs. Common types include:

- **Range-Based Partitioning:**
  - Divides data based on a defined range of values. Each partition stores data within a specific range, making it suitable for ordered data, such as time series or numeric data.

  Example: A time series database might use range-based partitioning to store data from January to March in one partition and April to June in another, allowing efficient retrieval of time-specific data.
- **Hash-Based Partitioning:**
  - Uses a hash function to assign data to partitions. The hash function maps data evenly across partitions, distributing data more uniformly and reducing hotspots.

  Example: An e-commerce application could hash customer IDs to distribute user profiles across multiple partitions, balancing the load evenly.
- **List-Based Partitioning:**
  - Organizes data based on a predefined list of categories or values. Each partition holds data corresponding to specific values or groups, allowing targeted data access.

  Example: In a multi-tenant application, data can be partitioned based on user regions, with each region assigned to a separate partition.
- **Composite Partitioning:**
  - Combines two or more partitioning strategies, such as hash and range, to address complex data requirements.

  Example: A social media platform might partition data by geographic region (list partitioning) and further partition each region's data by time (range partitioning) to optimize both region-based and time-based access.

Sharding in Distributed Systems

Sharding is a specific form of partitioning applied to entire databases or collections. Each shard operates as an independent database with a subset of the data, enabling large-scale systems to distribute data across multiple storage units and handle massive data volumes.

Benefits of sharding include:

- **Scalability:** Allows horizontal scaling by adding more shards as data grows, rather than requiring a single, large database.
- **Load Distribution:** Reduces the load on each shard, improving query performance and response times.
- **Fault Isolation:** Limits the impact of failures to specific shards, enhancing resilience.

However, sharding also introduces complexities, including:

- **Data Rebalancing:** As data grows or access patterns shift, shards may need to be rebalanced to maintain even distribution.
- **Cross-Shard Transactions:** Coordinating transactions across multiple shards can be challenging, impacting data consistency and query performance.

Example: In a large-scale application such as Twitter, user data may be sharded based on user ID, with each shard storing information for a subset of users. This setup enables Twitter to handle millions of users and queries simultaneously by distributing data across numerous shards.

Choosing Between Partitioning and Sharding

The choice between partitioning and sharding depends on the scale of the data and the structure of the application:

- **Partitioning** is often suitable for moderate-scale datasets that can be managed within a single database. It provides flexibility in organizing data for improved query performance.
- **Sharding** is necessary for large-scale applications with vast datasets that exceed the storage or performance capacity of a single database. Sharding distributes data across multiple databases, enabling horizontal scaling.

Example: A weather monitoring system might use partitioning to organize data by date ranges, while a global social network with billions of users would implement sharding to handle its vast dataset across multiple storage units.

Partitioning vs Sharding: Database Scaling Strategies

Criteria	Partitioning	Sharding
Definition	Divides data within a single database instance	Distributes data across multiple database instances
Scale	Moderate (Terabytes)	Large to Very Large (Petabytes)
Infrastructure	Single database server	Multiple database servers
Example Use Case	E-commerce orders by date: - 2023_orders - 2024_orders	Social media user data: - users_shard_1 (IDs 1-1M) - users_shard_2 (IDs 1M-2M)
Query Performance	- Fast partition-specific queries - Cross-partition queries possible - Single server bottleneck	- Excellent shard-specific queries - Cross-shard queries complex - Distributed processing power
When to Choose	Choose when: - Data size 5TB - Single server handles load - Need simple management - Strong consistency required	Choose when: - Data size > 5TB - High concurrent user load - Geographic distribution needed - Can handle eventual consistency
Real-world Examples	- Time-series data - Historical records	- Instagram - Twitter/Facebook

Figure 3.1: *Partitioning versus Sharding*

Challenges in Implementing Partitioning and Sharding

Partitioning and sharding provide scalability and performance benefits but also introduce challenges:

- **Data Rebalancing**: As the dataset grows, some partitions or shards may hold more data than others, requiring rebalancing to maintain even distribution.
- **Cross-Partition or Cross-Shard Queries**: Queries that span multiple partitions or shards can be complex and time-consuming, impacting performance.
- **Consistency Management**: Ensuring data consistency across partitions or shards, especially in transactions, requires additional mechanisms such as distributed locking.
- **Complexity in Maintenance**: Managing multiple shards or partitions involves more complex monitoring, backup, and recovery processes.

Example: An online marketplace that sharded its product data by category experienced uneven data growth, with some categories (for example, electronics) growing faster than others. The platform needed to rebalance shards to prevent slowdowns in high-demand categories.

Partitioning Strategies in Distributed Systems

Partitioning strategies define how data is divided and distributed across nodes in a distributed system, with the goal of improving data management, scalability, and performance. Choosing an appropriate partitioning strategy involves analyzing data access patterns, distribution requirements, and system goals.

Partitioning strategies can be tailored to specific application needs, such as read-heavy workloads, high write throughput, or geographically distributed users. In distributed systems, common partitioning strategies include **range-based**, **hash-based**, **list-based**, and **composite partitioning**.

Range-Based Partitioning

Range-based partitioning divides data based on a defined range of values. Each partition stores data within a specific range, such as time intervals or numeric sequences. This approach is effective for ordered data or queries that need to access specific ranges of data.

Advantages:

- **Efficient Range Queries**: Ideal for applications that frequently query data within a certain range, such as time-series data.
- **Data Locality**: Related data is stored together, reducing the need for cross-partition queries.

Disadvantages:

- **Hotspots**: Range-based partitioning can lead to imbalances if certain ranges are accessed more frequently.
- **Manual Repartitioning**: As data grows, partitions may need manual reconfiguration to maintain performance.

Example: A temperature monitoring system might use range-based partitioning to store data by month, allowing efficient retrieval of temperature data for specific time periods. If data is partitioned by date, the partition for a record with date can be assigned based on ranges:

$$P = \begin{cases} P_1 \; if \; D \; is \; in \; January \; to \; March \\ P_2 \; if \; D \; is \; in \; April \; to \; June \\ P_n \; otherwise \end{cases}$$

Figure 3.2 shows the range-based partitioning:

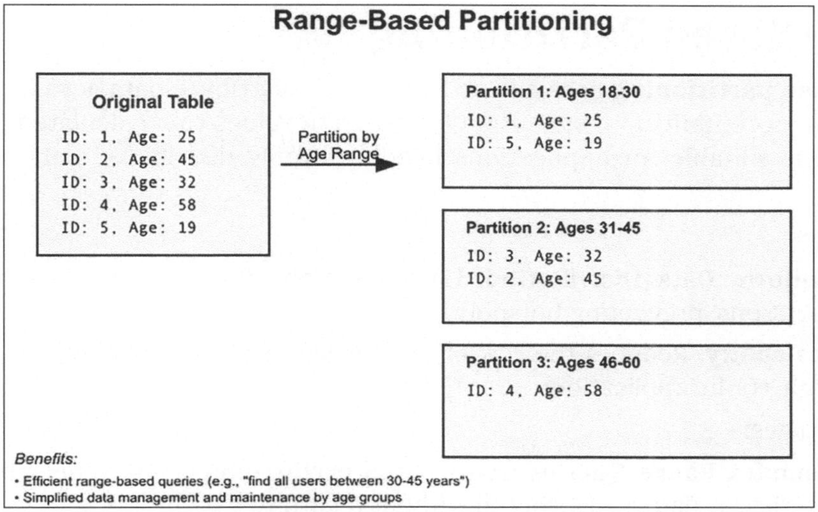

Figure 3.2: *Range-Based Partitioning*

And the code is shown in *Figure* 3.3:

```
def range_partitioner(data, num_partitions):
    """Partitions the range of data into equal intervals.

    Args:
        data (list): List of numeric data points.
        num_partitions (int): Number of partitions to divide the range into.

    Returns:
        list: A list of partitions represented as tuples (start, end).
    """
    if not data:
        return []
    min_val, max_val = min(data), max(data)
    range_size = (max_val - min_val) / num_partitions
    partitions = [
        (min_val + i * range_size, min_val + (i + 1) * range_size)
        for i in range(num_partitions)
    ]
    return partitions

# Example usage
data = [10, 20, 30, 40, 50]
num_partitions = 3
partitions = range_partitioner(data, num_partitions)

print("Input data:")
print(data)
print()

print("Number of partitions:")
print(num_partitions)
print()

print("Partitions:")
for partition in partitions:
    print(partition)

# Output:
# Input data:
# [10, 20, 30, 40, 50]
#
# Number of partitions:
# 3
#
# Partitions:
# (10.0, 23.333333333333336)
# (23.333333333333336, 36.66666666666667)
# (36.66666666666667, 50.0)
```

Figure 3.3: *Range-Based Partitioning code*

Hash-Based Partitioning

Hash-based partitioning uses a hash function to distribute data across partitions, creating a more uniform distribution by mapping values to a calculated hash. This approach is suitable for applications needing evenly distributed data to balance load.

Advantages:

- **Uniform Data Distribution**: Hash functions distribute data evenly across partitions, preventing hotspots.
- **Scalability**: Reduces the risk of overloaded partitions, making it suitable for high-traffic applications.

Disadvantages:

- **Complex Range Queries**: Hash-based partitioning is less efficient for range queries, as data is distributed without regard to data ordering.
- **Difficulty in Adding Partitions**: Changing the number of partitions may require rehashing existing data, leading to data migration overhead.

Example: In a social media application, user data can be partitioned by hashing user IDs, ensuring that user profiles are distributed uniformly across partitions.

For data D with an *ID x*, the partition P can be assigned based on a hash function *H(x)*:

$$P = H(x)\ mod\ N$$

Where N is the number of partitions. This ensures that data is uniformly distributed across N partitions.

Figure 3.4 shows the hash-based partitioning:

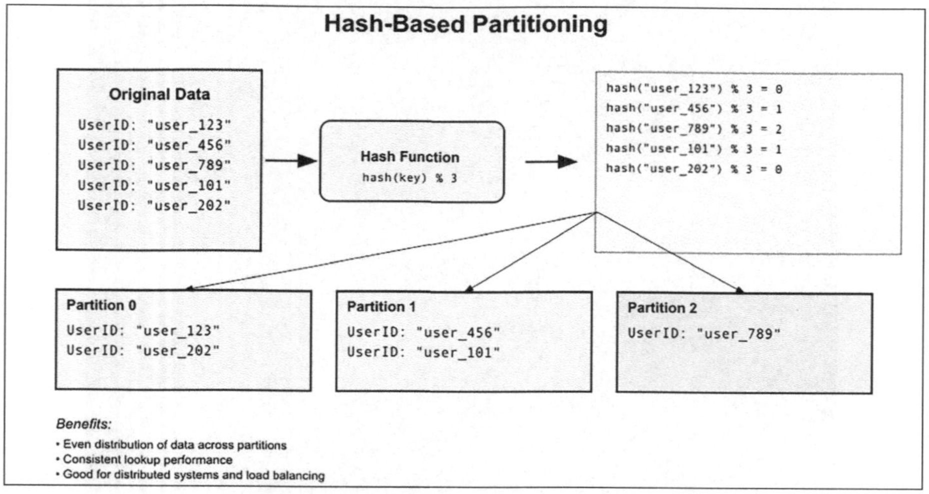

Figure 3.4: *Hash-Based Partitioning*

Figure 3.5 depicts the code:

```
def hash_partitioner(data, num_partitions):
    """Partitions data into groups based on hash values.

    Args:
        data (list): List of data points to partition.
        num_partitions (int): Number of partitions.

    Returns:
        dict: A dictionary where keys are partition indices and values are lists of data points.
    """
    if not data or num_partitions <= 0:
        return {}
    partitions = {i: [] for i in range(num_partitions)}
    for item in data:
        partition_index = hash(item) % num_partitions
        partitions[partition_index].append(item)
    return partitions

# Example usage
data = [10, 20, 30, 40, 50]
num_partitions = 3
partitions = hash_partitioner(data, num_partitions)

print("Input data:")
print(data)
print()

print("Number of partitions:")
print(num_partitions)
print()

print("Partitions:")
for key, value in partitions.items():
    print(f"Partition {key}: {value}")

# Output:
# Input data:
# [10, 20, 30, 40, 50]
#
# Number of partitions:
# 3
#
# Partitions:
# Partition 0: [30]
# Partition 1: [10, 40]
# Partition 2: [20, 50]
```

Figure 3.5: *Hash-Based Partitioning code*

List-Based Partitioning

List-based partitioning organizes data based on a predefined list of values or categories, with each partition holding data for specific values. This approach allows data to be stored according to distinct attributes, improving targeted access and retrieval.

Advantages:

- **Efficient Access for Specific Categories:** Enables targeted queries on specific categories or attributes.
- **Flexibility:** Useful for applications with clearly defined segments or categories.

Disadvantages:

- **Uneven Distribution:** Some categories may grow faster than others, leading to imbalances and hotspots.

- **Limited Scalability:** Adding new categories may require creating new partitions, which can be cumbersome.

Example: An online retail platform might use list-based partitioning to organize product data by category (for example, electronics, clothing, furniture), allowing efficient retrieval based on product type.

For a record with a category attribute, the partition is assigned based on the category list:

$$P = \textit{partition assigned to category } C$$

Figure 3.6 shows the list-based partitioning:

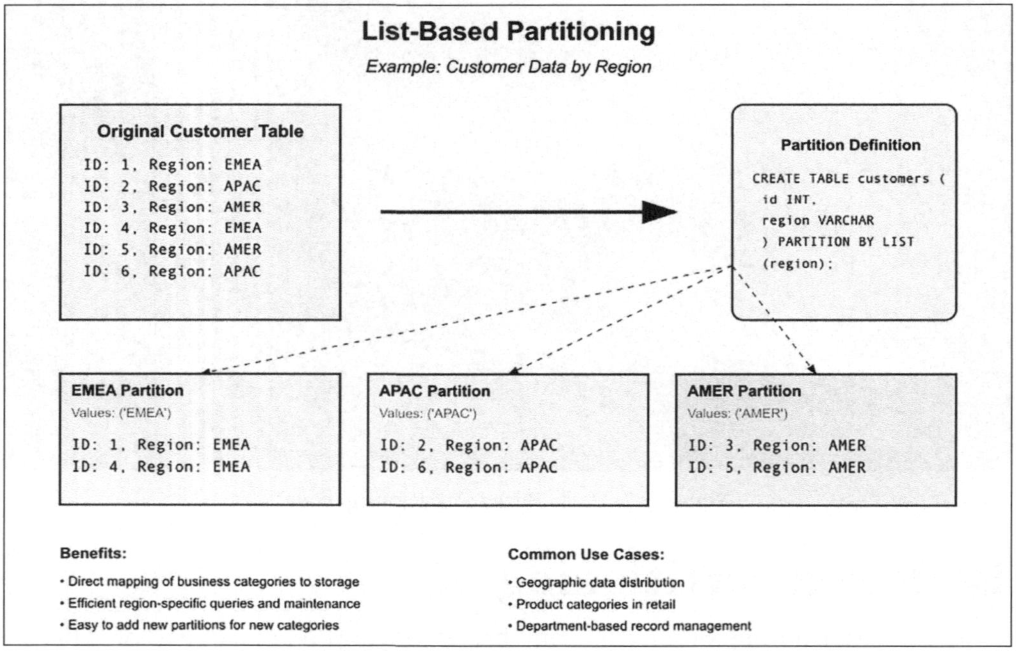

Figure 3.6: *List-Based Partitioning*

Here is the code in *Figure* 3.7:

```
def list_partitioner(data, num_partitions):
    """Divides a list of data into approximately equal-sized partitions.

    Args:
        data (list): List of data points to partition.
        num_partitions (int): Number of partitions.

    Returns:
        list: A list of partitions where each partition is a list of data points.
    """
    if not data or num_partitions <= 0:
        return []
    partition_size = len(data) // num_partitions
    partitions = [data[i * partition_size: (i + 1) * partition_size] for i in range(num_partitions)]

    # Add remaining elements to the last partition
    if len(data) % num_partitions != 0:
        partitions[-1].extend(data[num_partitions * partition_size:])
    return partitions

# Example usage
data = [10, 20, 30, 40, 50, 60, 70, 80, 90]
num_partitions = 4
partitions = list_partitioner(data, num_partitions)

print("Input data:")
print(data)
print()

print("Number of partitions:")
print(num_partitions)
print()

print("Partitions:")
for i, partition in enumerate(partitions):
    print(f"Partition {i}: {partition}")

# Output:
# Input data:
# [10, 20, 30, 40, 50, 60, 70, 80, 90]
#
# Number of partitions:
# 4
#
# Partitions:
# Partition 0: [10, 20]
# Partition 1: [30, 40]
# Partition 2: [50, 60]
# Partition 3: [70, 80, 90]
```

Figure 3.7: *List-Based Partitioning code*

Composite Partitioning

Composite partitioning combines multiple partitioning strategies, such as hash and range-based partitioning, to address complex data access patterns or optimize both read and write performance. Composite partitioning is useful when a single partitioning strategy is insufficient.

Advantages:

- **Enhanced Flexibility**: Enables tailored data distribution by combining partitioning methods.
- **Supports Complex Queries**: Optimizes performance for applications requiring both range and categorical data access.

Disadvantages:

- **Complexity**: Implementation and maintenance can be complex due to multiple partitioning schemes.

- **Costly Repartitioning**: Adding partitions may involve reconfiguring multiple partition layers, increasing complexity.

Example: A global logistics application could use composite partitioning by first dividing shipments by region (list partitioning) and then by delivery date within each region (range partitioning), improving efficiency for regional and time-based queries.

Composite Partition Assignment: For data with attributes and , where determines the list partition and determines the range within the partition, the partition assignment can be defined as:

$$P = \textit{partition based on A, then further partitioned by B}$$

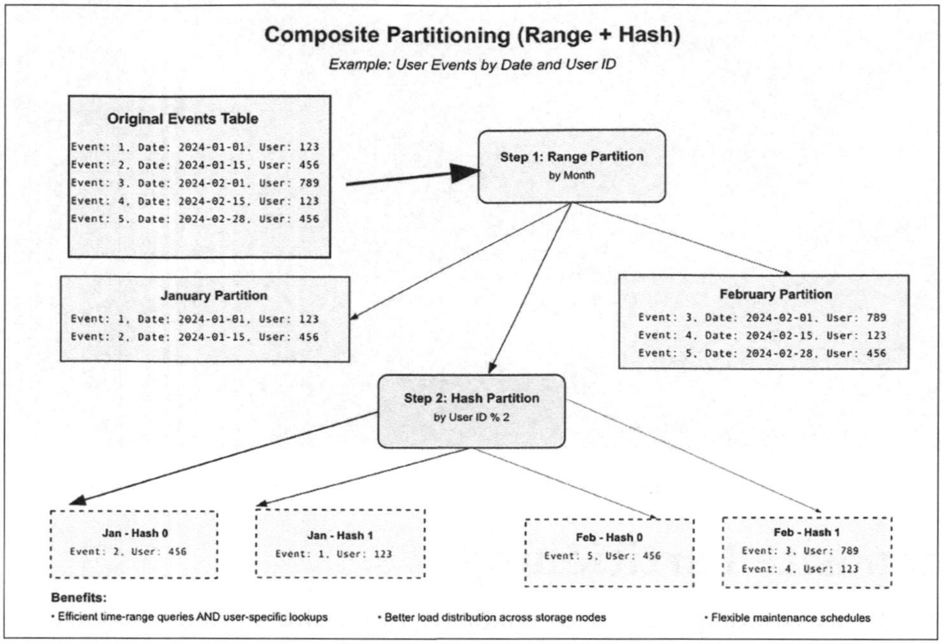

Figure 3.8: *Composite Partitioning (Range + Hash)*

Choosing the Right Partitioning Strategy

The choice of partitioning strategy depends on the application's data characteristics, query patterns, and scalability requirements:

- **Range-Based Partitioning**: Suitable for applications with range-based queries, such as time-series data or log data.
- **Hash-Based Partitioning**: Ideal for high-traffic applications requiring balanced data distribution, such as user profiles or account information.
- **List-Based Partitioning**: Effective for applications with well-defined categorical data, such as product catalogs or customer segments.

- **Composite Partitioning**: Best for complex use cases that benefit from multiple partitioning dimensions, such as geographic and time-based data access.

Example Comparison: A weather data application may benefit from range-based partitioning for temperature readings by date, while a multi-tenant SaaS platform might use list-based partitioning to organize customer data by account type.

Database Partitioning Strategies Comparison

Strategy	Key Characteristics	Use Cases	Example Implementation

Range-Based	• Sequential division
	• Natural ordering
	• Predictable ranges
	• Easy maintenance
		• Time-series data
		• Historical records
		• Temperature readings
		• Financial transactions
			`PARTITION BY RANGE (year) (`
			`p2023 VALUES 2024,`
			`p2024 VALUES 2025`
			`)`

Hash-Based	• Even distribution • Load balancing • Scalable • Parallel processing	• User profiles • Session data • High-traffic systems • Distributed databases	`PARTITION BY HASH(user_id)` `PARTITIONS 4;`

List-Based	• Categorical division
	• Discrete values
	• Business categories
	• Logical grouping
		• Product catalogs
		• Regional data
		• Customer segments
		• Service tiers
			`PARTITION BY LIST(region) (`
			`p_eu VALUES ('EU'),`
			`p_us VALUES ('US')`
			`)`

Composite	• Multiple strategies
	• Complex patterns
	• Flexible access
	• Multi-dimensional
		• IoT sensor data
		• E-commerce orders
		• Social media posts
		• Geographic + temporal
			`PARTITION BY RANGE(date)`
			`SUBPARTITION BY HASH(region)`
			`SUBPARTITIONS 4;`

Note: Selection should be based on data access patterns, scalability needs, and maintenance requirements

Figure 3.9: *Database Partitioning Strategies Comparison*

Challenges in Managing Partitioning in Distributed Systems

Partitioning provides scalability and performance improvements but also introduces challenges:

- **Data Rebalancing**: As data grows, partitions may become imbalanced, requiring rebalancing to maintain even data distribution and avoid hotspots.
- **Cross-Partition Queries**: Queries that span multiple partitions are complex and may impact performance, especially in range-based or list-based partitioning.
- **Partition Key Design**: Choosing an optimal partition key is crucial to avoid data skew and achieve balanced distribution.
- **Data Migration**: Adding new partitions or adjusting partition boundaries often requires data migration, which can disrupt operations.

Example: An IoT system partitioned by device type encountered rapid data growth in certain device categories, causing hotspots. The system needed rebalancing to distribute data more evenly.

Implementing Sharding in Cloud-Based Distributed Systems

Sharding is a method of distributing data across multiple databases or nodes, each containing a subset of the data. This approach enables distributed systems to handle large-scale data by dividing it into more manageable, isolated segments, or "*shards*." In cloud-based environments such as AWS, sharding enhances scalability and load balancing, enabling applications to grow without compromising performance.

Key components of a sharded architecture include:

- **Shard Key**: The attribute used to determine where each piece of data is stored.
- **Routing Layer**: Directs incoming queries to the appropriate shard based on the shard key.
- **Replication**: Each shard may have replicas to improve availability and fault tolerance.

Sharding Strategies

Several sharding strategies are commonly used in distributed systems, each designed to address different data distribution needs:

- **Range-Based Sharding**
    - Data is divided based on specific ranges. For instance, one shard might contain data from January to March, while another holds data from April to June.
    - **Use Case**: Time-series data and ordered data sets where range-based queries are common.

  Example: A financial system could shard transaction records by date, allowing efficient retrieval of recent transactions by querying only the relevant shard.
- **Hash-Based Sharding**
    - A hash function distributes data evenly across shards. This approach prevents hotspots and ensures even load distribution.
    - **Use Case**: High-traffic applications needing a balanced load, such as user profiles or account data.

Example: An e-commerce platform might hash customer IDs, ensuring that customer data is spread evenly across all shards.

- **Directory-Based Sharding**
  - A central directory maintains a mapping of each data item to its corresponding shard, allowing for flexible and customizable shard assignments.
  - **Use Case**: Applications with complex data access patterns that require specialized shard distribution.

Example: A SaaS provider could use directory-based sharding to assign each customer to a specific shard, with the directory managing query routing.

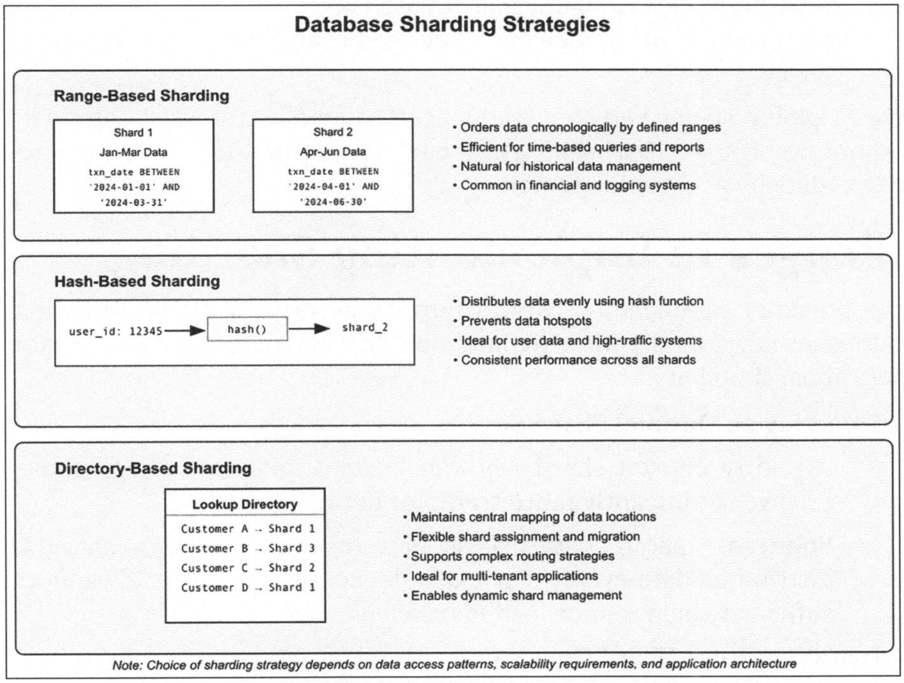

Figure 3.10: *Database Sharding strategies*

Sharding on AWS

AWS offers several options for implementing sharding, either through managed services or custom configurations:

- **Amazon DynamoDB Partitioning**
  - DynamoDB automatically handles sharding and partitioning. Data is distributed across partitions based on the primary key, with DynamoDB managing load and rebalancing.

  - **Best Practice**: Select a primary key that evenly distributes data, such as a combination of user ID and timestamp, to avoid hotspots.
- **Custom Sharding with Amazon RDS**
  - RDS does not provide built-in sharding, but custom sharding can be implemented by splitting data across multiple RDS instances.
  - **Best Practice**: Use a load balancer or application-level routing logic to direct queries to the correct shard.
- **Amazon OpenSearch Service**
  - OpenSearch (formerly Elasticsearch) supports sharding for search workloads, allowing data to be divided across multiple nodes.
  - **Best Practice**: Configure shards based on expected data volume and query patterns, ensuring a balance between search performance and resource usage.

Example: A global social network might use DynamoDB for user data, with hash-based sharding on user IDs, while using custom-sharded RDS instances to handle transaction data by geographic region.

Challenges in Implementing Sharding

Sharding presents significant technical hurdles as organizations attempt to scale their databases horizontally while maintaining data consistency, query performance, and operational simplicity.

- **Selecting an Optimal Shard Key**
  - A poorly chosen shard key can lead to *hotspots*, where some shards receive significantly more traffic or data.
  - **Solution**: Analyze data access patterns and choose a shard key that distributes data evenly. For example, combining a user ID and a random suffix may help reduce load imbalances.
- **Handling Cross-Shard Queries**
  - Queries spanning multiple shards can become slow and complex, impacting overall performance.
  - **Solution**: Design the application to limit cross-shard queries and use query aggregators to collect results from multiple shards when necessary.
- **Data Rebalancing**
  - As data grows, some shards may need rebalancing to maintain even distribution.
  - **Solution**: Use a scalable architecture that allows for easy addition of shards. DynamoDB handles automatic rebalancing, while custom sharding setups may require periodic rebalancing scripts.

- **Consistency and Transactions Across Shards**
    - Maintaining consistency across shards can be challenging, particularly for distributed transactions.
    - **Solution**: Implement a distributed transaction model, such as a two-phase commit, or relax consistency requirements if the application can tolerate it.

Example Challenge: A media company that sharded user-generated content by user ID encountered an imbalanced load due to a few high-traffic users. They restructured the shard key to use a hash of user ID and a timestamp, improving distribution.

Best Practices for Sharding in Cloud-Based Systems

Strategic implementation of sharding in cloud environments requires careful consideration of data distribution patterns, cross-shard operations, and infrastructure requirements.

- **Monitor and Adjust Shard Key Regularly**
    - Continually monitor data distribution to ensure a balanced load and adjust the shard key as data patterns evolve.
- **Automate Rebalancing with Managed Services**
    - Use managed services such as DynamoDB, which handle rebalancing automatically, reducing the operational burden.
- **Minimize Cross-Shard Transactions**
    - Design the application to minimize dependencies between shards. For scenarios requiring transactions across shards, use distributed transaction protocols such as the two-phase commit.
- **Implement Read Replicas for Load Distribution**
    - In read-heavy applications, create read replicas to offload read requests from the primary shard and distribute the read load.
- **Use Application-Level Routing for Custom Sharding**
    - For custom-sharded solutions on RDS or other non-managed databases, implement a routing layer to direct queries to the correct shard based on the shard key.

Example: An online gaming platform with read-intensive user data set up read replicas for each shard, ensuring that gameplay data is always accessible even during high-demand periods.

Case Study: Implementing Sharding for a Video Streaming Service on AWS

Scenario: A video streaming service with millions of users worldwide requires sharding to handle user data, playback histories, and content metadata.

- **Hash-Based Sharding for User Data**: User data, such as profiles and preferences, is stored in DynamoDB with hash-based sharding on user ID, ensuring even distribution and low latency.
- **Directory-Based Sharding for Content Metadata**: Content metadata, such as video descriptions and tags, is sharded using directory-based sharding, with a central directory routing query to the correct shard based on content type and popularity.
- **Custom Sharding for Playback Histories in RDS**: Playback histories are stored in a custom-sharded RDS setup, with data split by geographic region to provide localized access.

This sharding approach allows the streaming service to handle massive volumes of user data and content information efficiently, balancing load and minimizing latency.

Challenges and Best Practices for Managing Partitioning and Sharding

While partitioning and sharding improve scalability and performance in distributed systems, they also introduce complexities in data management, maintenance, and consistency. Here, we explore some common challenges and solutions to help manage partitioned and sharded systems effectively.

- **Data Skew and Imbalance**
  - Data skew occurs when partitions or shards are unevenly populated, leading to hotspots where certain nodes receive disproportionately higher traffic or data volumes.
  - **Solution**: Use hash-based partitioning or sharding to distribute data more evenly. For high-growth applications, monitor data distribution regularly and adjust the partition or shard keys as necessary to maintain balance.

  Example: In an e-commerce platform with list-based partitioning by product category, categories such as electronics may experience higher traffic. The platform might re-evaluate the partitioning strategy or introduce a secondary hash partition within these categories.

- **Cross-Partition and Cross-Shard Queries**
  - Queries spanning multiple partitions or shards are often slower and more complex to execute, as they require data aggregation across nodes.
  - **Solution**: Design applications to minimize cross-partition or cross-shard queries and consider caching frequently accessed aggregated data. Use a query aggregator to handle cross-shard queries efficiently if unavoidable.

  Example: A social media application minimizes cross-shard queries by limiting the scope of queries to individual users' data, avoiding cross-shard joins. For cases where cross-sharding of data is needed, the system uses an external aggregation service.

- **Data Rebalancing**
  - As data grows or access patterns change, some partitions or shards may become overloaded, requiring rebalancing to maintain even data distribution and performance.
  - **Solution**: Implement automatic rebalancing where possible, or plan for regular data redistribution. In managed services such as DynamoDB, AWS handles rebalancing, reducing the need for manual intervention.

  Example: A time-series database with range-based partitioning rebalances data periodically to keep partitions from growing disproportionately. This allows consistent performance over time.

- **Consistency and Transactions Across Shards**
  - Ensuring data consistency across shards can be challenging, particularly for applications with high transaction volumes or strict ACID requirements.
  - **Solution**: For applications with strict consistency needs, consider distributed transaction protocols such as two-phase commit. Alternatively, relax consistency requirements with eventual consistency for non-critical data.

  Example: In a payment processing system, cross-shard transactions are managed with a two-phase commit protocol to ensure consistency across shards, while a shopping cart service with eventual consistency tolerates slight delays in data synchronization.

- **Data Migration and Scaling**
  - Adding or removing partitions or shards may require migrating existing data, which can lead to downtime and increased operational costs.
  - **Solution**: Choose a scalable architecture that supports dynamic addition or removal of partitions or shards. Using AWS services such as DynamoDB, which automatically scales partitions, can reduce the need for manual data migration.

Best Practices for Partitioning and Sharding in Distributed Systems

To manage partitioned and sharded systems effectively, several best practices can help optimize data distribution, minimize disruptions, and maintain performance.

- **Choose a Well-Designed Partition or Shard Key**
    - Selecting an effective partition or shard key is essential for even data distribution. Analyze data access patterns to identify an attribute that ensures a balanced load.
    - **Tip**: *For applications with unpredictable growth, consider composite keys that combine multiple attributes (for example, user ID + timestamp) to avoid hotspots.*
- **Use Read Replicas for Load Distribution**
    - In read-heavy applications, create read replicas to offload read requests from the primary partitions or shards, distributing the read load and improving performance.
    - **Tip**: AWS *services such as RDS allow for read replicas, enabling horizontal scaling for read requests and reducing load on primary instances.*
- **Implement Monitoring and Alerts for Skew Detection**
    - Regularly monitor data distribution, query performance, and replication lag to identify potential imbalances or hotspots.
    - **Tip**: Use *Amazon CloudWatch to track metrics such as CPU utilization, request rates, and replication latency. Set up alerts to notify administrators of imbalances or latency spikes.*
    - **Example**: A financial service monitors shard utilization metrics with CloudWatch, allowing the team to detect and correct data imbalances before they impact performance.
- **Leverage Caching for Frequently Accessed Data**
    - Cache frequently accessed data to reduce the load on partitions or shards, improving performance and reducing query latency.
    - **Tip**: Use AWS *ElastiCache with Redis or Memcached to cache results from cross-shard or cross-partition queries, reducing the need to query underlying data repeatedly.*
- **Design Applications to Minimize Cross-Shard Transactions**
    - Structuring applications to avoid cross-shard dependencies can reduce the need for complex transaction protocols and improve performance.

- **Tip**: *Where cross-shard transactions are necessary, use a query aggregator or distributed transaction protocol, such as two-phase commit, to manage consistency.*
- **Example**: A multi-tenant SaaS application isolates each customer's data to a specific shard, eliminating the need for cross-shard transactions and ensuring faster query responses.

- **Plan for Scaling with Data Growth**
  - Design a scalable architecture that allows for easy addition or removal of partitions or shards as data grows. Consider both vertical and horizontal scaling options to support data growth.
  - **Tip**: AWS *DynamoDB's automatic partitioning and scaling features simplify scaling management by adjusting partitions dynamically as data grows.*
- **Use Versioning and Backups for Data Integrity**
  - For systems requiring strict data integrity, enable versioning and backup policies to ensure data can be recovered or rolled back if issues arise during partitioning or sharding changes.
  - **Tip**: *Amazon S3 offers versioning to track changes to data, and* AWS Backup *provides centralized backup management, enabling quick recovery in case of data corruption.*

Applying Best Practices for Sharding in a Global E-Commerce Platform

Scenario: A global e-commerce platform with millions of users and products requires a scalable sharding strategy to handle user data, orders, and product catalog information efficiently.

- **Shard Key Design**: User data is sharded by hashing user IDs, ensuring balanced distribution across regions. Product catalog data is range-sharded by category, grouping related items together for efficient access.
- **Read Replicas for High-Read Workloads**: Read replicas are created for each shard to handle read-heavy workloads, ensuring that product details and user information can be accessed quickly during high-traffic periods.
- **Monitoring and Alerting with CloudWatch**: The platform uses CloudWatch to monitor shard utilization and replication lag, alerting the team to potential imbalances or latency spikes.
- **Caching for Popular Products**: Frequently accessed product data is cached in ElastiCache, reducing load on the primary shards and ensuring quick response times for popular items.

- **Scaling and Rebalancing**: As new products are added, the system automatically scales the product catalog shards to maintain a balanced load, with periodic rebalancing to distribute data evenly.

This setup allows the e-commerce platform to handle high traffic volumes, scale with data growth, and maintain performance across regions.

Conclusion

In this chapter, we navigated the vital concepts of partitioning and sharding, uncovering how these techniques form the backbone of scalable and efficient data management in distributed systems. By dividing large datasets into smaller, more manageable segments, partitioning and sharding allow systems to distribute workload evenly across nodes, improving performance and responsiveness under heavy demand. We explored a range of partitioning strategies—such as range-based, hash-based, and composite approaches—and their role in handling different data patterns and access requirements, providing a toolkit for optimizing data distribution.

Sharding takes partitioning to a broader level, enabling horizontal scaling that is essential for applications with high traffic and vast datasets. Through AWS examples and best practices, we learned how to design resilient architectures capable of handling complex workloads while maintaining performance and data integrity. As data volumes continue to expand, mastering partitioning and sharding becomes increasingly important to meet the evolving demands of distributed systems. With these foundational strategies in place, you are well-prepared to address the challenges of large-scale data management, ensuring your system can scale efficiently and remain resilient in any data landscape.

Building upon these sharding principles, we will now explore how consensus mechanisms and consistency models work together to ensure data reliability across distributed partitions. Understanding these foundational concepts is crucial for maintaining data integrity while scaling horizontally, especially when implementing sharding strategies in production environments.

CHAPTER 4
Ensuring Consistency: Consensus Mechanisms and Models

Introduction

In distributed systems, consistency and consensus are critical elements that ensure data accuracy and coherence across multiple nodes, even in the presence of failures and network partitions. Achieving consistency in a system where data is replicated across various nodes can be challenging, especially when nodes operate independently. Consensus mechanisms play an essential role in maintaining agreement across nodes, allowing distributed systems to function reliably even in unpredictable environments.

This chapter delves into the complexities of consistency models, exploring how distributed systems handle data updates and synchronization to maintain a unified view. We will also examine consensus algorithms such as Paxos and Raft, the building blocks of fault-tolerant distributed architectures. By understanding the principles of consistency and consensus, readers will gain insight into the sophisticated techniques that allow distributed systems to ensure data integrity, even in the most complex setups.

Structure

In this chapter, we will cover the following topics:

- Understanding Consistency Models
  - CAP Theorem and its Implications
  - Strong versus Eventual Consistency
- Consensus Mechanisms in Distributed Systems
  - Overview of Consensus Algorithms
  - Detailed Explanation of Paxos and Raft
- Implementing Consensus on AWS
  - Using AWS Aurora with Multi-Master Setup
  - AWS Services and Consistency Trade-offs
- Practical Considerations for Consistency in the Cloud
  - Network Latency and Availability Zones
  - When to Choose Strong Consistency Over Eventual

The CAP Theorem and Consistency Models

The CAP theorem, formulated by Eric Brewer, states that in a distributed data store, it is impossible to simultaneously guarantee **Consistency, Availability, and Partition Tolerance**. This theorem is fundamental to understanding trade-offs in distributed systems, where each of the three properties affects how data is managed and accessed across nodes.

- **Consistency:** Ensures that all nodes in the system see the same data at the same time. In other words, a read request will return the most recent write.
- **Availability:** Guarantees that every request receives a response, even if it cannot return the most recent data.
- **Partition Tolerance:** Allows the system to continue functioning despite network partitions, where nodes cannot communicate with each other.

According to the CAP theorem, a distributed system can only provide two of these three guarantees at any given time. For example, a system prioritizing consistency and availability may suffer during network partitions, while a system focusing on availability and partition tolerance may relax consistency during high-traffic events.

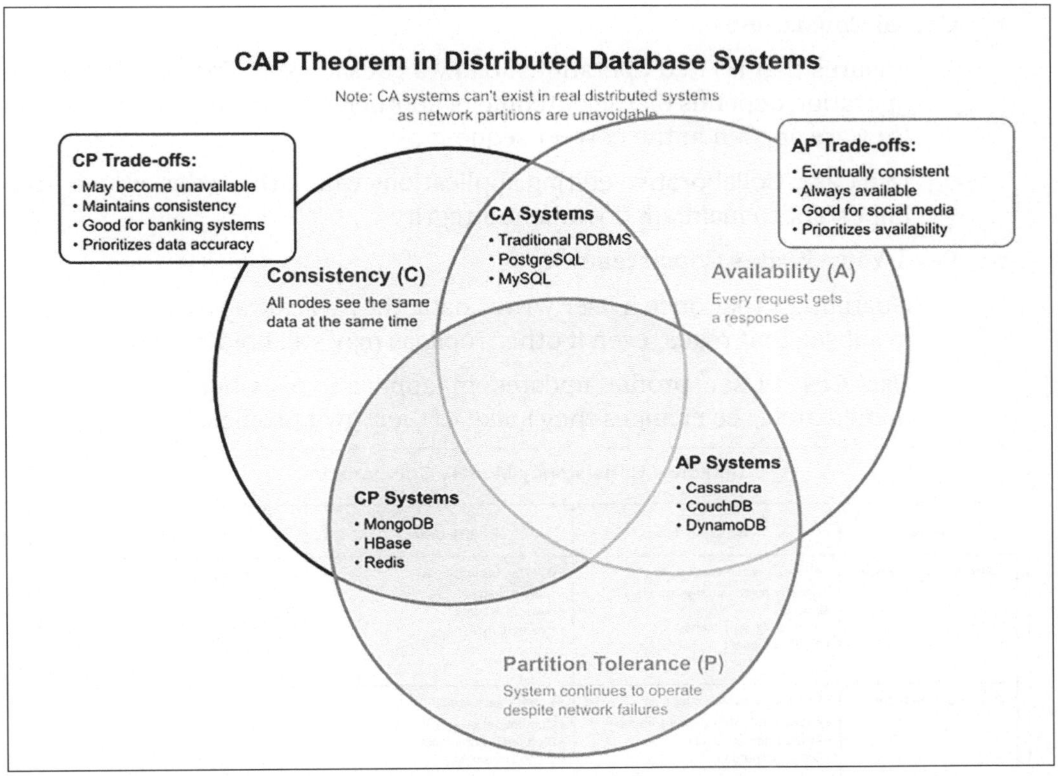

Figure 4.1: *CAP Theorem in Distributed Database Systems*

Types of Consistency Models

Consistency models define how data updates propagate across nodes and how soon replicas reflect the most recent data. Choosing a suitable consistency model depends on the application's requirements for data accuracy and performance.

- **Strong Consistency**
  - Guarantees that every read returns the most recent write. This model ensures that data is always accurate. However, it can introduce latency, as updates must be propagated to all nodes before responding to reads.
  - **Use Case**: Financial applications where transaction accuracy is critical.
- **Eventual Consistency**
  - Allows replicas to return stale data, with the guarantee that, over time, all nodes will converge to the same state. This model prioritizes availability and performance over immediate accuracy.
  - **Use Case**: Social media platforms where a slight delay in reflecting new posts across users is acceptable.

- **Causal Consistency**
  - Ensures that related operations follow a causal order. For instance, if one operation depends on the outcome of another, causal consistency ensures they are applied in the correct sequence.
  - **Use Case**: Collaborative editing applications where the order of updates is important to maintain document integrity.
- **Read-Your-Writes Consistency**
  - Guarantees that once a user writes data, they will always see their update in subsequent reads, even if other replicas may still hold stale data.
  - **Use Case**: User profile updates in applications, where users should immediately see changes they make to their own profiles.

Database Consistency Models Comparison

Model	Characteristics	Use Cases	Trade-offs
Strong Consistency	• All reads return latest write • Synchronized updates across all nodes • Immediate consistency • ACID compliant	• Banking transactions • Stock trading • Medical records • Payment systems	✓ Highest accuracy ✓ Data integrity ✗ Higher latency ✗ Reduced availability
Eventual Consistency	• Replicas converge over time • Allows temporary inconsistencies • Asynchronous updates • BASE properties	• Social media feeds • Content delivery • Blog posts/comments • Video streaming	✓ High availability ✓ Low latency ✗ Temporary inconsistencies ✗ Complex conflict resolution
Causal Consistency	• Preserves operation order • Maintains dependencies • Partial ordering of events • Tracks causal relationships	• Collaborative editing • Chat applications • Version control • Discussion threads	✓ Ordered updates ✓ Logical consistency ✗ Metadata overhead ✗ Complex implementation
Read-Your-Writes	• User sees own updates • Session consistency • Client-centric model • Per-user guarantees	• User profiles • Personal settings • Document editing • User preferences	✓ Good user experience ✓ Session guarantee ✗ Session tracking overhead ✗ Complex session management

✓ Advantage *✗ Disadvantage*

Figure 4.2: *Database Consistency models comparison*

Applying Consistency Models in AWS

AWS provides various services with configurable consistency models, enabling users to align data handling with specific application needs.

- **Amazon DynamoDB**
  - Offers both eventual consistency and strong consistency for read operations. By default, DynamoDB uses eventual consistency to provide

faster reads, but users can opt for strong consistency when accuracy is essential.

- **Amazon S3**
  - Provides eventual consistency for overwriting PUTS and DELETES in the US Standard region, while newer regions offer strong read-after-write consistency for objects. This model is suitable for applications needing fast access to updated data.
- **Amazon RDS**
  - Ensures strong consistency across replicas in Multi-AZ deployments, making it suitable for transactional applications that require accurate data across zones.

Example: An e-commerce application may use DynamoDB's eventual consistency model for inventory data to ensure high availability and performance while using RDS for payment transactions where strong consistency is critical.

Trade-offs in Consistency Models

Choosing a consistency model involves trade-offs between performance, availability, and data accuracy. For instance:

- **Strong Consistency** provides data accuracy but may reduce availability during network issues.
- **Eventual Consistency** offers high availability and performance but can introduce data staleness.

These trade-offs highlight that the "*best*" model depends on specific application requirements and tolerance for inconsistency. Systems such as Amazon DynamoDB allow developers to choose the desired consistency level per read operation, providing flexibility to balance consistency needs on a case-by-case basis.

Consensus Mechanisms in Distributed Systems

In distributed systems, achieving **consensus**—or agreement—among multiple, independent nodes is essential to maintain data consistency and coordinate actions. Consensus mechanisms ensure that all nodes agree on a particular data value or state, even in the presence of failures or network issues. Consensus algorithms are the foundation of fault-tolerant distributed systems, enabling nodes to function reliably and cohesively.

Consensus mechanisms play a critical role in applications requiring strong data integrity, such as financial systems, database replication, and blockchain networks. In this section, we will explore two widely used consensus algorithms—**Paxos** and

Raft–both of which ensure that distributed systems reach agreement in a reliable and consistent manner.

Paxos: A Foundation of Consensus

The **Paxos** algorithm, introduced by Leslie Lamport, is one of the earliest and most influential consensus mechanisms. Paxos is designed to handle failures while ensuring that most nodes reach agreement on a proposed value.

- **Working of Paxos:**
  - Paxos divides consensus into three roles: **Proposers**, **Acceptors**, and **Learners**.
  - Proposers suggest values, Acceptors vote on proposals, and Learners receive the agreed-upon value.
  - Consensus is achieved when most Acceptors agree on a value, allowing the system to proceed.
- **Phases of Paxos:**
  - **Prepare Phase**: The Proposer sends a prepare request with a proposal ID to all Acceptors. Acceptors promise not to accept proposals with lower IDs than the one received.
  - **Accept Phase**: If most Acceptors respond positively, the Proposer sends an accept request with the proposal value. Acceptors who have promised to accept the proposal ID will accept the value.
  - **Commit Phase**: Once a majority accepts the proposal, the value is committed, and Learners are informed of the final decision.
- **Strengths and Limitations:**
  - Paxos is highly reliable and fault-tolerant, capable of functioning with most nodes operational.
  - However, Paxos is known for its complexity and high messaging overhead, making it challenging to implement in practical systems.

Example: Google's **Chubby** lock service, used internally for coordination within distributed systems, relies on a variant of Paxos to ensure consistency and prevent conflicts in distributed locks.

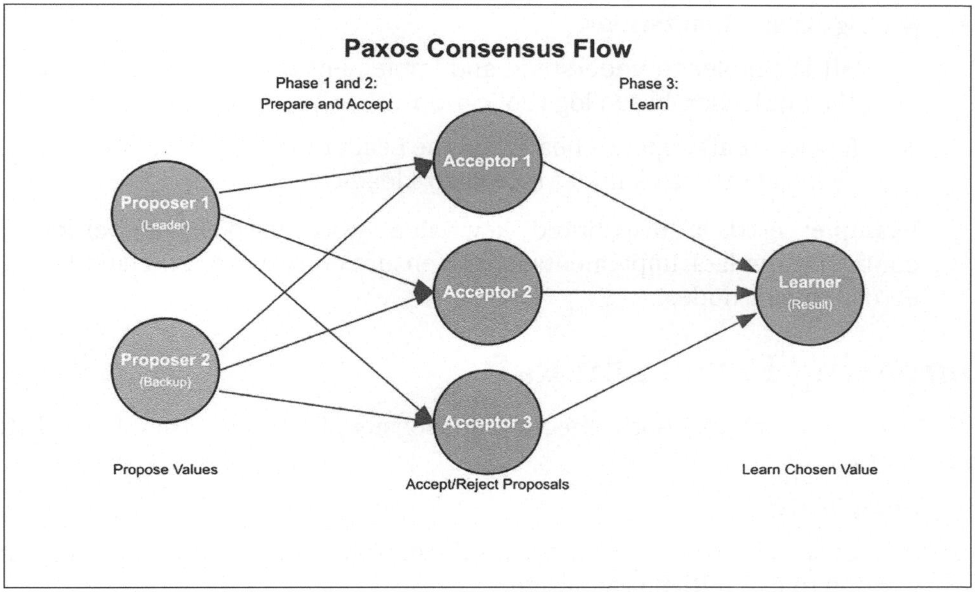

Figure 4.3: *Paxos Consensus Flow*

Raft: A Simpler Alternative to Paxos

The Raft algorithm, developed by Diego Ongaro and John Ousterhout, was designed to provide a more understandable and implementable alternative to Paxos. Raft simplifies the process of reaching consensus, making it more accessible for practical use in distributed systems.

- **Working of Raft:**
  - Raft divides the system into three roles: **Leaders**, **Followers**, and **Candidates**.
  - The Leader is responsible for managing all client interactions and directing Followers. Followers accept instructions from the Leader, while Candidates arise during leader elections.
- **Phases of Raft:**
  - **Leader Election**: When a system starts or the Leader fails, an election is triggered. Followers can become Candidates, requesting votes to become the new Leader. Once most nodes agree, a new Leader is elected.
  - **Log Replication**: The Leader replicates log entries (data updates) to all Followers, who then acknowledge the entries. The Leader commits entries once the majority acknowledge them, ensuring consistency.
  - **Commit and Apply**: Once entries are committed, they are applied to the system's state, allowing all nodes to reflect the most recent data.

- **Strengths and Limitations:**
  - Raft is simpler to understand and implement than Paxos, and it provides efficient leader-based log replication.
  - However, Raft depends heavily on the Leader for log replication, which can create a bottleneck under heavy workloads.

  Example: etcd, a distributed key-value store used by Kubernetes for configuration data, implements Raft to ensure consistency and fault tolerance across cluster nodes.

Comparing Paxos and Raft

While Paxos and Raft are both effective consensus algorithms, they have distinct characteristics:

- **Complexity:**
  - Paxos is known for its theoretical rigor but can be difficult to implement due to its multi-phase design.
  - Raft is designed for simplicity, providing a structured approach to leader election and log replication, making it easier to deploy.
- **Performance:**
  - Paxos requires more messaging overhead as it relies on multiple rounds of agreement, which can impact performance in high-latency environments.
  - Raft's leader-based replication is efficient, though it can suffer from single-point bottlenecks if the Leader becomes overloaded.
- **Reliability:**
  - Both algorithms are fault-tolerant, able to operate with most nodes available, and both handle network partitions effectively.

Feature	Paxos	Raft
Complexity	High, more difficult to implement	Low, easier to understand
Performance	High messaging overhead	Leader-based, efficient replication
Role Structure	Proposers, Acceptors, Learners	Leader, Followers, Candidates
Use Case	Highly critical, complex systems	Systems prioritizing simplicity

Table 4.1: *Paxos versus Raft comparison*

Applications of Consensus Mechanisms in Distributed Systems

Here are some applications of Consensus Mechanisms in Distributed Systems:

- **Distributed Databases:**
  - Consensus mechanisms are essential in distributed databases, where nodes must agree on the order and content of data updates. For example, databases such as **Google Spanner** use consensus algorithms to ensure that all replicas reflect consistent data.
- **Distributed Coordination Services:**
  - Services such as **ZooKeeper** use consensus to manage distributed locks, configuration data, and leader election. Consensus ensures that even during network failures, only one node holds a lock or acts as the primary.
- **Blockchain and Cryptocurrency Networks:**
  - Consensus algorithms such as **Proof of Work** or **Proof of Stake** in blockchain networks share similarities with Paxos and Raft by ensuring agreement across a decentralized system. These mechanisms allow nodes to maintain a single view of the blockchain ledger.

Example: In financial services, consensus mechanisms are used to maintain consistent transaction records across globally distributed databases, ensuring that financial transactions are accurately recorded and synchronized across multiple nodes.

Practical Applications of Consistency and Consensus Mechanisms in AWS

AWS provides a robust platform for building distributed systems, supporting various consistency and consensus models to meet the needs of scalable applications. By implementing consistency models and consensus mechanisms, AWS enables organizations to balance data accuracy, availability, and fault tolerance in distributed environments. This section explores practical applications of these principles in AWS services such as **Amazon DynamoDB**, **Amazon RDS**, and **Amazon ElastiCache**, showcasing how consistency and consensus are applied in real-world scenarios.

Consistency in Amazon DynamoDB

Amazon DynamoDB offers configurable consistency models, allowing users to choose between **eventual consistency** and **strong consistency** based on their application's requirements:

- **Eventual Consistency:**
  - DynamoDB's default consistency model is eventual consistency, providing faster read operations with potential data staleness.
  - **Use Case**: E-commerce platforms often use eventual consistency for

product catalog data, ensuring availability while tolerating slight delays in updates across regions.

- **Strong Consistency:**
  - For applications needing accurate, real-time data, DynamoDB offers strongly consistent reads, ensuring that each read reflects the latest committed write.
  - **Use Case**: Financial applications using DynamoDB for transaction records benefit from strong consistency, ensuring that all updates are immediately available to users.

Example: A gaming platform uses DynamoDB for player profiles, opting for strong consistency to ensure players' recent game achievements are reflected in real-time. This consistency model guarantees a seamless experience for users interacting with sensitive or fast-changing data.

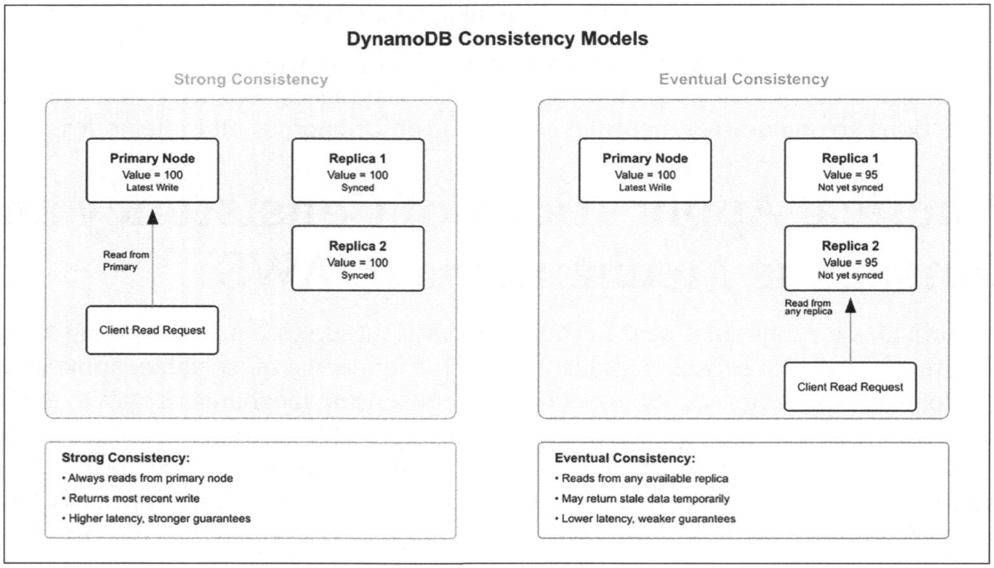

Figure 4.4: *DynamoDB consistency models*

Consensus in Amazon RDS Multi-AZ

In Amazon RDS, Multi-AZ deployments rely on a consensus-like mechanism to ensure high availability and data consistency. This setup automatically replicates data across multiple Availability Zones (AZs) and performs automatic failover in case of a primary instance failure:

- **Synchronous Replication:**
  - RDS Multi-AZ uses synchronous replication, which keeps a secondary

replica up-to-date with the primary instance. This ensures data consistency across the primary and standby replicas.

- **Automatic Failover:**
  - If the primary instance becomes unavailable, the secondary instance is automatically promoted to primary, maintaining service continuity with minimal disruption.

Example: An online banking application uses Amazon RDS Multi-AZ with synchronous replication to maintain transaction consistency across zones. If the primary instance in one AZ fails, the system seamlessly shifts to the standby instance, ensuring consistent and reliable access to critical financial data.

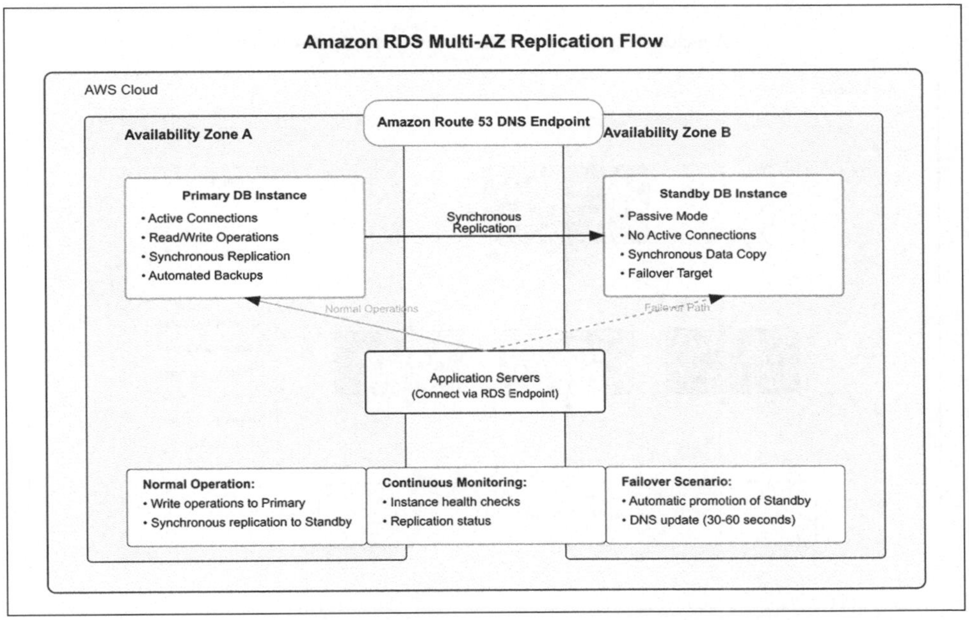

Figure 4.5: *Amazon RDS Multi-AZ Replicated Flow*

Distributed Cache Consistency with Amazon ElastiCache

Amazon ElastiCache provides caching solutions that enhance performance for read-heavy applications, with options for ensuring data consistency across distributed cache nodes.

- **Read Replicas for Consistency:**
  - ElastiCache Redis supports read replicas to distribute read requests while maintaining data consistency. Updates to the primary cache node are

replicated across read replicas, ensuring that frequently accessed data remains consistent.

- **Cluster Mode for Horizontal Scalability:**
  - In ElastiCache Redis Cluster mode, data is sharded across multiple nodes with replicas for fault tolerance. Redis Cluster mode employs a consensus mechanism to promote replicas to primary in case of node failure, maintaining both availability and consistency.

Example: A social media platform uses ElastiCache with Redis Cluster mode for caching user feeds. The cluster configuration allows high scalability, with consistent data available across replicas to provide users with up-to-date content.

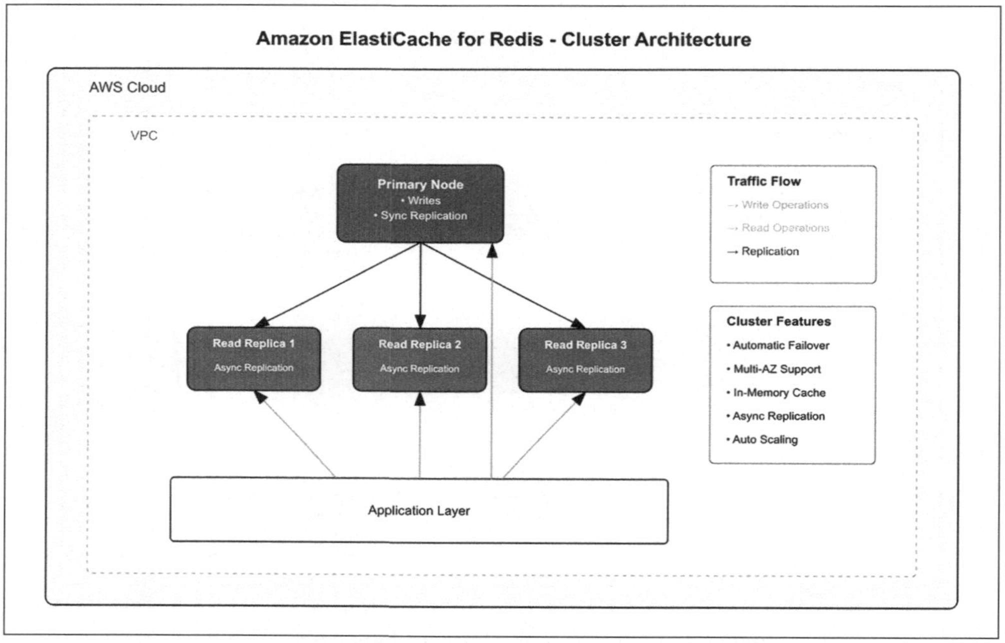

Figure 4.6: *Amazon ElastiCache for Redis - Cluster Architecture*

Amazon QLDB and Blockchain-Like Consensus Mechanisms

Amazon Quantum Ledger Database (QLDB) offers an immutable and cryptographically verifiable transaction log, ensuring data consistency and integrity akin to blockchain networks. QLDB achieves consensus through its unique journal structure, maintaining an ordered, append-only record of all changes:

- **Immutable Ledger:**
  - QLDB's ledger structure prevents tampering, allowing businesses to

maintain a transparent history of transactions. Each transaction is cryptographically chained to the previous one, preserving the integrity of data.

- **Verification of Data Integrity:**
  - QLDB uses cryptographic hashing to ensure that data cannot be altered or removed once committed to the ledger. This provides a trust layer for applications requiring verified data history, such as auditing and compliance.

Example: A supply chain management application uses QLDB to track product movements. QLDB's built-in consistency and verification mechanisms enable the application to ensure data accuracy across distributed participants in the supply chain, preventing tampering and maintaining an auditable trail of activities.

Implementing Consensus and Consistency in Microservices with AWS Step Functions

For complex workflows involving multiple microservices, AWS Step Functions enable orchestration with integrated support for maintaining data consistency and reliability:

- **State Management and Coordination:**
  - Step Functions coordinate multiple services, ensuring each step in a workflow is completed before proceeding to the next. This consistency mechanism prevents data inconsistencies in interdependent processes.
- **Error Handling and Rollbacks:**
  - Step Functions offer built-in error handling and retry policies, providing a level of fault tolerance similar to consensus mechanisms. In cases of failure, workflows can roll back to a previous state, ensuring consistent outcomes.

Example: A healthcare platform orchestrates patient records processing using Step Functions. If a step in the workflow fails (for example, data validation), Step Functions can trigger a retry or rollback to a consistent state, ensuring the integrity of patient data throughout the process.

Summary of AWS Consistency and Consensus Applications

AWS offers a range of services tailored for various levels of consistency and consensus, allowing architects to design applications that meet specific needs for data accuracy, availability, and fault tolerance:

Service	Consistency Model	Consensus Mechanism	Use Case
DynamoDB	Eventual and Strong Consistency	N/A	Scalable NoSQL database with configurable consistency
RDS Multi-AZ	Strong Consistency	Automatic Failover	High-availability database with transactional consistency
ElastiCache	Strong Consistency via Replicas	Replica Promotion in Clusters	Caching with read replicas and horizontal scalability
QLDB	Immutable Ledger with Consistency	Cryptographic Verification	Applications needing tamper-proof data integrity
Step Functions	Consistency via Workflow states	Error Handling and Rollbacks	Orchestration of microservices with consistency controls

Table 4.2: *AWS Consistency and Consensus applications*

Example Summary: A financial application might use RDS Multi-AZ for transaction data, DynamoDB for scalable user data storage, and Step Functions for orchestrating interdependent processes, ensuring data accuracy and consistency across services.

Trade-offs and Design Considerations in Consistency and Consensus

In distributed systems, maintaining consistency and achieving consensus across nodes requires navigating a series of trade-offs. These trade-offs arise because improving one aspect of the system–such as availability or speed–often impacts another, such as data accuracy or fault tolerance. This section delves into these trade-offs, guiding architects in making informed decisions that balance the needs of their applications.

One of the fundamental trade-offs is between **strong consistency** and **high availability**. Strongly consistent systems ensure that all nodes reflect the most recent data, which is critical in applications such as financial services. However, this consistency can come at the cost of availability or latency, as nodes may need to wait for each other to synchronize. Meanwhile, eventually consistent systems prioritize availability, allowing nodes to serve data even if updates have not yet propagated across the entire network. This approach is suitable for applications where data staleness is tolerable, such as social media platforms.

Key Considerations When Choosing Consistency Levels:

- Application Requirements:

  - Assess whether the application demands real-time data accuracy or if it can tolerate eventual consistency. Mission-critical applications such as healthcare systems often require strict consistency, while applications such as e-commerce catalog browsing can work with eventual consistency.
- **Latency Tolerance:**
  - Strong consistency generally introduces latency, as nodes must synchronize before responding to requests. For applications prioritizing low latency (for instance, gaming), eventual consistency may be more suitable to ensure responsive performance.
- **Network Stability and Partition Tolerance:**
  - In systems where network partitions are likely, eventual consistency allows the system to remain available, even if updates are temporarily out of sync. Applications in geographically distributed environments may prefer eventual consistency to ensure that users in different regions can continue accessing services during partitions.
- **Scalability Needs:**
  - Strong consistency can limit scalability, as each node may need to participate in data synchronization. For applications requiring massive scalability, such as IoT systems, eventual consistency or partial consistency can enhance performance while reducing synchronization overhead.

Example: An IoT platform with devices distributed worldwide may use eventual consistency for sensor data, allowing devices to report data without waiting for network confirmation. For control settings that impact device behavior, strong consistency may be applied to ensure accurate commands.

Balancing Consensus and System Performance

Consensus mechanisms such as Paxos and Raft are essential for ensuring that distributed nodes agree on a single source of truth, especially during failures. However, achieving consensus can introduce overhead, impacting performance and scalability. When designing systems with consensus mechanisms, it is essential to weigh these factors carefully.

- **Performance Impact of Consensus:**
  - Consensus mechanisms require multiple communication rounds to confirm agreement among nodes. This overhead can increase latency, which is a critical consideration for applications that prioritize speed and responsiveness.

- **Choosing Between Paxos and Raft:**
  - For applications requiring high fault tolerance and strict data integrity, Paxos offers a reliable yet complex solution. However, if the application prioritizes simplicity and performance, Raft's leader-based approach may provide a more practical choice.
  - **Example**: A distributed file storage service may use Paxos to maintain data consistency across nodes, while a simpler microservices architecture might opt for Raft to coordinate service instances with minimal messaging overhead.
- **Read and Write Patterns:**
  - Systems with heavy read and write demands may face bottlenecks if consensus mechanisms are applied universally. Selective use of consensus, only focusing on critical data, can reduce load while maintaining data integrity where it matters most.
- **Cost Considerations:**
  - Achieving consensus in distributed systems can drive up costs due to the increased need for messaging, storage, and processing resources. For cost-sensitive applications, consider designing a hybrid approach that uses consensus selectively, applying it only to crucial parts of the system.

Designing for Consistency and Consensus in Real-World Applications

Building applications that maintain data consistency and achieve consensus across distributed systems demands a delicate balance between theoretical guarantees and practical performance requirements in production environments.

- **Hybrid Consistency Models:**
  - Many modern systems adopt a hybrid approach, where critical components operate with strong consistency, and less critical data uses eventual or causal consistency. This design enables a balance between accuracy and efficiency.
  - **Example**: In an online retail platform, the inventory management system might enforce strong consistency to prevent overselling, while the product recommendation engine operates with eventual consistency to prioritize speed.
- **Using AWS Services for Trade-off Optimization:**
  - AWS offers various services to help manage consistency and consensus, enabling flexible design choices:

1. **DynamoDB**: Allows users to choose between strong and eventual consistency on a per-request basis.
2. **RDS Multi-AZ**: Provides strong consistency for failover scenarios, suitable for transactional applications.
3. **ElastiCache**: Supports read replicas to distribute load and maintain data consistency across multiple cache nodes.

- **Consistency Tuning Based on User Requirements:**
  - For applications with varied user needs, tuning consistency levels based on user profiles or operational context can optimize both experience and performance.
  - **Example**: A news platform might serve breaking news with strong consistency to paid subscribers while providing eventually consistent data to free users, balancing performance with service tiers.

Summary: Making Informed Design Choices

Balancing consistency and consensus mechanisms in distributed systems requires a deep understanding of application demands, user expectations, and resource constraints. Strong consistency and strict consensus provide reliability but can hinder performance and increase costs, while eventual consistency and selective consensus improve scalability but may introduce temporary data staleness.

Choosing the right mix of consistency and consensus depends on the specific requirements of each application component. By leveraging the flexible service configurations offered by AWS, architects can design distributed systems that achieve a well-rounded balance, meeting performance goals while ensuring data accuracy where it matters most.

Conclusion

In this chapter, we examined the essential role of consistency and consensus in distributed systems, exploring the CAP theorem, various consistency models, and consensus algorithms such as Paxos and Raft. Consistency ensures data accuracy across nodes, while consensus mechanisms enable distributed systems to reach agreement on data values, even in the presence of network failures or node outages. Through this chapter, we have seen how these foundational principles support fault tolerance, data integrity, and operational continuity in complex, large-scale systems.

By leveraging AWS services such as DynamoDB, RDS, and ElastiCache, developers can apply these principles practically, choosing consistency and consensus models tailored to their application's needs. We also discussed the trade-offs involved in selecting different models, from the strict accuracy of strong consistency to the performance-focused benefits of eventual consistency. Understanding these trade-offs empowers architects to design distributed systems that balance availability, accuracy, and efficiency—ensuring data reliability without compromising on scalability or performance.

Building upon these principles of consistency and consensus, the next chapter examines the foundations of load balancing and scaling strategies in distributed systems. From basic algorithms like Round Robin to advanced AWS implementations using Elastic Load Balancing and Auto Scaling Groups, we'll explore both horizontal and vertical scaling approaches. The chapter provides practical insights into optimizing resource distribution and cost efficiency, essential for architects designing systems that dynamically adapt to varying workloads.

CHAPTER 5
Balancing the Load: Achieving Performance and Efficiency

Introduction

As data-driven applications expand in scope and scale, efficiently distributing workloads becomes essential to maintaining performance and user experience. Load balancing and horizontal scaling are key strategies in distributed systems, enabling the distribution of incoming requests across multiple servers, preventing bottlenecks, and supporting applications that handle heavy traffic or complex computations. Load balancing ensures that no single server is overwhelmed, while horizontal scaling enables systems to increase capacity by adding more nodes rather than upgrading existing ones. Together, these techniques allow distributed systems to achieve reliability, high availability, and scalability, even under dynamic and fluctuating demand.

In this chapter, we will explore the mechanisms and strategies for load balancing and horizontal scaling, focusing on design patterns, best practices, and real-world implementations. We will examine various load-balancing algorithms, scaling strategies, and specific tools available within AWS that support seamless scaling and traffic distribution. By understanding these foundational concepts, you will gain insight into designing systems capable of handling both predictable growth and sudden surges in demand.

Structure

In this chapter, we will cover the following topics:

- Introduction to Load Balancing
    - Role of Load Balancers in Distributed Systems
    - Types of Load Balancing Strategies (Round Robin, Least Connections)
- Horizontal versus Vertical Scaling
    - Benefits of Horizontal Scaling
    - Challenges in Achieving True Scalability
- Implementing Load Balancing on AWS
    - Elastic Load Balancing (ELB) Types and Use Cases
    - Auto Scaling Groups and EC2 Scaling Strategies
- Optimizing Load Balancing and Scaling
    - Best Practices for Load Distribution
    - Cost-Efficiency and Resource Management

Load Balancing Fundamentals

Load balancing is the process of distributing incoming network traffic across multiple servers, ensuring that no single server bears too much load. It improves system performance, availability, and reliability by distributing requests efficiently and preventing any one server from becoming a bottleneck. Load balancing is especially critical in distributed systems, where workloads are spread across a network of nodes to handle large volumes of traffic and high availability requirements.

Key objectives of load balancing include:

- **Improving Availability:** Ensures that services remain accessible by distributing requests, reducing the impact of server failures.
- **Enhancing Performance:** Prevents overload on individual servers, maintaining optimal response times for users.
- **Ensuring Fault Tolerance:** If a server goes down, the load balancer redirects traffic to healthy servers, maintaining continuous service.

Types of Load Balancing

There are three types of load balancing:

- **Hardware load balancers:** Hardware load balancers are physical devices placed between client requests and servers, responsible for directing traffic based on defined algorithms. These devices offer robust performance but can be costly and lack the flexibility of software-based solutions.

Example: In a financial trading platform, a hardware load balancer ensures low-latency processing of trade transactions, leveraging dedicated hardware to deliver the performance required for high-speed operations.

- **Software Load Balancers:** Software load balancers are virtual solutions that distribute traffic across servers based on load balancing algorithms. They are highly flexible, scalable, and easier to configure compared to hardware solutions.

  Example: An e-commerce application uses a software load balancer to direct incoming requests to the least-busy server, allowing the application to handle variable traffic loads efficiently.

- **Cloud Load Balancers:** Cloud load balancers are managed services provided by cloud platforms such as AWS, Google Cloud, and Azure. These load balancers offer automatic scaling, ease of management, and integration with other cloud services.

  Example: A content delivery network (CDN) might use AWS Elastic Load Balancing (ELB) to route traffic based on geographic proximity, ensuring users receive content from the closest server, minimizing latency.

Types of Load Balancers Comparison

Type	Characteristics	Benefits	Use Cases
Hardware Load Balancers	• Physical devices • Dedicated hardware • Fixed capacity • Hardware-based processing	• Robust performance • Low latency • High reliability • Dedicated resources	• Financial trading • High-frequency trading • Enterprise apps • Mission-critical systems
Software Load Balancers	• Virtual solutions • Software-based algorithms • Configurable setup • Dynamic capacity	• High flexibility • Easy scalability • Simple configuration • Cost-effective	• E-commerce platforms • Web applications • Content delivery • Medium-sized businesses
Cloud Load Balancers	• Managed services • Cloud platform integration • Auto-scaling capability • Pay-as-you-go model	• Automatic scaling • Easy management • Cloud integration • Global availability	• Microservices • Cloud-native apps • Startups • Dynamic workloads

Figure 5.1: *Load Balancer Types Comparison*

Load Balancing Algorithms

Load balancers use algorithms to decide how to distribute incoming requests across servers. Common algorithms include:

- **Round Robin:**
  - Distributes requests sequentially across all available servers in a circular order.
  - **Use Case:** Suitable for applications with servers that have similar configurations and can handle an equal share of traffic.
- **Least Connections:**
  - Directs traffic to the server with the fewest active connections, balancing load based on real-time server demand.
  - **Use Case:** Ideal for applications with varying request durations, ensuring servers with fewer connections receive more requests.
- **Weighted Round Robin:**
  - Assigns weights to each server based on its capacity, directing more traffic to servers with higher capacity.
  - **Use Case:** Used in heterogeneous environments where servers have different performance levels, such as a mix of large and small instance types.
- **IP Hash:**
  - Routes requests based on the client's IP address, ensuring that subsequent requests from the same client are directed to the same server.
  - **Use Case:** Useful for applications that require session persistence, such as online gaming or video streaming.

Example: A video streaming service might use IP Hash to ensure that a user's session is consistently routed to the same server, providing a smooth playback experience.

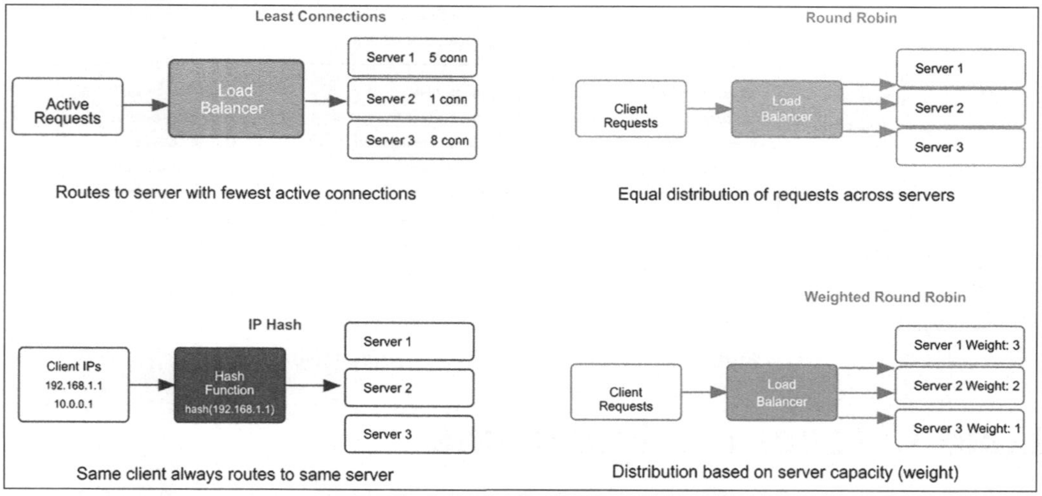

***Figure 5.2:** Load Balancing Algorithms*

AWS Load Balancing Solutions

AWS offers multiple load-balancing services that support flexible scaling and high availability for applications:

- **Elastic Load Balancing (ELB)**
  - ELB is a managed load-balancing service that distributes incoming traffic across multiple targets, such as EC2 instances, containers, and IP addresses. ELB supports different load balancers for specific needs:
    - **Application Load Balancer (ALB)**: Operates at the application layer (Layer 7) and is ideal for web applications that require content-based routing.
    - **Network Load Balancer (NLB)**: Operates at the network layer (Layer 4) and is optimized for applications requiring high throughput and low latency.
    - **Gateway Load Balancer (GLB)**: Manages and scales virtual appliances, such as firewalls or intrusion detection systems, for traffic inspection.
- **Amazon Route 53**
  - Route 53 is a managed DNS service of AWS with built-in load-balancing capabilities. It directs users to the closest endpoint based on geographic location, providing low-latency access for global users.
  - **Use Case**: Route 53 is commonly used with global applications, allowing users from different regions to connect to the nearest data center or edge location.
- **AWS Global Accelerator**
  - AWS Global Accelerator improves the availability and performance of applications by directing traffic across the global network of AWS, offering intelligent routing that bypasses congested areas in public internet routing.
  - **Use Case**: High-performance applications, such as gaming or media streaming, use Global Accelerator to reduce latency and improve user experience by leveraging the AWS backbone network.

Example Scenario: A global e-commerce platform may use ALB for routing traffic to microservices, NLB for low-latency database access, and Route 53 for geographic load balancing to ensure that users worldwide experience minimal latency.

Benefits and Challenges of Load Balancing

Load balancing provides significant advantages but also introduces unique challenges:

Benefits:

- **Improved Performance and Scalability**: Distributing requests across servers prevents individual nodes from overloading, allowing the system to scale as traffic increases.
- **Enhanced Fault Tolerance**: Load balancers detect and redirect traffic away from failed servers, maintaining service continuity.
- **Optimized Resource Utilization**: Load balancing ensures that resources are used efficiently, maximizing application performance across the infrastructure.

Challenges:

- **Session Persistence**: Some applications require users to interact with the same server throughout a session. Managing this persistence in a distributed setup can be complex.
- **Latency Overheads**: Load balancers introduce slight delays as they process and direct traffic, which can impact latency-sensitive applications.
- **Cost Considerations**: Using multiple load-balancing services or instances may increase operational costs, particularly in cloud environments.

Example Case Study: Load Balancing for a Social Media Application

Scenario: A social media platform with millions of active users requires a load balancing strategy to support its global audience. The platform handles various services, such as content feeds, real-time messaging, and profile management.

- **Application Load Balancer (ALB)**: The platform uses ALB to route traffic based on URL paths, directing requests for different services (for example, feeds, messages) to separate backend targets.
- **Network Load Balancer (NLB)**: For the messaging service, NLB routes traffic at low latency, ensuring real-time interactions between users.
- **Amazon Route 53**: Route 53 directs users to the nearest data center, reducing latency and improving user experience.
- **AWS Global Accelerator**: The platform uses Global Accelerator for high-demand content delivery, ensuring users receive quick access to multimedia content without network delays.

This multi-layered load-balancing architecture allows the social media application to provide a seamless experience, balancing load effectively while minimizing latency and maintaining high availability.

Horizontal Scaling Techniques

Horizontal scaling, also known as **scaling out**, involves adding more nodes to a system rather than upgrading existing nodes (vertical scaling). This approach allows distributed systems to increase capacity and handle growing demand by adding resources to a cluster, enhancing performance and fault tolerance without disrupting existing services. Horizontal scaling is foundational for achieving high availability and scalability, particularly in cloud environments, where adding nodes is more cost-effective and flexible than upgrading physical servers.

Horizontal scaling is often used in conjunction with load balancing, which distributes traffic across multiple nodes to prevent bottlenecks. Together, these techniques enable distributed systems to meet the demands of high-traffic applications and maintain consistent performance during usage spikes.

Techniques for Horizontal Scaling

Here are the techniques used for Horizontal Scaling:

- **Stateless Architecture**
    - Stateless architectures separate application logic from the data stored, allowing nodes to handle requests independently. This approach enables seamless scaling by adding more nodes, each capable of serving requests without needing to retain state.
    - **Use Case**: Stateless architecture, which allows any node in the cluster to process each request, benefits web applications that serve static content like HTML or images.
- **Microservices Architecture**
    - Microservices break down applications into smaller, self-contained services that communicate over APIs. Each microservice can be scaled independently, allowing horizontal scaling to target specific services with high demand.
    - **Use Case**: E-commerce platforms with separate services for product catalog, payments, and user accounts can scale each service individually based on usage patterns.
- **Auto Scaling Groups (ASG)**
    - Auto Scaling Groups dynamically add or remove instances based on predefined metrics, such as CPU utilization or network traffic. This ensures that the system scales according to real-time demand, optimizing resource usage and cost.
    - **Use Case**: Media streaming services often use ASGs to scale instances

during peak hours and reduce capacity during off-peak times, maintaining cost-efficiency while supporting fluctuating demand.

- **Containerization and Orchestration**
    - Containers allow applications to run consistently across different environments. By using orchestration platforms such as Kubernetes, distributed systems can automatically scale containers to meet demand, providing efficient resource utilization.
    - **Use Case**: Cloud-native applications that rely on containerized microservices can use Kubernetes to manage scaling automatically, ensuring that resources match the current workload

Example: A mobile gaming platform uses a stateless architecture to handle game sessions, scaling out nodes as player demand increases. The system deploys Auto Scaling Groups for game servers and containerized services orchestrated by Kubernetes to maintain performance.

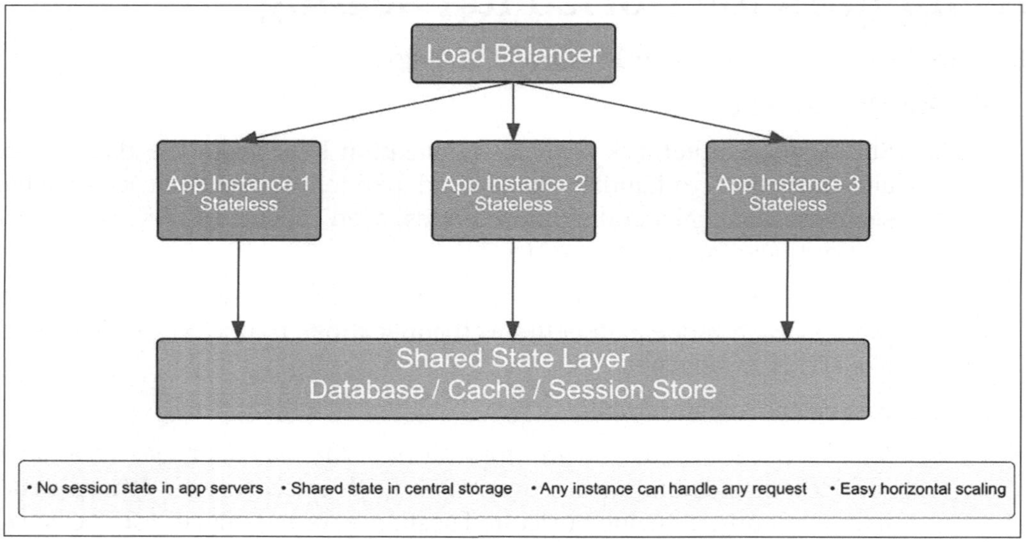

***Figure 5.3:** Stateless Architecture Scaling*

Figure 5.4 shows the architecture of microservices and containers:

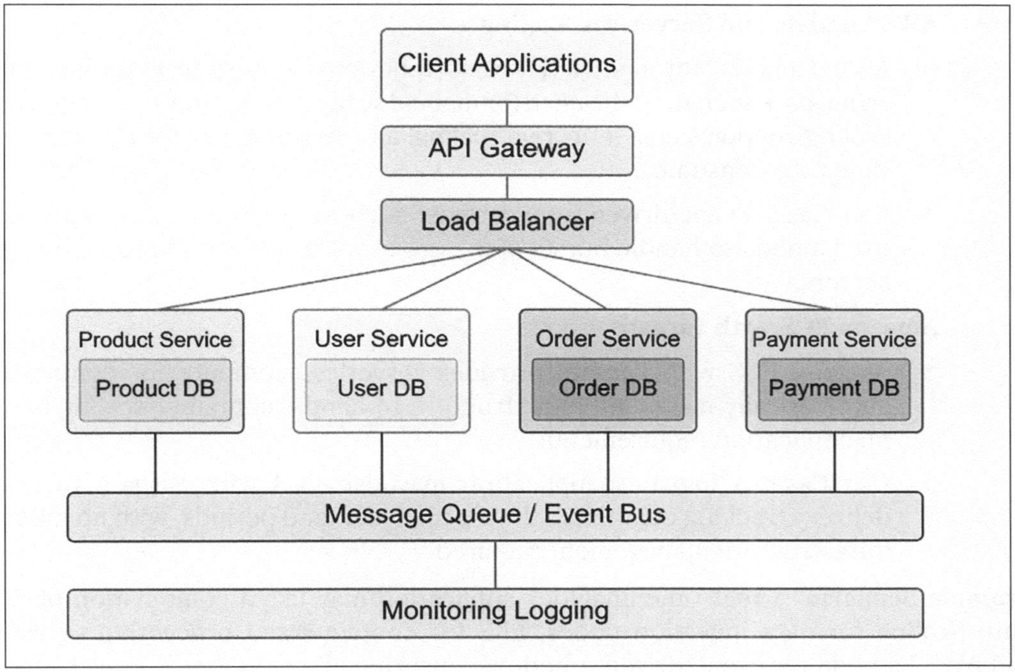

***Figure 5.4:** Microservices and Containers Architecture*

AWS Solutions for Horizontal Scaling

AWS provides a range of services designed to facilitate horizontal scaling, enabling applications to adapt to traffic spikes and meet growing demand.

- **Amazon EC2 Auto Scaling**
  - EC2 Auto Scaling allows applications to add or remove instances automatically based on demand. With customizable scaling policies, EC2 Auto Scaling helps optimize costs by adjusting instance counts based on real-time metrics.
  - **Use Case**: A SaaS application might use EC2 Auto Scaling to expand compute resources during peak hours and reduce instances during quieter periods.
- **AWS Elastic Kubernetes Service (EKS)**
  - Amazon EKS is a managed Kubernetes service that automates the deployment, scaling, and operation of containerized applications. EKS enables horizontal scaling of containers based on load, making it ideal for microservices-based applications.
  - **Use Case**: A healthcare platform can use EKS to handle patient data processing, scaling containers up or down as data intake fluctuates.

- **AWS Lambda and Serverless Scaling**
    - AWS Lambda automatically scales functions in response to incoming requests, eliminating the need for manual scaling configurations. Serverless scaling supports cost-effective scaling, as users only pay for the compute time they consume.
    - **Use Case**: Event-driven applications, such as notification systems, can use Lambda to handle bursts of messages without the need for dedicated servers.
- **Amazon ECS with Fargate**
    - Amazon ECS with Fargate provides serverless compute for containers, automatically managing infrastructure to handle container scaling based on application requirements.
    - **Use Case**: A logistics application may use ECS with Fargate to scale delivery tracking containers during high-demand periods, with no manual infrastructure management required.

Example Scenario: A real-time analytics application may use a combination of EC2 Auto Scaling for data ingestion nodes, EKS for containerized processing services, and AWS Lambda for event-driven functions, ensuring all components scale to meet varying data loads.

Best Practices for Horizontal Scaling

Here are the best practices:

- **Design for Failure and Redundancy**
    - In a horizontally scaled environment, designing for failure is critical. Each component should be able to fail without affecting the overall system. Redundancy ensures that if one node goes down, others can take over, maintaining uninterrupted service.
    - **Tip**: *Use EC2 Auto Scaling health checks and configure instances to automatically replace any failed nodes.*
- **Optimize Cost with Right-Sizing**
    - Right-sizing involves selecting instance types and sizes that match the application's workload. For cost-effective scaling, ensure that resources are neither underutilized nor oversized.
    - **Tip**: *Use AWS Cost Explorer to analyze usage patterns and adjust instance types or configurations accordingly.*
- **Implement Load Testing and Monitoring**
    - Before deploying horizontal scaling solutions, load testing helps identify

bottlenecks and ensures that scaling configurations meet performance goals. Continuous monitoring detects any potential issues as they arise.

    - **Tip**: *Use Amazon CloudWatch to monitor metrics such as CPU utilization, memory usage, and response time to evaluate the effectiveness of scaling policies.*

- **Employ Graceful Shutdown for Instance Termination**
    - When instances are scaled down, a graceful shutdown ensures that no requests are abruptly terminated. Configure applications to complete active requests before shutting down, maintaining a seamless experience.
    - **Tip**: *Configure EC2 Auto Scaling termination policies to allow instances to finish requests before they are terminated.*
- **Use Caching for Enhanced Performance**
    - Caching reduces the load on backend servers by storing frequently accessed data. This technique complements horizontal scaling by reducing repetitive database queries and speeding up response times.
    - **Tip**: *Use AWS ElastiCache to cache frequently requested data and reduce the load on horizontally scaled instances.*

Example Case Study: Horizontal Scaling for an E-Commerce Application

Scenario: An e-commerce platform needs to scale horizontally to handle increased traffic during seasonal sales. The application includes multiple services, such as product browsing, checkout, and order processing, each with distinct scaling requirements.

- **EC2 Auto Scaling for Product Catalog:** The product catalog service is hosted on EC2 instances with Auto Scaling policies based on CPU usage, allowing more instances to be added as browsing activity increases.
- **AWS Lambda for Order Notifications:** Order confirmation emails are handled by Lambda functions, which automatically scale to send notifications based on incoming orders, without requiring dedicated servers.
- **Amazon EKS for Checkout Microservices:** The checkout service runs on Amazon EKS, allowing the application to scale specific microservices, such as payment processing and inventory checks, independently to meet demand during high-traffic periods.
- **ElastiCache for Frequently Accessed Data:** The application uses ElastiCache to cache frequently accessed data, such as product details and user profiles, reducing load on backend instances and improving response times.

This horizontally scaled architecture allows the e-commerce platform to maintain performance and availability even during high-demand events, while optimizing costs and resource usage.

Auto Scaling Strategies and Best Practices

Auto Scaling is a dynamic scaling technique that automatically adjusts resources in response to real-time demand. By adding or removing instances based on predefined metrics, auto scaling ensures that applications maintain performance without over-provisioning resources. This approach optimizes cost-effectiveness by scaling out during traffic surges and scaling in during low-demand periods. AWS provides robust auto- scaling tools, such as **EC2 Auto Scaling**, **AWS Lambda scaling**, and **ECS/Fargate auto-scaling**, each designed to support different application architectures and scaling requirements.

Auto scaling is particularly valuable in cloud environments where traffic patterns can fluctuate unpredictably, enabling distributed systems to remain responsive and resilient under varying loads.

Types of Auto Scaling Policies

Following are the types of Auto Scaling Policies, detailing how each addresses specific scaling needs.

- **Dynamic Scaling**
    - Dynamic scaling policies adjust resources based on real-time metrics such as CPU usage, memory, or network traffic. These policies trigger resource changes only when demand thresholds are met.
    - **Example**: An online news platform with variable traffic loads can use dynamic scaling based on CPU utilization to ensure enough instances are running during peak hours.
- **Scheduled Scaling**
    - Scheduled scaling predefines scaling activities based on known traffic patterns, such as daily, weekly, or seasonal demand. This approach is ideal for applications with predictable usage trends.
    - **Example**: An e-commerce site anticipating high traffic during a holiday sale might use scheduled scaling to increase resources in advance, maintaining performance throughout the event.
- **Predictive Scaling**
    - Predictive scaling uses machine learning algorithms to anticipate future demand based on historical data, allowing the system to prepare for anticipated surges before they occur.
    - **Example**: A financial trading application with predictable peaks at market opening and closing times might use predictive scaling to add resources proactively, minimizing latency.

Auto Scaling Policies Comparison

Policy Type	Characteristics	Triggers	Use Cases
Dynamic Scaling	• Real-time adjustments • Reactive to current load • Metric-based decisions • Immediate response • Resource optimization	• CPU utilization • Memory usage • Network traffic • Request count • Queue length	• News websites • Social media platforms • Gaming servers • API services • Streaming platforms
Scheduled Scaling	• Planned adjustments • Time-based patterns • Proactive scaling • Regular intervals • Known peak handling	• Time of day • Day of week • Seasonal events • Business hours • Regular maintenance	• E-commerce sales • Business applications • Batch processing • Development environments • Regular backups
Predictive Scaling	• ML-based forecasting • Historical analysis • Pattern recognition • Proactive preparation • Continuous learning	• Historical patterns • Usage trends • Load forecasts • Seasonal variations • Growth trends	• Financial trading • Retail platforms • IoT applications • Ad serving systems • Content delivery

Figure 5.5: *Auto Scaling Policies comparison*

Auto Scaling in AWS

AWS provides a suite of auto-scaling solutions tailored to various services and architectures, allowing users to implement effective scaling strategies for different applications.

- **EC2 Auto Scaling**
  - EC2 Auto Scaling enables scaling based on demand, using metrics from Amazon CloudWatch to trigger actions. Policies can be configured for dynamic, scheduled, or predictive scaling.
  - **Use Case**: A SaaS platform running on EC2 instances might use EC2 Auto Scaling to automatically increase compute resources during onboarding spikes or software updates.
- **Application Auto Scaling for AWS Lambda**
  - AWS Lambda automatically scales to handle incoming requests, with no need for predefined instance counts. This serverless auto-scaling model adjusts the number of concurrent executions based on demand.
  - **Use Case**: A notification service using Lambda functions can handle bursts of messages by automatically scaling functions as request volumes fluctuate.

- **Amazon ECS and Fargate Auto Scaling**
  - For containerized applications, Amazon ECS and Fargate provide auto-scaling capabilities that adjust container counts based on demand. ECS also integrates with Elastic Load Balancing to distribute traffic evenly across containers.
  - **Use Case**: A machine learning inference service can use ECS auto-scaling to launch additional containers during intensive processing periods, scaling down once the workload decreases.
- **DynamoDB Auto Scaling**
  - Amazon DynamoDB can automatically adjust read and write throughput capacity based on application demand, ensuring efficient database operations.
  - **Use Case**: An IoT platform capturing sensor data in real-time can rely on DynamoDB auto-scaling to handle sudden spikes in data ingestion without manual adjustments.

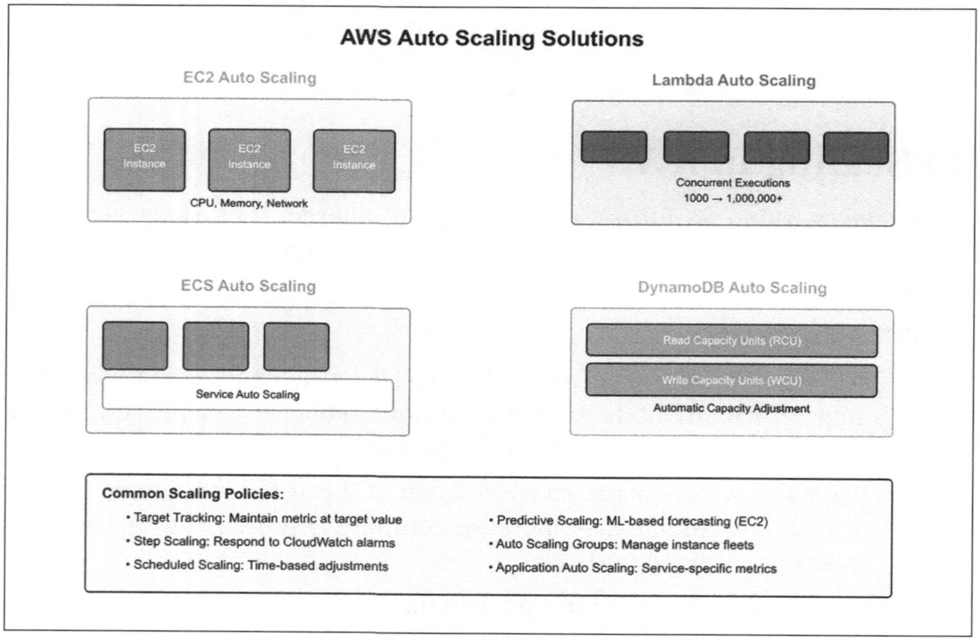

Figure 5.6: *AWS Auto Scaling Solutions*

Best Practices for Implementing Auto Scaling

Here are the best practices for implementing Auto Scaling:

- **Set Appropriate Scaling Policies and Thresholds**

  - Define scaling policies that match application requirements and usage patterns. Avoid overly sensitive thresholds that could lead to frequent scaling, which may increase costs without a significant performance gain.
  - **Tip**: *Use historical data to establish realistic thresholds for metrics such as CPU and memory utilization, balancing responsiveness with cost-effectiveness.*
- **Monitor and Optimize with CloudWatch Metrics**
  - Monitor metrics such as average response time, CPU utilization, and memory usage to assess the effectiveness of auto-scaling policies. AWS CloudWatch provides detailed insights that can help optimize scaling parameters.
  - **Tip**: *Set up CloudWatch alarms to notify you of unexpected spikes or drops in utilization, allowing for timely adjustments to scaling configurations.*
- **Avoid Over-Provisioning with Predictive Scaling**
  - Predictive scaling can help prevent over-provisioning by accurately forecasting demand based on historical data. This approach reduces idle resource costs while maintaining readiness for anticipated demand.
  - **Tip**: *Use predictive scaling in conjunction with other scaling policies, applying it to high-demand periods and relying on dynamic scaling for unpredictable fluctuations.*
- **Test Scaling Configurations with Load Testing**
  - Regular load testing helps ensure that scaling configurations perform as expected under various demand scenarios. Testing can reveal potential bottlenecks and ensure that resources scale appropriately.
  - **Tip**: *Use AWS Load Testing with simulated traffic to evaluate performance, refining scaling configurations based on test results.*
- **Implement Graceful Scaling for User Experience**
  - Graceful scaling prevents disruption by gradually adding or removing resources, ensuring that applications continue to serve requests seamlessly during scaling activities.
  - **Tip**: *Configure instances to complete ongoing tasks before scaling in, using lifecycle hooks for services such as EC2 Auto Scaling to manage transitions smoothly.*

Example Case Study

Auto Scaling is crucial for video streaming platforms to handle fluctuating user demand while maintaining performance and cost-efficiency. The following Example Case

Study—Auto Scaling for a Video Streaming Platform—demonstrates its implementation in a real-world scenario.

Auto Scaling for a Video Streaming Platform

Scenario: A video streaming platform needs to manage dynamic traffic loads, especially during major live events. The application must support both video-on-demand and live-streaming services, which have different demand patterns.

- **EC2 Auto Scaling for Streaming Servers**: The platform uses EC2 Auto Scaling to dynamically adjust the number of streaming servers based on CPU usage. During live events, the system adds instances to handle peak traffic, scaling down once the event concludes.
- **AWS Lambda for Event Notifications**: Notifications for new content releases are handled by AWS Lambda, which scales automatically to handle bursts of requests as users receive notifications and start streaming.
- **ECS Auto Scaling for Content Delivery**: Content delivery services run on Amazon ECS, with auto-scaling configured to add containers based on network traffic. The system uses Elastic Load Balancing to distribute user requests across containers efficiently.
- **Predictive Scaling for Demand Forecasting**: During popular show releases, the platform relies on predictive scaling to prepare resources in advance, ensuring a smooth user experience by proactively scaling streaming servers.

This layered auto-scaling strategy enables the video streaming platform to maintain high availability and responsiveness, even during high-traffic events, while optimizing costs and resource usage.

Monitoring and Optimizing Load Balancing and Scaling

In distributed systems, monitoring is crucial for maintaining performance, reliability, and cost-efficiency. Load balancing and scaling solutions are only effective when continuously monitored and optimized to match evolving workloads and traffic patterns. By observing real-time metrics and analyzing historical data, system administrators can detect performance bottlenecks, address under-utilized resources, and adjust scaling policies proactively. AWS provides a suite of monitoring tools, such as **Amazon CloudWatch**, **AWS CloudTrail**, and **AWS X-Ray**, that enable granular insights into application performance.

Effective monitoring not only supports efficient scaling but also enhances the overall user experience by reducing latency, preventing resource wastage, and maintaining high availability.

Key Metrics for Monitoring Load Balancing and Scaling

Monitoring load balancing and scaling requires tracking a set of critical metrics to ensure resources are used efficiently and requests are distributed effectively. Key metrics include:

- **CPU and Memory Utilization:**
  - Measures the workload on individual instances or containers. High utilization may indicate the need for more resources, while low utilization suggests over-provisioning.
  - **Example**: An application with consistent high CPU utilization may need to adjust its auto-scaling policy to add instances earlier, preventing resource saturation.
- **Request Latency and Response Time:**
  - Monitors the time taken for requests to be processed. Increased latency may signal bottlenecks, indicating that more instances or optimized routing is needed.
  - **Example**: An e-commerce site noticing rising response times during flash sales could optimize latency by adding instances or caching frequently requested data.
- **Instance or Container Health Status:**
  - Tracks the health of each instance or container, ensuring only healthy nodes receive traffic. Instances in unhealthy states should be automatically replaced by the load balancer or scaling group.
  - **Example**: In a microservices application, unhealthy containers can be terminated and replaced automatically, maintaining continuous service availability.
- **Network Throughput and Bandwidth:**
  - Measures the amount of data transferred across the network. Monitoring bandwidth ensures that applications remain within network limits, preventing throttling.
  - **Example**: A video streaming platform might monitor network throughput closely, scaling up servers when data transfer volumes peak to handle increased traffic smoothly.
- **Auto Scaling Activity and Scaling Actions:**
  - Provides insight into how often and when scaling actions are triggered, helping identify patterns or unnecessary scaling events that could be optimized.

- **Example**: A SaaS provider analyzing frequent scaling events could refine thresholds to reduce the frequency of scale-outs and scale-ins, balancing responsiveness and cost.

AWS Tools for Monitoring Load Balancing and Scaling

- **Amazon CloudWatch**
  - CloudWatch enables monitoring of performance metrics, setting alarms, and creating dashboards to visualize data. CloudWatch also integrates with Auto Scaling and Elastic Load Balancing, allowing metrics-based scaling and alert configurations.
  - **Use Case**: A media streaming service might set up CloudWatch alarms for high latency, triggering scaling events or notifications to administrators for real-time action.
- **AWS CloudTrail**
  - CloudTrail records account activity across AWS services, offering visibility into API calls and changes made to scaling and load-balancing configurations. This audit trail is invaluable for security and troubleshooting.
  - **Use Case**: A financial institution uses CloudTrail to monitor changes in Auto Scaling policies and ensure that no unauthorized modifications occur, maintaining regulatory compliance.
- **AWS X-Ray**
  - X-Ray provides end-to-end tracing, helping developers analyze and debug distributed applications. It identifies bottlenecks, traces request paths, and highlights areas where load balancing or scaling improvements are needed.
  - **Use Case**: A retail application may use X-Ray to trace customer requests through multiple services, identifying areas with high latency and optimizing load-balancing routes to improve performance.
- **Elastic Load Balancing (ELB) Access Logs**
  - ELB access logs capture detailed information about requests, including client IP addresses, response times, and load balancer actions. These logs provide insights into traffic patterns, helping optimize routing and scaling decisions.
  - **Use Case**: An online gaming platform could analyze ELB logs to identify high-traffic periods and pre-scale instances to ensure smooth performance for players.

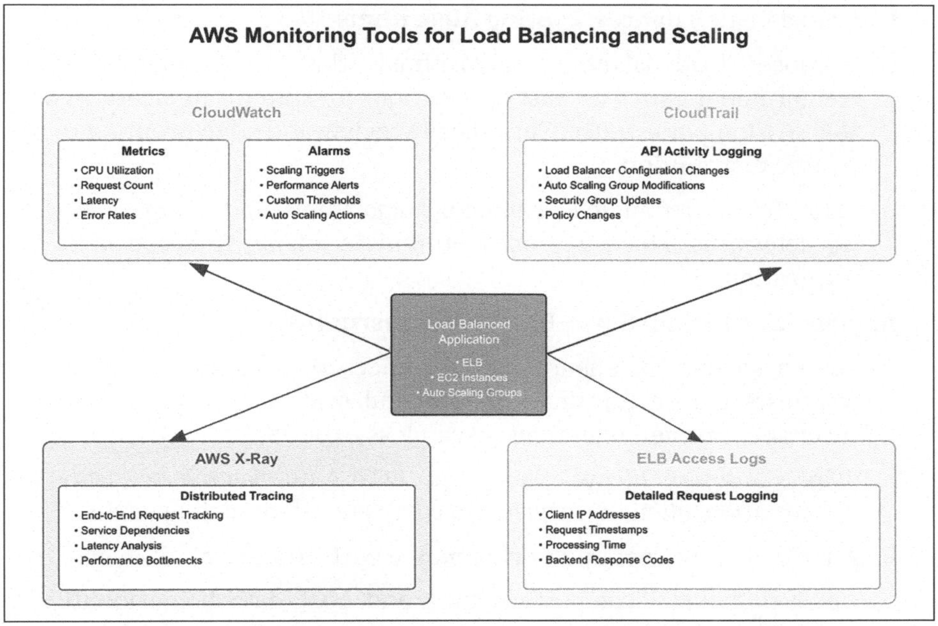

***Figure* 5.7:** *AWS Monitoring Tools for Load Balancing and Scaling*

Best Practices for Optimizing Load Balancing and Scaling

Optimizing load balancing and scaling is vital for ensuring application availability, performance, and cost-efficiency in dynamic environments.

- **Define and Refine Scaling Policies Based on Usage Patterns**
  - Regularly review and adjust scaling policies to align with real-time usage data and historical trends. Overly sensitive policies can lead to frequent scaling actions, while underresponsive policies may impact user experience.
  - **Tip**: *Use Amazon CloudWatch to analyze usage patterns, refining scaling policies to ensure that they are neither too conservative nor overly aggressive.*
- **Set Up Alarms and Alerts for Key Metrics**
  - Configuring alarms on critical metrics such as CPU utilization, latency, and instance health allows proactive management. Alerts provide real-time insights, enabling administrators to act before issues affect user experience.
  - **Tip**: *Create composite alarms for scenarios where multiple metrics signal potential problems, reducing the risk of false positives and unnecessary scaling actions.*

- **Optimize Load Balancer Routing Algorithms**
  - Choose load-balancing algorithms that best match application requirements, such as least connections for stateful applications or IP hash for session persistence. Periodically review and adjust routing to optimize traffic distribution.
  - **Tip**: *Test different load-balancing algorithms and compare performance to determine which approach minimizes latency and optimizes resource utilization.*
- **Implement Graceful Scale-In to Avoid Disruptions**
  - When scaling in, ensure that instances or containers complete active requests before termination. Graceful scale-in prevents disruptions in user sessions and maintains a seamless experience.
  - **Tip**: *Configure lifecycle hooks in* EC2 Auto Scaling *to delay instance termination, allowing requests to complete before scaling down.*
- **Regularly Review Cost and Performance with Historical Analysis**
  - Analyzing historical performance and cost data helps identify trends, providing insights into resource usage patterns. This data-driven approach allows optimization of scaling policies to balance cost-efficiency with performance.
  - **Tip**: *Use* AWS Cost Explorer *to track scaling costs and* Amazon CloudWatch *for performance metrics, enabling data-driven adjustments to improve cost-effectiveness.*

Example Case Study

Effective load balancing and scaling are critical for HealthTech applications to ensure reliability and responsiveness during peak usage. The following example case study highlights a practical implementation.

Optimizing Load Balancing and Scaling for a HealthTech Application

Scenario: A HealthTech application handling patient records and real-time data from medical devices requires efficient load balancing and scaling to ensure reliability and compliance.

- **Monitoring CPU and Memory with CloudWatch**: The application monitors CPU and memory usage on EC2 instances via CloudWatch, setting alarms for high utilization to trigger scale-outs. During off-peak hours, scale-in events reduce resource usage, optimizing costs.
- **End-to-End Tracing with AWS X-Ray**: AWS X-Ray traces patient data requests across multiple services to help identify bottlenecks in data processing

services. Optimizations are made based on X-Ray data to minimize latency and improve the patient experience.

- **ELB Access Logs for Compliance Monitoring**: ELB access logs track all incoming requests, providing an audit trail for regulatory compliance. The logs also identify peak times, allowing administrators to schedule scaling events to match predictable high-traffic periods.
- **Refining Scaling Policies with Historical Analysis**: Using CloudWatch's historical data, the application adjusts scaling thresholds to minimize frequent scaling actions, maintaining a stable environment while reducing costs.

This proactive monitoring and optimization strategy enables the HealthTech application to maintain high availability and compliance while ensuring that resources scale in alignment with real-time demand and usage patterns.

Conclusion

In this chapter, we explored the critical concepts of load balancing and horizontal scaling, two foundational techniques that empower distributed systems to handle fluctuating demand while maintaining high availability and performance. By distributing workloads across multiple nodes, load balancing prevents bottlenecks, enhances fault tolerance, and ensures that applications remain responsive even during peak traffic. Horizontal scaling, on the other hand, allows systems to grow by adding resources instead of upgrading individual components, enabling applications to scale seamlessly in response to demand.

Through practical examples and AWS solutions such as Elastic Load Balancing, EC2 Auto Scaling, AWS Lambda, and Amazon EKS, we examined strategies and best practices for implementing scalable and resilient architectures. We also emphasized the importance of monitoring and optimizing these solutions to maintain efficiency, minimize costs, and ensure a consistent user experience. Together, these techniques form a robust framework for designing distributed systems that can adapt to dynamic workloads, providing a reliable foundation for scalable, cloud-based applications.

In the next chapter, we will build upon these scaling concepts by exploring fault-tolerant architectures, focusing on how to design systems that can withstand and recover from various types of failures while maintaining service availability.

CHAPTER 6
Building Fault-Tolerant Architectures

Introduction

In distributed systems, monitoring and fault tolerance are essential components that safeguard applications against failures and ensure high availability. Distributed environments are inherently complex, with nodes spread across multiple locations and interconnected by networks that are vulnerable to latency, outages, and unexpected disruptions. Monitoring enables real-time visibility into the health, performance, and reliability of system components, allowing administrators to detect and resolve issues before they impact users. Fault tolerance, on the other hand, involves designing systems capable of continuing operation even when parts of the system fail, ensuring resilience and uninterrupted service.

This chapter explores the principles and practices of monitoring and fault tolerance in distributed systems, focusing on techniques to detect, diagnose, and mitigate issues effectively. We will also cover AWS tools and services, such as Amazon CloudWatch, AWS X-Ray, and AWS Elastic Load Balancing, which provide automated monitoring, fault detection, and recovery mechanisms. Through real-world examples and best practices, this chapter aims to equip readers with the skills to build and maintain resilient, self-healing systems capable of withstanding the challenges of distributed environments.

Structure

In this chapter, we will cover the following topics:

- Principles of Monitoring in Distributed Systems
  - Identifying Performance Bottlenecks
  - Role of Monitoring in Ensuring Reliability

- Fault Tolerance in Distributed Systems
  - Fault Detection
  - Redundancy and Failover Strategies
- Designing Self-Healing Systems in Distributed Architectures
  - Amazon Beanstalk for building Self-Healing Distributed Systems
  - Best Practices for Designing Self-Healing Distributed Systems
- Best Practices for Building Resilient Architectures
  - Strategies for Minimizing Downtime
  - Testing and Disaster Recovery in AWS

Principles of Monitoring in Distributed Systems

Monitoring is the process of collecting, analyzing, and visualizing data from system components to track performance, detect anomalies, and diagnose issues. In distributed systems, where services are often spread across multiple nodes, monitoring is crucial for maintaining visibility into each layer, from infrastructure to application performance. Effective monitoring provides insight into the health and availability of resources, allowing teams to respond quickly to issues, optimize performance, and make informed decisions.

Key objectives of monitoring include:

- **Ensuring System Health:** Monitoring helps maintain system uptime by identifying issues before they escalate into failures.
- **Optimizing Performance:** Performance metrics highlight areas for improvement, enabling teams to fine-tune resources and reduce latency.
- **Supporting Scalability:** By monitoring usage trends and bottlenecks, administrators can adjust scaling policies to ensure resources meet demand.
- **Enhancing Security and Compliance**: Monitoring logs and system activity provides a security layer, helping detect unauthorized access and maintain compliance with data regulations.

Key Metrics for Effective Monitoring

To effectively monitor distributed systems, it is essential to track a set of core metrics that provide insight into system health, performance, and reliability:

- **Infrastructure Metrics**
  - **CPU and Memory Utilization**: Tracks the processing and memory usage

of instances or containers, helping identify under-utilized or over-utilized resources.

  - **Disk I/O and Network Traffic**: Measures the read/write rates to storage and network data transfer, which can reveal potential bottlenecks.
  - **Instance Health**: Monitors the health status of instances, alerting administrators to failing or unresponsive nodes.

- **Application Metrics**
  - **Response Time and Latency**: Monitors the time taken to process requests, providing insight into user experience and potential slowdowns.
  - **Request Rate (Throughput)**: Tracks the number of requests served per second, helping gauge the system's capacity to handle load.
  - **Error Rates**: Monitors the frequency of errors in the application, such as failed transactions or database connection issues, signaling underlying problems.
- **Business Metrics**
  - **User Engagement**: Tracks user interactions with the system, providing insight into feature usage and performance impact on user experience.
  - **Transaction Success Rate**: Monitors successful versus failed transactions, especially critical for e-commerce, finance, and other transactional systems.
  - **Revenue Impact Metrics**: Tracks metrics tied to revenue, such as completed checkouts or subscriptions, helping assess the financial health and operational impact of the system.

Key Metrics for Effective Monitoring

Metric Type	Key Metrics	Purpose	Impact Areas
Infrastructure Metrics	• CPU utilization • Memory usage • Disk I/O • Network traffic	• Resource optimization • Bottleneck detection • Capacity planning • Health monitoring	• System performance • Resource allocation • Cost optimization • System stability
Application Metrics	• Response time • Request rate • Error rates • Service latency	• Performance tracking • Error detection • Load monitoring • User experience	• Application reliability • Service quality • User satisfaction • System availability
Business Metrics	• User engagement • Transaction success • Revenue metrics • Conversion rates	• Business impact • Revenue tracking • User behavior • Growth monitoring	• Business growth • Financial health • Customer satisfaction • Market performance

Figure 6.1: *Key Monitoring Metrics*

Monitoring Levels in Distributed Systems

Monitoring can be categorized into several levels, each focusing on different system components to provide comprehensive visibility:

- **Infrastructure-Level Monitoring**
  - Focuses on the underlying hardware or virtualized infrastructure, including servers, storage, and networking. Key metrics include resource utilization, instance health, and network throughput.
  - **Example**: Monitoring CPU utilization in an EC2 cluster to ensure optimal performance, scaling out resources if necessary.
- **Application-Level Monitoring**
  - Targets application performance, tracking metrics such as response time, error rates, and request volume. Application-level monitoring helps detect performance bottlenecks and application-specific failures.
  - **Example**: A web application monitoring request latency and error rates to ensure smooth, responsive user experience.
- **Service-Level Monitoring**
  - In microservices architectures, service-level monitoring focuses on individual services, tracking inter-service communications, dependency health, and latency between services.
  - **Example**: Monitoring inter-service API latency in a microservices-based e-commerce platform to identify bottlenecks in the checkout process.
- **End-to-End User Experience Monitoring**
  - Provides a holistic view of the user experience by tracking the entire journey across multiple services and components. This level includes tracking metrics from the user's perspective, such as page load times and session success rates.
  - **Example**: An online banking application tracking the time taken from user login to completing a transaction to optimize the user journey.

AWS Tools for Monitoring Distributed Systems

AWS provides several tools to support comprehensive monitoring, from infrastructure to application layers, empowering teams to detect and resolve issues quickly:

- **Amazon CloudWatch**
  - CloudWatch enables monitoring of system metrics, setting alarms, and creating dashboards. It integrates with AWS services such as EC2, RDS, and Lambda, providing visibility into performance and resource utilization.

- **Use Case**: An online education platform uses CloudWatch to monitor resource utilization across EC2 instances, setting alarms for CPU spikes during exam periods to trigger scaling actions.

- **AWS X-Ray**
  - X-Ray offers end-to-end tracing for distributed applications, enabling root cause analysis by tracking requests across services. X-Ray highlights performance bottlenecks and dependencies, offering insights for optimization.
  - **Use Case**: A travel booking application uses X-Ray to trace user requests from search to checkout, identifying latency issues between microservices and optimizing inter-service communication.
- **AWS CloudTrail**
  - CloudTrail provides detailed logs of API calls and activity across AWS accounts, supporting audit, compliance, and security monitoring. CloudTrail logs also help track changes that impact monitoring configurations.
  - **Use Case**: A healthcare application uses CloudTrail to audit access to patient data, ensuring compliance with data privacy regulations and logging unauthorized access attempts.
- **Amazon Managed Service for Prometheus and Grafana**
  - Amazon Managed Service for Prometheus and Amazon Managed Grafana offer open-source monitoring and visualization tools. Prometheus collects metrics from infrastructure, and Grafana provides a flexible, interactive dashboard for visualizing performance data.
  - **Use Case**: A DevOps team uses Prometheus and Grafana to monitor Kubernetes clusters, creating custom dashboards for tracking container resource usage and scaling needs.

Best Practices for Effective Monitoring

Following are some of the best practices we could leverage for effective monitoring:

- **Set Clear SLAs and SLOs**
  - Define Service Level Agreements (SLAs) and Service Level Objectives (SLOs) for key metrics, setting performance standards and establishing benchmarks. SLAs provide a baseline for monitoring, helping teams respond proactively to deviations.
  - **Tip**: *Align SLAs and SLOs with business priorities, such as response time targets for high-value transactions or uptime requirements for customer-facing services.*

- **Use Threshold-Based Alarms and Anomaly Detection**
  - Configure alarms for critical metrics with threshold-based triggers, ensuring prompt alerts when values exceed acceptable ranges. Anomaly detection can be applied to identify unusual behavior, providing early warning of potential issues.
  - **Tip**: *For metrics with fluctuating baselines, consider AWS CloudWatch's anomaly detection feature, which adapts to typical patterns and highlights deviations.*
- **Create Centralized Dashboards for Visibility**
  - Centralized dashboards provide a unified view of system health and performance, facilitating real-time monitoring. Group metrics by category or priority to simplify monitoring across levels and services.
  - **Tip**: *Use Amazon Managed Grafana to create interactive dashboards, allowing teams to track and filter metrics dynamically.*
- **Implement Log Aggregation for Troubleshooting**
  - Log aggregation consolidates logs from multiple sources, aiding troubleshooting and incident response. Aggregated logs allow for faster analysis of errors and failures, streamlining the troubleshooting process.
  - **Tip**: *Use Amazon CloudWatch Logs Insights for log aggregation and querying, helping identify trends and root causes of performance issues.*
- **Review and Refine Monitoring Strategies Regularly**
  - Periodically evaluate and update monitoring strategies to align with changes in application architecture, user behavior, or scaling policies. Regular reviews ensure monitoring remains relevant as the system evolves.
  - **Tip**: *Conduct quarterly reviews of monitoring configurations, ensuring that metrics, alarms, and dashboards reflect current system requirements and priorities.*

Fault Tolerance in Distributed Systems

Fault tolerance is the ability of a distributed system to continue functioning even when parts of it fail. In distributed environments, where applications are spread across multiple nodes, networks, and data centers, failures are inevitable—whether from hardware issues, network partitions, or software bugs. Fault tolerance enables systems to detect, isolate, and recover from these failures without disrupting overall service, ensuring high availability, data integrity, and user satisfaction.

Designing for fault tolerance involves both proactive and reactive strategies. Proactive strategies include redundancy and failover mechanisms, while reactive strategies involve monitoring and automated recovery processes. This section explores core principles and techniques for achieving fault tolerance, focusing on redundancy, failover, data replication, and self-healing mechanisms in AWS environments.

Core Principles of Fault Tolerance

Here are the main principles of fault tolerance:

- **Redundancy:**
  - Redundancy involves duplicating critical components or resources to ensure continuity in case of failure. This could include multiple instances, storage replicas, or network paths.
  - **Example**: A database can be set up with read replicas, allowing the system to continue serving data if the primary database fails.
- **Isolation and Containment:**
  - Fault isolation limits the impact of failures by isolating faulty components from the rest of the system. Containment prevents cascading failures, ensuring that other components remain unaffected.
  - **Example**: In a microservices architecture, individual services run in isolated containers, so if one service fails, it does not affect the others.
- **Failover and Recovery:**
  - Failover automatically redirects traffic or workloads to backup resources when a primary component fails, maintaining service continuity. Recovery processes focus on restoring failed resources to normal operation.
  - **Example**: An application hosted on AWS might use Elastic Load Balancing to automatically route traffic to healthy instances when one becomes unresponsive.
- **Graceful Degradation:**
  - Fault-tolerant systems should be designed to degrade gracefully, continuing to offer partial functionality when full service is not possible. This approach maintains a basic level of service even under failure conditions.
  - **Example**: A streaming service might reduce video quality during high-traffic periods rather than cutting off access, ensuring a continuous user experience.

Techniques for Achieving Fault Tolerance

Following are some of the techniques that assist in achieving fault tolerance to maintain functionality and reliability despite unexpected failures or disruptions.

- **Data Replication and Redundancy**
  - Replicating data across multiple nodes or regions ensures that even if one location experiences an outage, the data remains available. AWS offers data replication features in services such as RDS Multi-AZ and DynamoDB Global Tables, supporting fault tolerance in case of regional failures.
  - **Use Case**: A global e-commerce platform might replicate customer data across multiple AWS regions, ensuring high availability and low-latency access worldwide.
- **Automatic Failover with Load Balancers**
  - Load balancers automatically redirect traffic from failed instances to healthy ones, enabling applications to remain operational despite instance outages. AWS Elastic Load Balancing (ELB) supports failover across multiple AZs, providing automatic recovery during failures.
  - **Use Case**: An online gaming application may use ELB to redirect player sessions to available servers if a particular server fails, preserving the gameplay experience.
- **Multi-AZ and Multi-Region Deployments**
  - Distributing resources across multiple Availability Zones (AZs) or regions provides resilience against localized failures. Multi-AZ deployments improve fault tolerance within a region, while multi-region setups enhance disaster recovery and global availability.
  - **Use Case**: A financial services application could deploy its database in a Multi-AZ configuration within a single region, while critical backup data is stored in another region to support disaster recovery.
- **Self-Healing Architectures**
  - Self-healing systems detect failures and initiate automated recovery processes. This could involve restarting failed components, replacing unhealthy instances, or reallocating resources. AWS Auto Scaling, for instance, enables self-healing by automatically replacing instances marked as unhealthy.
  - **Use Case**: A SaaS platform might configure Auto Scaling to replace any EC2 instance that fails a health check, ensuring that resources remain available with minimal manual intervention.

AWS Services for Fault Tolerance

AWS offers a range of services to support fault tolerance in distributed systems, enabling applications to maintain continuity and resilience:

- **Amazon RDS Multi-AZ**
  - Amazon RDS Multi-AZ deployments replicate data synchronously across Availability Zones, ensuring that a standby instance is always available for failover if the primary instance fails.
  - **Use Case**: An online transaction processing system might use RDS Multi-AZ to ensure uninterrupted access to its database, maintaining data consistency and availability.
- **Amazon S3 Cross-Region Replication**
  - S3 Cross-Region Replication (CRR) copies objects across AWS regions, providing high availability and disaster recovery. In case of a regional failure, the replicated data is accessible from other regions.
  - **Use Case**: A media storage platform might use S3 CRR to replicate user-uploaded content across regions, ensuring content availability despite regional disruptions.
- **AWS Auto Scaling with Health Checks**
  - Auto Scaling can automatically replace instances that fail health checks, ensuring that the desired instance count is always maintained. Combined with Elastic Load Balancing, this provides a self-healing system for high availability.
  - **Use Case**: A web application with fluctuating traffic can configure Auto Scaling to add instances during peak times and replace unhealthy instances to maintain consistent performance.
- **AWS Route 53 for DNS Failover**
  - Route 53 enables DNS-based failover, directing traffic to alternate endpoints when primary resources become unavailable. This is particularly useful for multi-region setups, where Route 53 can redirect users to an alternate region in case of failure.
  - **Use Case**: A content delivery network (CDN) uses Route 53 to route user requests to the nearest available server, ensuring low latency and high availability even if a primary server goes down.

Example Scenario: A healthcare application handling sensitive patient data could use RDS Multi-AZ for database failover, S3 Cross-Region Replication for secure data backups, and Route 53 DNS failover to ensure uninterrupted access to patient records across regions.

Best Practices for Building Fault-Tolerant Distributed Systems

We can implement the following best practices for building fault-tolerant systems:

- **Design for Failure with Redundancy**
  - Implement redundancy for all critical components, ensuring that each layer of the architecture has a backup resource ready to take over if needed.
  - **Tip**: *Use a Multi-AZ setup for databases and Auto Scaling for compute resources, ensuring redundancy in each system layer.*
- **Automate Failover and Recovery**
  - Automate failover processes with load balancers and use services such as Auto Scaling for automated recovery. This minimizes downtime and reduces the need for manual intervention during failure events.
  - **Tip**: *Enable health checks for all instances and configure auto-scaling groups to replace unhealthy instances promptly.*
- **Implement Graceful Degradation for Essential Services**
  - Ensure that critical services degrade gracefully when failures occur, maintaining core functionality even if some features are disabled temporarily.
  - **Tip**: *In e-commerce applications, ensure checkout functions remain operational, even if some non-critical services such as recommendations or reviews are temporarily unavailable.*
- **Test Fault Tolerance Regularly**
  - Conduct regular testing to verify fault tolerance mechanisms, including failover processes, backup and recovery, and redundancy systems. Simulated failure testing helps validate resilience.
  - **Tip**: *Implement "chaos engineering" practices, such as intentionally terminating instances, to test the system's fault-tolerant capabilities and identify areas for improvement.*
- **Use Distributed and Decentralized Data Storage**
  - For critical data, employ distributed storage solutions that replicate data across multiple regions or availability zones, ensuring continuous access and disaster recovery.
  - **Tip**: *Use S3 Cross-Region Replication or DynamoDB Global Tables to ensure data availability across regions.*

Example Case Study: Fault Tolerance for a Financial Services Application

Scenario: A financial services application handling user transactions requires high availability and reliability, as any downtime could result in significant revenue loss and affect the user's trust.

- **Multi-AZ Database for Transaction Data**: The application uses Amazon RDS Multi-AZ for storing transactional data, ensuring automatic failover to a standby instance if the primary instance fails.
- **S3 Cross-Region Replication for Data Backups**: Critical transaction logs and user data are stored in Amazon S3 with cross-region replication, providing redundancy and disaster recovery in case of a regional outage.
- **Route 53 DNS Failover for Global Availability**: Route 53 directs users to the nearest available server, rerouting to alternate regions if primary servers become inaccessible.
- **Auto Scaling with Health Checks**: The application's frontend servers are configured with Auto Scaling and health checks, automatically replacing any failed instances to ensure consistent performance.

This fault-tolerant architecture allows the financial application to maintain high availability, data security, and resilience, even during failures or unexpected traffic spikes.

Designing Self-Healing Systems in Distributed Architectures

A **self-healing system** is a distributed architecture that can automatically detect and respond to issues without human intervention. Self-healing systems rely on monitoring, automation, and fault-tolerance mechanisms to identify failures, restart or replace failed components, and maintain system health. In dynamic distributed environments, where applications must handle high traffic and frequent updates, self-healing capabilities are essential for ensuring high availability, reducing downtime, and enhancing the user experience.

Self-healing involves several components, including proactive monitoring, automated recovery workflows, and adaptive scaling. AWS provides a variety of tools and services, such as Auto Scaling, Lambda, and CloudWatch, that enable systems to recover from failures and continue operations seamlessly.

Key Components of a Self-Healing System

A self-healing system must incorporate the following components to ensure effective detection, diagnosis, and recovery from failures:

- **Automated Monitoring and Alerting**
    - Continuous monitoring is essential for detecting anomalies, errors, or failures in real-time. Automated alerts enable prompt responses to issues, while data from monitoring tools feeds into self-healing workflows.

    - **Example**: An e-commerce application uses Amazon CloudWatch to monitor CPU utilization and response times across EC2 instances. When a threshold is exceeded, an alert triggers an automated action to investigate or resolve the issue.

- **Health Checks and Instance Replacement**
    - Health checks regularly evaluate the status of instances or containers. If a resource is flagged as unhealthy, it can be replaced automatically, ensuring that only functioning resources are available to handle traffic.
    - **Example**: In a microservices application, health checks in AWS Elastic Load Balancing identify failing instances and redirect traffic to healthy instances, while Auto Scaling replaces the failing instances.
- **Automated Scaling and Recovery**
    - Automated scaling adds or removes resources based on demand, and automated recovery processes restart or replace failed instances. These mechanisms reduce manual intervention, helping the system maintain availability.
    - **Example**: A SaaS application with variable traffic volumes uses Auto Scaling to add instances during peak times. If an instance fails, Auto Scaling detects the issue and launches a new instance to replace it.
- **Logging and Root Cause Analysis**
    - Logs provide detailed records of system events, enabling root cause analysis (RCA) when failures occur. RCA helps identify recurring issues, feeding back into the self-healing process to prevent similar failures.
    - **Example**: AWS CloudTrail logs record configuration changes and API calls. When an issue arises, the logs allow the team to trace the sequence of events that led to the problem, adjusting configurations to prevent reoccurrence.

AWS Services for Building Self-Healing Systems

AWS provides a comprehensive suite of services and tools that enable architects to build resilient, self-healing systems, from automated instance recovery with EC2 Auto Scaling to sophisticated health monitoring with Amazon CloudWatch and AWS Systems Manager.

- **AWS Auto Scaling**
    - AWS Auto Scaling monitors resource usage and automatically adjusts capacity to maintain application availability. It can replace unhealthy instances based on health checks, ensuring that workloads always run on functioning resources.

  - **Use Case**: A streaming service uses Auto Scaling to manage its EC2 instances, adding capacity during peak viewing hours and replacing failed instances without manual intervention.

- **AWS Lambda for Event-Driven Recovery**
  - AWS Lambda enables serverless, event-driven responses to issues. Lambda functions can execute automated recovery actions, such as restarting services, clearing cache, or adjusting configurations in response to monitoring alerts.
  - **Use Case**: In a data pipeline, a Lambda function automatically restarts data processing jobs if they fail, ensuring that processing continues without delays.

- **Amazon CloudWatch Alarms and Events**
  - CloudWatch Alarms monitor metrics and trigger actions when specific thresholds are exceeded. CloudWatch Events enable automated workflows by initiating recovery steps based on detected events.
  - **Use Case**: An IoT platform uses CloudWatch Alarms to monitor device connectivity. When a device goes offline, a CloudWatch Event triggers a workflow that attempts to reconnect the device or alert the administrator.

- **AWS Systems Manager Automation**
  - AWS Systems Manager Automation automates repetitive maintenance and recovery tasks. Automation runbooks provide predefined procedures to handle common issues, reducing manual effort in managing infrastructure.
  - **Use Case**: A financial application uses Systems Manager Automation to restart services, apply patches, and perform failover testing, ensuring operational continuity with minimal manual input.

- **AWS Elastic Load Balancing (ELB)**
  - ELB distributes traffic across multiple resources and reroutes traffic when instances are detected as unhealthy. This ensures that only healthy instances receive traffic, improving reliability and minimizing service disruptions.
  - **Use Case**: A multi-region web application relies on ELB to route traffic based on instance health, maintaining high availability by redirecting users to healthy resources.

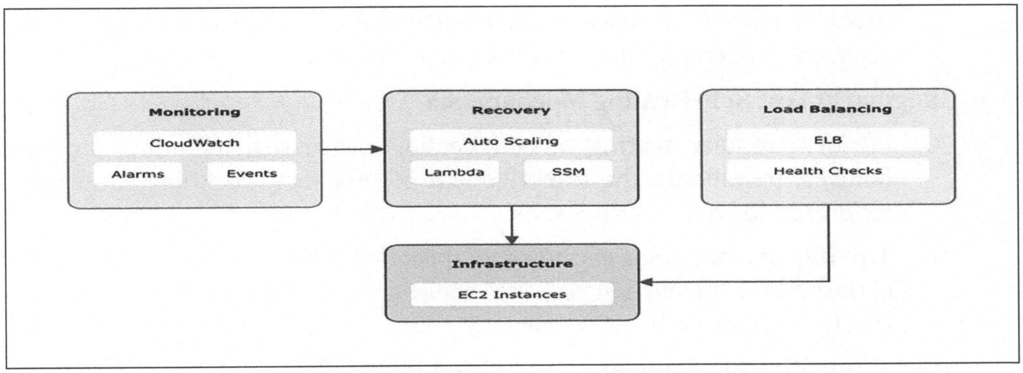

Figure 6.2: *Self-Healing Systems interactions*

Best Practices for Designing Self-Healing Architectures

Implementing robust self-healing architectures requires a systematic approach that combines automated health checks, recovery procedures, and intelligent failover mechanisms to ensure your systems can autonomously detect, respond to, and recover from failures.

- **Implement Multi-Layered Monitoring and Health Checks**
  - Design multi-layered monitoring for comprehensive visibility across infrastructure, applications, and services. Health checks should monitor critical system metrics, triggering automated recovery actions for failed resources.
  - **Tip**: *Configure health checks at both the infrastructure level (CPU, memory) and the application level (response time, error rates) for early detection of issues.*
- **Automate Failure Responses with Event-Driven Triggers**
  - Set up automated recovery workflows triggered by monitoring events. Event-driven recovery minimizes response times, ensuring prompt resolution without manual intervention.
  - **Tip**: *Use CloudWatch Events or Lambda functions to automatically restart services or replace instances based on specific error codes or threshold breaches.*
- **Design for Stateless and Independent Services**
  - Build applications as stateless and independent services whenever possible, enabling individual components to restart or scale without impacting the system.

- **Tip**: *Use a distributed caching layer such as ElastiCache to store session data separately, allowing instances to be replaced or scaled independently.*

- **Regularly Test Self-Healing Mechanisms**
  - Perform regular testing of self-healing processes, including simulated failures, to validate the effectiveness of recovery workflows and ensure readiness for real-world issues.
  - **Tip**: *Implement "chaos engineering" practices to intentionally disrupt parts of the system, testing how well self-healing mechanisms restore functionality and learning from the outcomes.*
- **Use Centralized Logging and Automated Root Cause Analysis**
  - Centralized logging and automated root cause analysis (RCA) enable quick identification and resolution of recurring issues. Logs provide context for failures, helping improve self-healing strategies.
  - **Tip:** *Use CloudWatch Logs Insights to centralize logs and configure automated workflows that trigger RCA when specific patterns or errors are detected.*

Using AWS Elastic Beanstalk for Self-Healing Applications

AWS Elastic Beanstalk is a Platform-as-a-Service (PaaS) solution that simplifies the deployment, management, and scaling of applications. Elastic Beanstalk manages the underlying infrastructure, automatically scaling resources based on demand, and provides built-in health monitoring and automated recovery features. For applications that require self-healing capabilities but benefit from simplified management, Elastic Beanstalk offers an ideal solution, combining ease of deployment with robust fault tolerance.

Elastic Beanstalk supports applications developed in a variety of languages, such as Java, Python, Node.js, and PHP, and abstracts infrastructure complexity. This makes it a popular choice for developers focused on building application logic without needing to manage underlying infrastructure manually. Elastic Beanstalk's self-healing features enable applications to remain highly available by automatically detecting failures, replacing unhealthy instances, and scaling resources dynamically.

Self-Healing Features in AWS Elastic Beanstalk

Here are the Self-Healing Features in AWS Elastic Beanstalk:

- **Automated Health Monitoring**
  - Elastic Beanstalk continuously monitors the health of deployed applications, automatically assessing metrics such as latency, error rates,

and resource utilization. If a health issue is detected, Elastic Beanstalk marks the instance as unhealthy and initiates recovery actions.

  - **Example**: A content management application hosted on Elastic Beanstalk uses automated health monitoring to detect instances with high latency. If performance issues persist, the platform automatically replaces these instances, ensuring consistent response times.

- **Automatic Instance Replacement and Scaling**
  - Elastic Beanstalk environments are configured to replace instances that fail health checks. With Auto Scaling enabled, Beanstalk ensures the right number of healthy instances are available, adding new ones or replacing failing instances as needed.
  - **Example**: An e-commerce application experiences high traffic during a flash sale. Elastic Beanstalk automatically scales out instances to handle the increased load and removes additional instances once demand normalizes.

- **Rolling Updates with Health Checks**
  - Elastic Beanstalk provides rolling updates to deploy new versions of an application without causing downtime. Health checks are performed on updated instances, and if issues are detected, the deployment process can automatically roll back to a stable version.
  - **Example**: A financial application deploys new features incrementally using rolling updates. If any deployment segment shows errors or fails health checks, Beanstalk halts the deployment and rolls back to a previous version, preventing disruption.

- **Integrated Load Balancing and Traffic Routing**
  - Elastic Beanstalk environments integrate with Elastic Load Balancing to distribute traffic evenly across instances and ensure that only healthy instances receive traffic. Load balancers reroute traffic to functional instances, maintaining application uptime.
  - **Example**: A social networking application relies on Elastic Load Balancing within Beanstalk to manage user traffic. When an instance fails, the load balancer automatically reroutes traffic to healthy instances, maintaining a seamless experience for users.

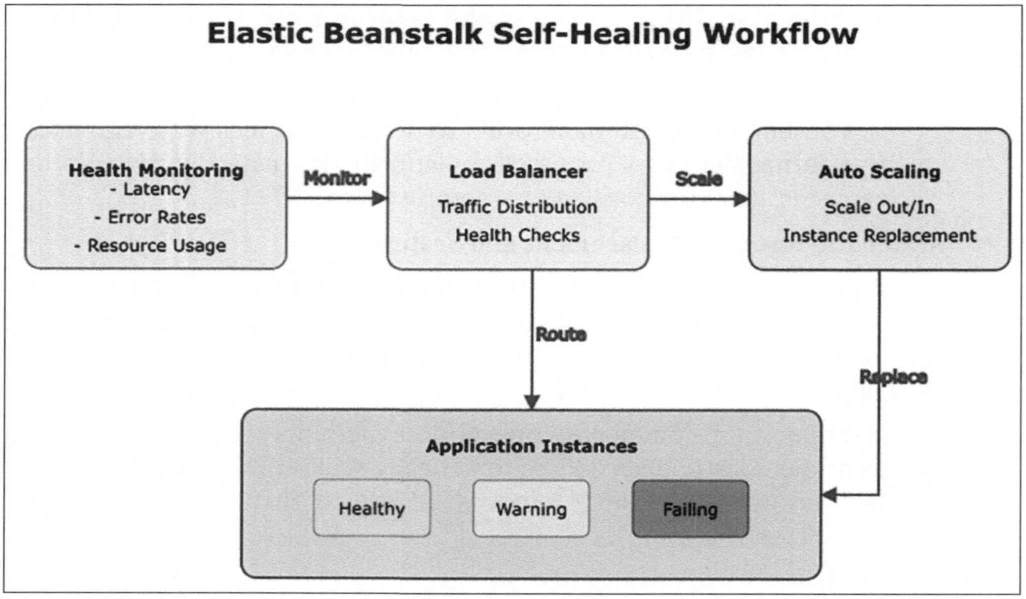

Figure 6.3: *Elastic Beanstalk Self-Healing Workflow*

Setting Up Self-Healing with Elastic Beanstalk

Amazon Elastic Beanstalk simplifies the implementation of self-healing capabilities by offering built-in health monitoring, automatic instance replacement, and environment management features that work together to maintain application availability with minimal manual intervention.

- **Enable Enhanced Health Monitoring**
  - Enhanced health monitoring in Elastic Beanstalk provides detailed insights into application health at instance and environment levels. This feature analyzes metrics such as latency, CPU usage, and application logs, proactively detecting issues.
  - **Tip**: *Enable enhanced health monitoring in the Elastic Beanstalk console to track application metrics in real-time and respond to potential failures faster.*
- **Configure Auto Scaling and Health Check Thresholds**
  - Elastic Beanstalk environments can be configured to scale automatically based on thresholds for CPU, memory, and other metrics. Define health check thresholds that balance performance with resource usage, triggering replacement or scaling events when necessary.
  - **Tip**: *Set lower thresholds for critical metrics to ensure proactive scaling and instance replacement, preventing application slowdowns during peak loads.*

- **Define Application Health Policies**
  - Elastic Beanstalk allows users to define application health policies with specific health statuses, such as "*Severe*," "*Degraded*," or "OK." These statuses can be configured to trigger alerts or initiate automated recovery steps when specific conditions are met.
  - **Tip**: *Customize health policies based on application requirements so the system can automatically respond to varying levels of performance degradation.*
- **Implement Regular Deployment Testing**
  - Elastic Beanstalk's rolling updates can be coupled with deployment testing to ensure new code deployments do not negatively impact application stability. Conduct tests during updates and configure Beanstalk to roll back changes if health issues are detected.
  - **Tip**: *Enable deployment testing in staging environments to validate changes before pushing updates to production, reducing the risk of unexpected failures.*

Best Practices for Using Elastic Beanstalk for Self-Healing

To maximize Elastic Beanstalk's self-healing capabilities, proper configuration of health checks, environment settings, and deployment automation ensures robust recovery with minimal downtime.

- **Leverage Health Monitoring for Proactive Management**
  - Use enhanced health monitoring to track application health continuously and take proactive actions. Custom alerts can notify administrators of issues before they impact user experience.
  - **Tip**: *Set up notifications for critical health statuses such as "Degraded" or "Severe," ensuring rapid intervention when needed.*
- **Use Rolling Updates with Health Checks for Safe Deployments**
  - Implement rolling updates to minimize downtime and test each deployment stage. Health checks during updates allow quick rollbacks if issues arise, maintaining stability.
  - **Tip**: *Use blue/green deployments for major updates to test new versions in parallel environments before shifting traffic.*
- **Configure Auto Scaling Based on Demand Patterns**
  - Define auto-scaling policies that align with typical traffic patterns, scaling out for peak times and scaling in during off-hours. This reduces resource costs while maintaining performance.

 - **Tip**: *Use predictive scaling if traffic patterns are predictable, allowing Elastic Beanstalk to adjust resources before peak times.*

- **Optimize Health Check Thresholds for Application Needs**
  - Set health check thresholds that reflect application-specific performance metrics, preventing unnecessary replacements while ensuring prompt response to real issues.
  - **Tip**: *Regularly review and adjust health check thresholds to align with changes in application performance requirements.*
- **Integrate with Logging and Root Cause Analysis Tools**
  - Combine Elastic Beanstalk with CloudWatch Logs and CloudTrail to track detailed logs and conduct root cause analysis. This enhances debugging and ensures that self-healing adjustments are informed by historical data.
  - **Tip**: *Configure CloudWatch alarms for common error patterns, allowing for faster resolution and improved system resilience.*

Example Case Study: Self-Healing Architecture for a Travel Booking Platform

Scenario: A travel booking platform with real-time availability and booking updates needs to ensure uptime and seamless functionality, even if some components fail.

- **Multi-Layer Monitoring and CloudWatch Alarms**: CloudWatch monitors resource utilization, error rates, and response times across the platform. Alarms trigger when thresholds are exceeded, activating automated recovery steps.
- **Auto Scaling for Redundancy**: The application's EC2 instances run in an Auto Scaling group that automatically replaces any instance failing a health check, ensuring that traffic is always directed to healthy resources.
- **Lambda for Event-Driven Recovery**: When a booking service experiences a failure, a CloudWatch Event triggers a Lambda function that reinitializes the service, allowing the platform to recover immediately.
- **Stateless Services with Distributed Cache**: The platform's session management is handled by ElastiCache, ensuring that each instance remains stateless. This setup enables independent instance replacement without disrupting user sessions.
- **AWS Systems Manager Automation for Incident Response**: Systems Manager Automation runbooks handle common recovery procedures, such as restarting database connections or clearing caches, ensuring prompt and consistent responses to known issues.

This self-healing architecture enables the travel booking platform to provide a reliable, uninterrupted service, ensuring that even if individual components fail, the overall system continues to operate smoothly.

Best Practices for Building Resilient Architectures and Disaster Recovery

Building a resilient architecture means designing systems that can withstand unexpected disruptions and continue to operate effectively. Resilience involves both **high availability** and **disaster recovery** (DR) planning, ensuring that applications can recover from regional outages, data loss, or infrastructure failures. Effective disaster recovery strategies aim to minimize downtime and data loss by implementing safeguards and recovery processes that allow quick restoration of services.

This section highlights best practices to create robust systems that can recover from severe incidents, focusing on proactive preparation, redundancy, and tailored recovery plans that meet business continuity requirements.

Best Practices for Building Resilient Architectures

Following are some of the best practices for building resilient architectures:

- **Design for Geographical Redundancy**
  - Deploy applications across multiple geographic regions to mitigate the impact of localized failures. By distributing resources across regions, services remain accessible even if a single region experiences an outage.
  - **Tip**: *Use multi-region architectures with load balancing and routing policies that automatically direct traffic to an alternate region in case of failure.*
- **Implement Data Backup and Cross-Region Replication**
  - Regularly back up critical data and configure cross-region replication for data stores. This approach ensures data availability in disaster recovery scenarios and allows seamless restoration of services in a different region if needed.
  - **Tip**: *Use* AWS *Backup for automated, policy-driven backups of key resources, and configure* Amazon RDS, DynamoDB, *or* S3 *cross-region replication for highly available data.*
- **Separate Dependencies with Fault Isolation Zones**
  - Design the architecture to contain failures within isolated zones or components, preventing cascading failures across the system. By isolating dependencies, the impact of one service's failure on other services is minimized.

  - **Tip**: *Use isolated VPCs for different services and apply security groups to limit cross-service dependencies. This setup prevents system-wide outages caused by single-component failures.*
- **Set Up Multi-Tier Architectures**
  - A multi-tier architecture (for example, web, application, and database layers) reduces system dependencies and enhances scalability. Each layer operates independently, so if one tier experiences issues, it does not directly impact the others.
  - **Tip**: *Separate each tier with load balancers, allowing each layer to scale independently. This approach minimizes bottlenecks and maintains performance even when certain tiers experience increased load.*
- **Use Automated Infrastructure-as-Code (IaaC) for Consistency**
  - Infrastructure-as-Code (IaaC) tools such as AWS CloudFormation and Terraform help maintain consistent configurations across environments, ensuring that recovery environments mirror production. IaaC also facilitates faster disaster recovery by automating the deployment of identical infrastructure in backup regions.
  - **Tip**: *Store IaaC templates in version-controlled repositories, enabling quick access and deployment during recovery and ensuring infrastructure configurations are consistent and reliable.*

Best Practices for Disaster Recovery (DR)

Following are some of the best practices for disaster recovery:

- **Define a Recovery Time Objective (RTO) and Recovery Point Objective (RPO)**
  - Establishing an RTO (maximum allowable downtime) and an RPO (acceptable data loss window) helps guide DR planning by setting realistic recovery goals. These objectives inform DR strategies, ensuring recovery aligns with business needs.
  - **Tip**: *Use RTO and RPO to define DR tiers, such as hot standby (for low RTO/RPO) or warm/cold backups (for higher RTO/RPO), enabling tailored recovery strategies based on application criticality.*
- **Implement Pilot Light Architecture for DR**
  - A pilot light DR architecture keeps core system components running at minimal capacity, ready to scale up when needed. This approach minimizes cost while enabling quick restoration by scaling up pre-configured resources in response to a disaster.
  - **Tip**: *For applications requiring rapid recovery, run critical components (for*

example, database or authentication services) in a pilot light configuration in a secondary region, ready for full-scale deployment as needed.

- **Regularly Test and Validate DR Plans**
  - Conduct regular DR drills to test recovery processes, infrastructure readiness, and staff preparedness. Testing identifies gaps in the recovery plan, ensuring continuous improvement and confirming the system's ability to meet recovery objectives.
  - **Tip**: *Schedule quarterly or semi-annual* DR *exercises, simulating various disaster scenarios and measuring recovery times to validate* RTO *and* RPO *requirements.*
- **Automate Failover and Recovery Processes**
  - Automate failover and recovery tasks to minimize manual intervention and reduce recovery times. Automated failover directs traffic to a secondary region or backup site when the primary location is unavailable, enabling seamless recovery.
  - **Tip**: *Configure* DNS*-based failover with* AWS Route 53 *or similar services, automating redirection of users to a backup region during primary region outages.*
- **Establish a Communication Plan for DR Scenarios**
  - A structured communication plan is essential for coordinating responses and providing stakeholders with timely updates during DR events. Define roles and responsibilities and ensure communication channels are ready for internal and external updates.
  - **Tip**: *Prepare templates and escalation protocols for different* DR *scenarios, ensuring that team members know whom to contact and that stakeholders are informed at each stage of the recovery.*

Example Scenario: Disaster Recovery Plan for an E-Learning Platform

Scenario: An e-learning platform requires continuous availability to serve students worldwide. To prepare for regional failures, the platform follows these DR best practices:

- **Multi-Region Deployment**: The application is hosted in two regions, with Route 53 set up for DNS failover, automatically redirecting traffic to the secondary region if the primary one fails.
- **Cross-Region Replication for Databases**: The platform's RDS and S3 instances use cross-region replication to ensure data consistency and availability, with regular backups scheduled via AWS Backup.

- **Pilot Light Architecture**: Core services, including authentication and user profiles, are always active in the secondary region, allowing rapid scaling in case of a primary region failure.
- **Quarterly DR Testing**: The team performs quarterly DR drills, verifying the ability to meet the platform's RTO of 30 minutes and RPO of 15 minutes.
- **Predefined Communication Protocols**: The DR plan includes communication templates and escalation contacts for prompt updates to stakeholders and users during any DR event.

Conclusion

In this chapter, we explored essential practices for building resilient distributed systems that can withstand failures, recover autonomously, and maintain high availability. Effective monitoring, fault tolerance, self-healing capabilities, and disaster recovery are vital components for achieving reliability in dynamic, distributed environments. Monitoring provides real-time insights into system health, enabling proactive issue detection and optimization. Fault tolerance ensures continuity by allowing systems to operate despite individual component failures, while self-healing mechanisms enable automated recovery without manual intervention.

We also discussed best practices for resilient architecture design and disaster recovery, including multi-region deployments, automated backups, and clearly defined recovery objectives. Together, these strategies form a comprehensive approach to achieving resilience, allowing systems to deliver uninterrupted service, maintain data integrity, and meet user expectations—even under challenging conditions. By combining proactive monitoring, fault-tolerant design, and robust disaster recovery planning, organizations can build distributed systems that are prepared to handle both expected and unexpected disruptions, ensuring a reliable and seamless user experience.

Moving forward, we will explore AWS's diverse data storage services, understanding how to choose and implement the right storage solutions that complement our resilient architectures while meeting specific application requirements for performance, durability, and cost-effectiveness.

CHAPTER 7
Exploring the Realm of AWS Data Storage Services

Introduction

Welcome to the Data Storage Frontier: Unleashing the Power of AWS.

In the ever-expanding data universe, the ability to securely and efficiently store information is paramount. This chapter serves as your gateway to the fascinating realm of AWS data storage solutions, designed to empower you to navigate this critical landscape with confidence.

As data volumes continue to soar, traditional storage methods struggle to keep pace. Fortunately, AWS provides a comprehensive suite of innovative storage services specifically tailored to meet the diverse needs of modern data-driven organizations. Whether you require a robust platform for massive datasets or a secure haven for sensitive information, AWS offers the perfect solution.

By the end of this chapter, you will emerge as a confident data storage master, ready to harness the power of AWS to achieve your data-driven goals. So, fasten your seatbelts and prepare to embark on an exhilarating exploration of the AWS data storage universe!

Structure

We will embark on a captivating journey, exploring the unique features and functionalities of each service, including:

- Amazon S3: The Object Storage Powerhouse
  - Limitless Scalability and Flexibility for Unstructured Data
- Amazon DynamoDB: The NoSQL Champion
  - Blazing-Fast Performance and Unmatched Scalability for Agile Data Models

- Amazon Redshift: The Data Warehousing Behemoth
  - Perfect Platform for Large-Scale Data Analysis and Business Intelligence
- Amazon RDS: The Trusted Choice for Relational Databases
  - Reliable and Secure Storage for Your Structured Data

Amazon Simple Storage Service (Amazon S3): The Object Storage Powerhouse

Amazon Simple Storage Service (Amazon S3) stands as the foundational powerhouse of object storage in the world of cloud computing within AWS.

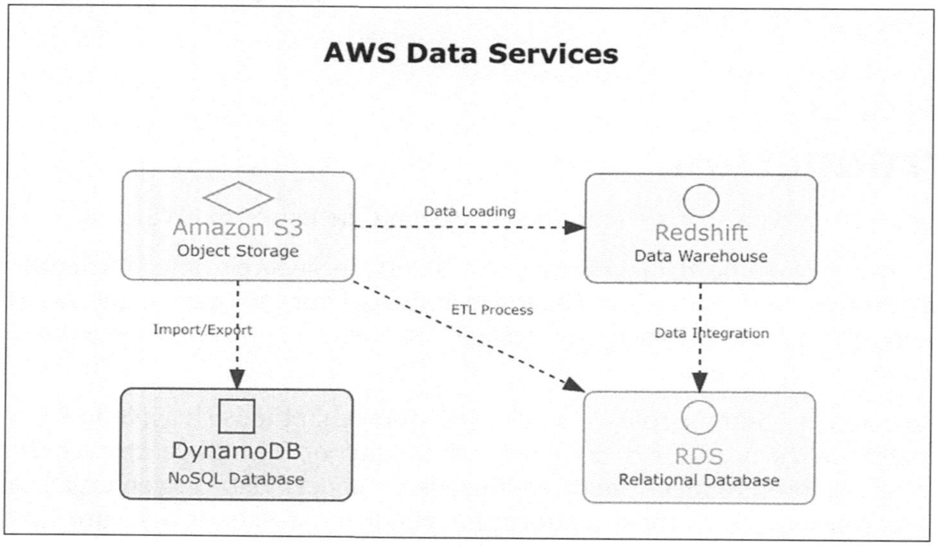

Figure 7.1: *AWS Data Services*

- **Choose the Right Storage Solution**: Identify the perfect fit for your specific data requirements and optimize for cost and performance.
- **Leverage Powerful Tools and APIs**: Master the tools and techniques provided by AWS to manage and access your data efficiently.
- **Scale with Confidence**: Design robust data architectures that can accommodate your evolving data needs and support future growth.

Understanding Object Storage: A New Paradigm

The traditional approach to data storage relied on file systems, where data was organized in a hierarchical structure. However, this approach faced limitations when dealing with vast amounts of data, particularly unstructured data such as images, videos, and logs. Enter object storage, a revolutionary paradigm that emerged as a game-changer.

Object storage, pioneered by Amazon S3, breaks away from the hierarchical structure and treats data as individual objects. Each object is assigned a unique identifier and metadata, allowing for independent storage and retrieval. This approach offers several key advantages:

- **Scalability**: Object storage is infinitely scalable, making it ideal for storing massive datasets with ease.
- **Flexibility**: Object storage can handle any type of data, regardless of size or format.
- **Durability**: Data stored in S3 replicates across multiple geographically dispersed data centers, ensuring high availability and data durability.
- **Cost-Effectiveness**: S3 offers various storage classes optimized for different data access patterns and lifecycle stages, allowing you to pay only for what you use.

Key Features of Amazon S3: Scalability, Durability, and Flexibility

Amazon S3 stands out as the leading object storage solution, offering a plethora of features that empower data-driven organizations:

- **Unlimited Storage**: S3 scales seamlessly to accommodate any amount of data, eliminating storage constraints.
- **Versioning**: S3 allows you to store multiple versions of the same object, enabling easy rollback and ensuring data integrity.
- **Lifecycle Management**: Automatically manage the lifecycle of your data with S3 lifecycle rules, transitioning data to different storage classes based on access patterns and time-based triggers.
- **Security and Access Control**: S3 offers robust security features such as object-level encryption and granular access controls, ensuring the confidentiality and integrity of your data.

Exploring S3 Storage Classes: Optimizing Cost and Performance

S3 provides various storage classes designed to optimize cost and performance based on your data access needs:

- **S3 Standard**: The most frequently accessed data, offering high performance and low latency.
- **S3 Standard-IA**: Infrequently accessed data, offering a balance between cost and performance.
- **S3 Glacier**: Archives and backups, offering the most cost-effective storage for data that requires long-term retention but infrequent access.
- **S3 Glacier Deep Archive**: The most cost-effective option for long-term archival data with extremely low access frequency.

Accessing and Managing S3 Data: The API and Tools at Your Disposal

S3 provides a comprehensive set of tools and APIs for accessing and managing your data:

- **S3 API**: The programmatic interface for interacting with S3, enabling automation and integration with other services.
- **AWS Management Console**: A user-friendly web interface for managing your S3 buckets, objects, and permissions.
- **AWS CLI**: A command-line tool for interacting with S3, allowing for scripting and automation tasks.
- **Third-Party Tools**: A rich ecosystem of third-party tools and libraries, providing additional functionality and integrations for specific use cases.

Use Cases for S3: From Archiving to Streaming and Analytics

S3's versatility makes it a vital tool for diverse use cases:

- **Archiving**: Securely store backups, historical data, and log files for long-term retention.
- **Static Website Hosting**: Host static websites directly from S3, leveraging its scalability and reliability.
- **Media Streaming**: Stream music, videos, and other media content directly from S3.
- **Data Lakes:** Build scalable data lakes for storing and analyzing unstructured data.
- **Backup and Disaster Recovery**: Create reliable backups of your data in S3 to ensure business continuity.

- **Machine Learning**: Store and manage training data for machine learning models.

As you can see, Amazon S3 is the ultimate object storage solution, offering unparalleled scalability, flexibility, and affordability. By understanding its key features, exploring storage class options, and leveraging the available tools and APIs, you can unlock the full potential of S3 and propel your data-driven initiatives to new heights.

Demystifying NoSQL: A Data Model Built for Agility

In the realm of data management, traditional relational databases have long reigned supreme, meticulously organizing structured data within defined schemas. However, the exponential growth of unstructured data and the rise of real-time applications demanded a paradigm shift. This is where NoSQL databases, such as Amazon DynamoDB, emerge as the champions of agility and scalability.

NoSQL databases break free from the rigid confines of relational databases, embracing a schema-less or document-oriented approach. This revolutionary shift offers unparalleled flexibility, allowing your data structures to adapt seamlessly to evolving requirements. No longer are you confined by pre-defined schema, empowering you to embrace the dynamic nature of modern data.

Imagine a world where your data can effortlessly adjust to your needs, regardless of its format or structure. This is the liberating power of NoSQL, paving the way for innovative applications and agile data management.

Types of NoSQL Databases

Within the vast and diverse world of NoSQL, several distinct types exist, each offering unique strengths and catering to specific needs. Let us explore some of the most popular categories:

- **Key-Value Stores:** These databases store data as simple key-value pairs, prioritizing speed and performance. They excel in storing simple data objects and facilitating quick retrieval based on the key. Examples include Amazon DynamoDB and Redis.
- **Document Databases**: These databases store data in flexible documents, accommodating complex data structures with embedded objects and nested arrays. They offer greater flexibility and richer data representation compared to key-value stores. Examples include MongoDB and Amazon DocumentDB.
- **Column-Oriented Databases:** These databases store data by columns instead of rows, enabling efficient retrieval of specific data elements across multiple documents. They are ideal for analytical workloads that involve querying

specific data points across large datasets. Examples include Apache Cassandra and Amazon HBase.

- **Graph Databases:** These databases store relationships between entities as nodes and edges, forming a graph-like structure. They excel at representing and analyzing complex relationships and are perfect for social networking applications and fraud detection. Examples include Neo4j and Amazon Neptune.

Understanding these primary types of NoSQL databases equips you with the knowledge to choose the right solution for your specific data needs and unlocks the full potential of the NoSQL paradigm. By considering the nature of your data, access patterns, and performance requirements, you can harness the power of the NoSQL universe to achieve your data-driven goals.

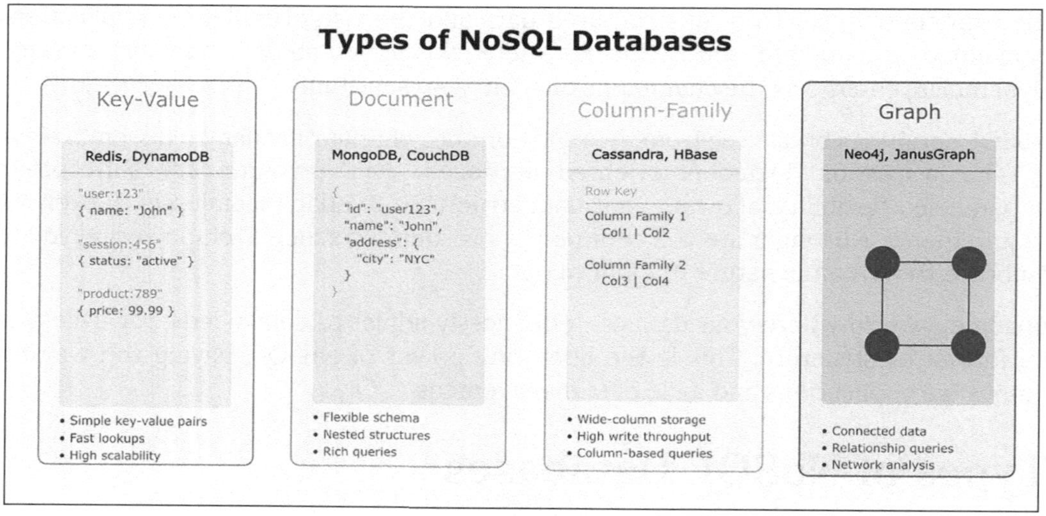

Figure 7.2: *Types of NoSQL Databases*

Amazon DynamoDB: NoSQL for Speed and Scalability

In the ever-evolving landscape of data, agility and performance are paramount. Enter DynamoDB, Amazon's fast and scalable NoSQL database service. Imagine a world where your data can seamlessly adapt to your needs, respond to queries in milliseconds, and handle massive workloads with unwavering stability. That is the power of DynamoDB—the ideal solution for modern applications demanding lightning-fast access and unmatched scalability.

Forget the limitations of traditional relational databases. DynamoDB offers a dynamic and flexible architecture, perfectly suited for today's data-driven world. Whether you are building real-time applications, managing large-scale mobile backends, or powering your next innovative project, DynamoDB is poised to unleash the full potential of your data.

Let us dive deeper into this revolutionary database and explore its key features, benefits, and how it can empower you to achieve your data-driven goals. Buckle up, because we are about to embark on a journey into the world of NoSQL and discover the power of DynamoDB!

Unveiling DynamoDB's Key Features: Fast Performance and High Availability

DynamoDB emerges as a leader in the NoSQL landscape, offering several key features that empower agile data management:

- **Blazing-Fast Performance**: DynamoDB delivers exceptional read and write throughput, making it ideal for real-time applications and high-traffic scenarios.
- **Automatic Scaling**: DynamoDB scales seamlessly to accommodate spikes in traffic and data volume, ensuring consistent performance.
- **High Availability**: DynamoDB replicates data across multiple geographically dispersed data centers, guaranteeing data availability even in the event of failures.
- **Flexible Data Modeling**: DynamoDB allows for flexible data modeling with primary keys and secondary indexes, enabling efficient querying and retrieval based on your specific needs.

Designing Data Models in DynamoDB

Crafting an effective DynamoDB data model requires a deep understanding of its fundamental building blocks:

Primary Keys

The cornerstone of any DynamoDB data model, primary keys uniquely identify each data item. They act as the entry point for data retrieval and ensure efficient access to your information. Choosing the right primary key is crucial, as it dictates the performance and scalability of your data model.

Factors to consider when selecting a primary key:

- **Access Patterns**: Identify how you will primarily access and retrieve data. Choose a primary key that aligns with these patterns for optimal performance.

- **Data Uniqueness**: Ensure your primary key guarantees unique identification for each item. This prevents data duplication and facilitates efficient retrieval.
- **Query Flexibility**: Consider whether you require additional query capabilities beyond the primary key. If so, you can utilize secondary indexes for broader data access.

Secondary Indexes

While primary keys provide the core access mechanism, secondary indexes unlock additional querying possibilities. They act as additional search paths for your data, allowing you to retrieve information based on attributes other than the primary key. Secondary indexes are especially beneficial when you need to:

- Query data based on frequently accessed attributes.
- Perform range queries on specific attribute values.
- Filter data based on multiple criteria.

Document Structure

DynamoDB stores data in JSON documents, offering a flexible and scalable format. This allows you to represent complex data structures with nested objects and arrays, catering to the diverse needs of modern applications.

Designing effective document structures:

- **Normalize your Data**: Break down complex data into smaller, manageable objects.
- **Employ Denormalization where Appropriate**: Pre-populate documents with frequently accessed data for faster retrieval.
- **Use Data Types Efficiently**: Choose the appropriate data type for each attribute to optimize storage and retrieval.

DynamoDB offers advanced features that further enhance your data modeling capabilities:

- **Global Secondary Indexes**: Provide query capabilities across multiple regions, ideal for globally distributed applications.
- **Provisioned Throughput**: Control the read and write capacity of your tables for optimal performance and cost-efficiency.
- **Time to Live (TTL)**: Automatically expire data after a predefined time, facilitating data lifecycle management.

By mastering the art of designing data models in DynamoDB, you can build efficient, scalable, and flexible data structures that unlock the full potential of this powerful NoSQL database. Remember, a well-designed data model is the foundation for successful data engineering and empowers you to extract valuable insights from your data with ease.

Building with DynamoDB: Tools and APIs for Efficient Data Access

DynamoDB empowers you to build robust and scalable data applications with its diverse array of tools and APIs. These resources equip you to efficiently manage your data, automate tasks, and integrate with other services seamlessly.

DynamoDB API

This programmatic interface serves as the core access point for interacting with DynamoDB. It empowers you to perform various operations, including:

- **Create and Manage Tables**: Define your data structure and configure read/write capacity.
- **Place and Get Data Items**: Store and retrieve individual items efficiently.
- **Perform Queries**: Utilize primary and secondary indexes to filter and retrieve specific data.
- **Update and Delete Data Items**: Modify or remove existing data based on your needs.

The DynamoDB API allows for automation and integration with other AWS services, facilitating the creation of complex data pipelines.

AWS Management Console

This web-based interface provides a user-friendly platform for managing your DynamoDB resources. You can:

- Visually create and manage tables.
- View and edit data items.
- Monitor table performance and utilize metrics for optimization.
- Configure access control and security settings.

The AWS Management Console offers a convenient way to manage your DynamoDB environment without requiring coding expertise.

AWS CLI

The command-line interface (CLI) provides a powerful tool for interacting with DynamoDB through scripts and commands. This allows you to:

- Perform batch operations on data items.
- Automate data import and export processes.
- Integrate DynamoDB with other command-line tools.
- Manage your DynamoDB environment from a shell script.

The AWS CLI offers advanced capabilities for scripting and automation, streamlining your data management workflow.

DynamoDB Mapper

This Python library simplifies data modeling and object-relational mapping for DynamoDB. It provides:

- Convenient class-based data modeling.
- Automatic conversion between Python objects and DynamoDB data items.
- Simplified query methods and data access.

DynamoDB Mapper eliminates the need for manual data serialization and deserialization, making development with DynamoDB more efficient and less error-prone.

Use Cases for DynamoDB: Powering Mobile Apps, Real-time Applications, and IoT

DynamoDB's speed and scalability make it ideal for diverse use cases:

- **Mobile Apps**: Store and manage user data, app state, and other information for mobile apps, ensuring responsive and smooth user experiences.
- **Real-Time Applications**: Power real-time applications such as chat services, gaming platforms, and financial trading systems.
- **Internet of Things (IoT)**: Manage the vast amount of data generated by IoT devices, providing real-time insights and enabling intelligent automation.
- **High-Traffic Websites**: Handle massive traffic spikes and ensure consistent performance for high-traffic websites and applications.
- **Social Media Platforms**: Manage user profiles, social interactions, and other data for large-scale social media platforms.

By embracing the agility and scalability of DynamoDB, you can unlock new possibilities for your data-driven initiatives and build applications that are fast, responsive, and always available.

Amazon Redshift: The Data Warehousing Champion

In today's data-driven world, extracting meaningful insights from vast quantities of data requires a powerful engine. Enter Amazon Redshift, the scalable, secure, and cost-effective data warehousing champion that empowers you to unlock the hidden treasures within your data.

Imagine a world where you can analyze petabytes of data with blazing speed, gain instant answers to complex queries, and uncover hidden patterns that were previously shrouded in obscurity. This is the transformative power of Redshift, a data warehouse built for the demands of the modern enterprise.

Forget the limitations of traditional on-premise data warehouses. Redshift offers unparalleled scalability, allowing you to handle massive datasets with ease. It seamlessly integrates with other AWS services, enabling you to build comprehensive data pipelines and streamline your analytics workflow.

But Redshift's strength goes beyond mere size and speed. It provides a secure and reliable environment for your valuable data, ensuring its protection and compliance with industry standards. And with its pay-as-you-go pricing model, you can optimize your costs and only pay for the resources you use.

Whether you are a data analyst, a data scientist, or a business leader, Redshift empowers you to make data-driven decisions with confidence. It is the ideal platform for:

- **Analyzing Large Datasets**: Extract valuable insights from petabytes of data.
- **Running Complex Queries**: Gain instant answers to your toughest data questions.
- **Uncovering Hidden Trends**: Discover patterns and correlations that were previously invisible.
- **Making Data-Driven Decisions**: Inform your business strategies with actionable insights.

Are you ready to unleash the power of your data? Join the countless organizations that have chosen Redshift as their data warehousing champion and unlock the full potential of your data-driven journey.

Unpacking Data Warehousing: A Foundation for Big Data Analytics

In the age of big data, extracting meaningful insights requires a dedicated platform for storing, processing, and analyzing vast amounts of information. Data warehousing is a specialized technology designed to facilitate efficient and comprehensive data analysis.

Data warehouses act as centralized repositories for historical and current data, often gathered from diverse sources. This consolidated data serves as a foundation for business intelligence, reporting, and advanced analytics, enabling organizations to uncover hidden patterns, make informed decisions, and drive business growth.

Introducing Amazon Redshift: Scalable Data Warehousing in the Cloud

Among the leading data warehousing solutions, Amazon Redshift stands out as a powerful and versatile tool. Built specifically for the cloud, Redshift offers unparalleled scalability, performance, and cost-effectiveness, making it ideal for tackling massive data sets.

Redshift boasts several key features that empower data-driven organizations:

- **Unleashing the Power of Massively Parallel Processing (MPP)**: Redshift's architectural brilliance lies in its MPP technology. By distributing data across multiple nodes, it unlocks the power of parallel processing, enabling lightning-fast query execution. Imagine extracting insights from petabytes of data in mere seconds, a feat unimaginable with traditional data warehouses. This translates to faster decision-making, quicker response times, and ultimately, a competitive edge for your organization.
- **Scalability**: Redshift can seamlessly scale up to handle terabytes or even petabytes of data, ensuring you have the capacity to analyze your growing data volumes.
- **SQL Compatibility**: Redshift supports standard SQL, allowing you to leverage existing SQL skills for querying and analyzing your data.

Querying Data with Redshift: SQL and Beyond for Efficient Analysis

Redshift's robust SQL engine empowers you to extract valuable insights from your data with exceptional efficiency. Its capabilities extend far beyond basic querying, unveiling a world where complex analysis becomes effortless and insightful discoveries are just a query away.

- **Unlocking Familiarity with Standard SQL**: Redshift embraces the power of standard SQL, allowing data analysts and scientists to leverage their existing SQL knowledge. By employing familiar syntax, you can readily transition to Redshift and begin querying your data without the burden of learning a new language. This seamless transition minimizes the learning curve and allows you to quickly unlock the potential of your data.
- **Delving Deeper with Advanced SQL Functions**: Redshift goes beyond basic SQL, offering a comprehensive arsenal of built-in functions for data manipulation, aggregation, and statistical analysis. These powerful functions empower you to perform complex calculations, identify trends and patterns, and uncover hidden correlations within your data. From calculating statistical measures such as mean, median, and standard deviation to performing sophisticated data manipulation tasks such as joins and aggregations, Redshift equips you with the tools necessary to tackle even the most intricate data analysis challenges.
- **Transforming Data into Visual Insights**: Redshift seamlessly integrates with various visualization tools, enabling you to transform your data insights into captivating visuals. By presenting complex data in clear and compelling formats, you can communicate your findings effectively and ensure that your insights resonate with your audience. Visualizations not only enhance communication but also unlock new perspectives on your data, allowing you to identify patterns and trends that might otherwise remain hidden within spreadsheets and tables.
- **Beyond the Basics**: Redshift's querying capabilities extend beyond standard SQL and visualizations to provide additional functionalities:
    - **Redshift Query Editor**: A web-based interface for writing and executing SQL queries, offering a user-friendly platform for data analysis.
    - **Redshift Spectrum**: Analyze data directly in Amazon S3 without the need to move it into Redshift, ideal for large datasets.
    - **Amazon QuickSight**: Create interactive dashboards and visualizations directly within Redshift for immediate insights and data exploration.

Optimizing Redshift Performance: Tuning Queries and Managing Costs

In today's competitive landscape, maximizing data insights while minimizing costs is crucial for success. Redshift empowers you to achieve this delicate balance through its powerful optimization techniques, allowing you to extract maximum value from your data while maintaining cost-efficiency.

Crafting efficient SQL queries is the cornerstone of Redshift optimization. By analyzing and optimizing your queries, you can minimize unnecessary processing and optimize data retrieval, resulting in faster query execution and improved overall performance. Redshift provides various tools and techniques for query optimization, including:

- **Query Explain Plans**: Analyze the execution plan for your queries to identify bottlenecks and areas for improvement.
- **Redshift Query Editor**: Leverage the built-in query editor to visualize and optimize your queries visually.
- **Best Practices**: Utilize best practices for query writing, such as avoiding unnecessary joins and filtering data before aggregation.

Data Partitioning and Clustering:

Partitioning and clustering your data based on commonly queried attributes can significantly improve query performance and reduce read times. This allows Redshift to efficiently locate and retrieve only the relevant data, minimizing unnecessary processing and maximizing performance.

- **Partitioning**: Divide your data into smaller, manageable partitions based on specific criteria such as date range or customer ID.
- **Clustering**: Group data based on frequently accessed attributes to further improve query performance.

Utilizing Compression to Reduce Costs:

Redshift offers automatic data compression techniques that help you reduce storage costs without compromising query performance. By compressing your data, you can store more information within the same storage space, significantly lowering your storage expenses.

Implementing Workload Management:

Workload management techniques allow you to optimize Redshift usage and ensure cost-efficiency. By utilizing features such as Amazon Redshift Spectrum and automatic workload management, you can:

- **Offload queries to Amazon S3**: Analyze data directly in S3, reducing costs associated with data movement and storage within Redshift.
- **Optimize resource allocation**: Automatically adjust Redshift resources based on workload demands, ensuring cost-efficiency and preventing overprovisioning.

By implementing these optimization strategies, you can unlock the full potential of Redshift and achieve remarkable results:

- **Faster Query Execution**: Extract insights from your data more quickly and efficiently.

- **Improved Data Analysis**: Perform complex analyses with greater ease and accuracy.
- **Reduced Storage Costs**: Minimize storage expenses without compromising performance.
- **Enhanced Cost-Efficiency**: Optimize resource usage and ensure value for your investment.

Note: *Redshift is not just a data warehouse; it is a platform for unlocking the true potential of your data while maintaining cost-efficiency. By embracing its optimization techniques, you can embark on a journey of data discovery without compromising your budget.*

Use Cases for Redshift: Business Intelligence, Reporting, and Advanced Analytics

Redshift's capabilities make it a valuable asset for diverse use cases:

- **Business Intelligence (BI)**: Analyze historical data trends and gain insights into business performance, enabling informed decision-making.
- **Reporting**: Generate comprehensive reports and dashboards to track key metrics and visualize data trends effectively.
- **Marketing Analytics**: Analyze customer behavior, campaign performance, and market trends to optimize marketing strategies.
- **Financial Analysis**: Analyze financial data, identify trends, and predict future performance.
- **Scientific Research**: Analyze large datasets generated from scientific experiments and simulations.

By leveraging the scalability, performance, and cost-effectiveness of Amazon Redshift, you can unlock valuable insights from your data, gain a competitive edge, and drive your organization towards data-driven success.

Amazon Relational Database Service (RDS): The Trusted Choice for Structured Data

In the ever-evolving data landscape, one fundamental need remains constant: the reliable and secure storage of structured data. Enter Amazon RDS, the trusted choice for relational database management within the AWS ecosystem. This fully managed service empowers you to easily operate and scale your database of choice, ensuring optimal performance and unparalleled reliability.

Forget the complexities of managing your own database infrastructure. RDS takes care of the heavy lifting, freeing you to focus on what matters most: extracting valuable insights from your data. Whether you choose the familiar MySQL, the versatile PostgreSQL, the robust Microsoft SQL Server, or the high-performance Aurora, RDS provides a seamless and efficient platform for your relational database needs.

- **Unparalleled Scalability**: As your data volume grows, RDS seamlessly scales to accommodate your evolving needs. No longer are you limited by the constraints of traditional on-premises solutions. With RDS, you can effortlessly scale your database up or down with just a few clicks, ensuring peak performance without sacrificing cost-efficiency.
- **Enhanced Security**: Protecting your sensitive data is paramount. RDS prioritizes security with industry-leading features such as encryption at rest and in transit, automated backups, and access control mechanisms. You can be confident that your data is safe and protected within the robust AWS security infrastructure.
- **Simplified Management**: RDS eliminates the complexities of database management. With automated patching, monitoring, and backups, you can focus on your core business objectives while RDS handles the mundane tasks. This simplified management translates to time saved, resources freed, and a more efficient data management workflow.
- **Cost Optimization**: RDS embraces a pay-as-you-go pricing model, allowing you to pay only for the resources you use. This ensures cost-efficiency and minimizes unnecessary expenses. You can further optimize costs by leveraging features such as reserved instances and automated scaling, ensuring you receive optimal value for your investment.

RDS empowers you to:

- Easily manage and scale your relational databases.
- Focus on your data instead of infrastructure management.
- Ensure the security and integrity of your sensitive information.
- Optimize costs with flexible pricing and resource management options.

Whether you are a small startup or a large enterprise, RDS provides the perfect platform for your relational database needs. Embrace the peace of mind, reliability, and scalability that RDS offers and unlock the full potential of your structured data.

Relational Databases: The Bedrock of Data Management

For decades, relational databases have served as the bedrock of data management, offering a structured and organized approach to storing and retrieving information.

Their adherence to the relational model, characterized by tables, columns, and defined relationships, ensures data integrity and facilitates efficient data manipulation.

Relational databases excel at managing structured data with clearly defined relationships. This makes them ideal for applications where data needs to be organized, categorized, and accessed in a predictable manner. Examples include:

- **Transactional Applications**: Online shopping platforms, financial systems, and other applications that require real-time data transactions and ACID compliance (Atomicity, Consistency, Isolation, and Durability).
- **Web Applications**: Dynamic websites and web applications rely on structured data for user authentication, content management, and other functionalities.
- **E-commerce Platforms**: Managing product information, customer data, and order details.

Exploring RDS: Diverse Database Engine Options and Flexible Deployment Choices

Amazon RDS empowers you to choose the perfect database engine for your specific needs, offering a diverse selection of options within its managed service environment. This eliminates the need for infrastructure management and allows you to focus on building and deploying your applications.

A Realm of Database Engine Options:

- **Amazon Aurora**: This MySQL and PostgreSQL-compatible relational database engine boasts high performance, scalability, and availability. It outperforms MySQL by up to five times, making it ideal for demanding workloads.
- **MySQL**: As the most popular open-source relational database engine, MySQL is a familiar choice for many developers and administrators. Its ease of use and flexibility make it perfect for web applications, e-commerce platforms, and other online endeavors.
- **PostgreSQL**: Widely used for enterprise applications and complex data models, PostgreSQL is an object-relational database engine known for its robust features and rich data types. Its support for advanced functionalities such as stored procedures and triggers makes it a powerful tool for data-intensive applications.
- **Microsoft SQL Server**: This popular relational database engine reigns supreme in the Windows-based world. Its integration with Microsoft tools and services makes it the preferred choice for many Windows applications and enterprise environments.
- **Oracle Database**: As the leading enterprise-grade relational database engine,

Oracle Database offers robust features, high performance, and scalability, making it ideal for mission-critical business applications.

AWS Solution	Database Engine
RDS for MySQL	MySQL
RDS for PostgreSQL	PostgreSQL
RDS for SQL Server	Microsoft SQL Server
RDS for Oracle	Oracle Database
Aurora MySQL	MySQL-Compatible Aurora
Aurora PostgreSQL	PostgreSQL-Compatible Aurora
Redshift	Proprietary MPP Engine
Athena	Presto

Table 7.1: *Databases counterparts*

RDS provides several deployment options to meet your specific needs and preferences:

- **Multi-AZ deployments**: Ensure high availability and disaster recovery by deploying your database across multiple Availability Zones within a region.
- **Read Replicas**: Enhance scalability and performance by creating read-only replicas of your database that can serve read-intensive queries.
- **Aurora Serverless**: Leverage a serverless option for Aurora that automatically scales based on your workload, eliminating the need to manage database servers.
- **Database Snapshots**: Backup your database at any point in time and restore it as needed for testing or disaster recovery purposes.
- **Customizable Configurations**: Configure your database instances with specific memory, CPU, and storage resources to optimize performance for your workloads.

Beyond the diverse engine options and deployment choices, RDS offers a wealth of features that enhance your data management experience:

- **Automatic Patching and Backups**: Reduce administrative overhead with automated patching and backups that ensure your database is always up-to-date and protected.
- **Security Features**: Secure your data with features such as encryption at rest and in transit, access control mechanisms, and audit logging.

- **Monitoring and Logging**: Gain insights into your database performance and identify potential issues with comprehensive monitoring and logging capabilities.
- **Performance Insights**: Optimize your database performance with detailed performance insights and recommendations.

RDS provides several additional features to enhance your data management experience:

- Automated backups and point-in-time recovery.
- Read replicas for improved read performance.
- Parameter groups for configuration management.
- Monitoring and logging for performance insights.
- Security features such as encryption and access control.

RDS offers various advanced features and capabilities, including:

- **Amazon RDS Proxy**: Simplifies database management and improves security.
- **Amazon RDS Performance Insights**: Provides detailed performance metrics and recommendations.
- **Amazon RDS Custom**: Allows you to deploy your own database engine images.
- **RDS Data API**: Enables programmatic access to your RDS databases.

Managing RDS Databases: Tools for Administration, Security, and Backup

RDS provides a comprehensive set of tools for managing your databases:

- **AWS Management Console**: A user-friendly interface for managing databases, users, security settings, backups, and monitoring.
- **AWS CLI**: A command-line tool for automation and scripting tasks.
- **Database Management Tools**: Compatible third-party tools, such as MySQL Workbench and pgAdmin, provide advanced features for database administration.

Security features include:

- **User Authentication and Authorization**: Control access to your databases and prevent unauthorized data access.
- **Encryption**: Encrypt data at rest and in transit to protect sensitive information.
- **Auditing and Logging**: Monitor database activity and identify potential security threats.

Backup and recovery capabilities ensure data availability:

- **Point-in-Time Recovery**: Restore your database to any point-in-time within a backup window.
- **Automated Backups**: Schedule automatic backups to protect your data from accidental deletion or hardware failures.

Scaling RDS: Meeting Your Growing Data Needs with Ease

RDS offers seamless scaling options to accommodate your evolving data needs:

- **Vertical Scaling**: Increase the compute resources for your database instance to improve performance.
- **Horizontal Scaling**: Add read replicas to improve read performance and distribute load across multiple instances.
- **Bursting**: Automatically scale up your database resources to handle temporary spikes in traffic.

Use Cases for RDS: Transactional Applications, Web Applications, and E-commerce

RDS's diverse engine options, flexible deployment choices, and robust management tools make it a valuable asset for:

- **Transactional Applications**: Ensure reliable and consistent data handling for financial transactions, online payments, and other critical processes.
- **Web Applications**: Build dynamic and scalable web applications that rely on structured data for content management, user authentication, and personalization.
- **E-commerce Platforms**: Manage product information, customer data, orders, and payments efficiently.
- **Content Management Systems**: Store and manage content for websites, blogs, and other online platforms.
- **Enterprise Applications**: Support complex business processes and manage vast amounts of structured data.

By leveraging the capabilities of Amazon RDS, you can manage your structured data efficiently, ensuring data availability, security, and scalability for your data-driven applications.

Choosing the Right Storage Solution: A Strategic Approach

Navigating the diverse landscape of AWS storage solutions can be overwhelming. Selecting the perfect storage option requires careful consideration of your specific data requirements, budget, and future growth plans. This section will guide you through a strategic approach to choosing the ideal storage solution for your needs.

Matching Data Requirements to Storage Options: Selecting the Perfect Fit

The first step in choosing the right storage solution is clearly understanding your data requirements. Consider the following factors:

- **Data Type**: Structured (relational databases) or unstructured (images, videos, logs)
- **Data Size**: Gigabytes, terabytes, or petabytes
- **Access Frequency**: Frequently accessed data requires higher performance storage.
- **Durability and Availability**: How critical is data integrity and uptime?
- **Security Requirements**: Does the data need encryption and access control?

By evaluating these factors, you can match your data requirements to the most suitable storage option:

- **Amazon S3:** Ideal for large, unstructured data with infrequent access, offering high scalability and cost-effectiveness.
- **Amazon DynamoDB**: Perfect for NoSQL data requiring fast performance and high availability, ideal for real-time applications.
- **Amazon Redshift:** The go-to solution for data warehousing and large-scale analytics, ideal for analyzing massive historical datasets.
- **Amazon RDS**: The trusted choice for structured data with frequent access, offering various database engine options and managed services.

Cost Analysis and Optimization: Balancing Performance with Affordability

While performance and functionality are important, cost is a crucial factor in choosing a storage solution. AWS offers a transparent pay-as-you-go model and various storage classes with varying cost structures:

- **S3 Storage Classes**: Standard, Standard-IA, Glacier, and Glacier Deep Archive offer different cost-performance trade-offs.
- **DynamoDB**: Provides pay-per-read and pay-per-write capacity units, allowing you to optimize costs based on your access patterns.
- **Redshift**: Charges based on the number of nodes you use and the amount of data you store.
- **RDS**: Offers various pricing tiers and instance types to fit your performance and budget needs.

To optimize your storage costs, consider:

- **Utilizing the Right Storage Class**: Analyze your data access patterns and choose the most cost-effective storage class for your needs.
- **Right-Sizing your Instances**: Choose the appropriate instance type or database size based on your expected data volume and workload.
- **Auto-Scaling**: Implement auto-scaling to automatically adjust resources based on your changing demands, preventing unnecessary costs.
- **Monitoring and Optimizing**: Regularly monitor your storage usage and identify opportunities for further optimization.

Combining Services for Enhanced Functionality: Building Hybrid Solutions

AWS storage solutions are not mutually exclusive. You can combine them to create a hybrid solution that leverages the strengths of each service:

- Use S3 for archiving long-term data and Redshift for analyzing large datasets stored in S3.
- Use DynamoDB for real-time applications and RDS for storing transactional data related to those applications.
- Use S3 for static website content and CloudFront for content delivery network (CDN) distribution for faster loading times.
- Building hybrid solutions allows you to tailor your storage architecture to your specific needs and enjoy the benefits of different services.

Planning for Future Growth: Choosing Scalable and Flexible Storage Options

As your data volume and access requirements grow, your storage solution needs to adapt. Choose services that offer:

- **Horizontal Scaling**: Ability to add additional nodes or instances to increase capacity and performance.
- **Vertical Scaling**: Ability to increase compute resources within an existing instance for a performance boost.
- **Easy Migration:** Ability to seamlessly migrate your data between different storage services as your needs evolve.

By choosing scalable and flexible storage options, you can ensure your solution can support your growth and adapt to changing demands efficiently.

Your Journey Begins Now: Embarking on the Path to Data Mastery

Consider exploring services such as:

- **Amazon EFS**: A scalable file system designed for cloud applications.
- **AWS Snowball**: A data transfer service for securely moving large datasets to AWS.
- **Amazon S3 Glacier Instant Retrieval**: Provides rapid access to archived data stored in the Glacier storage class.
- **Amazon FSx for Lustre**: A high-performance file system optimized for compute-intensive workloads.

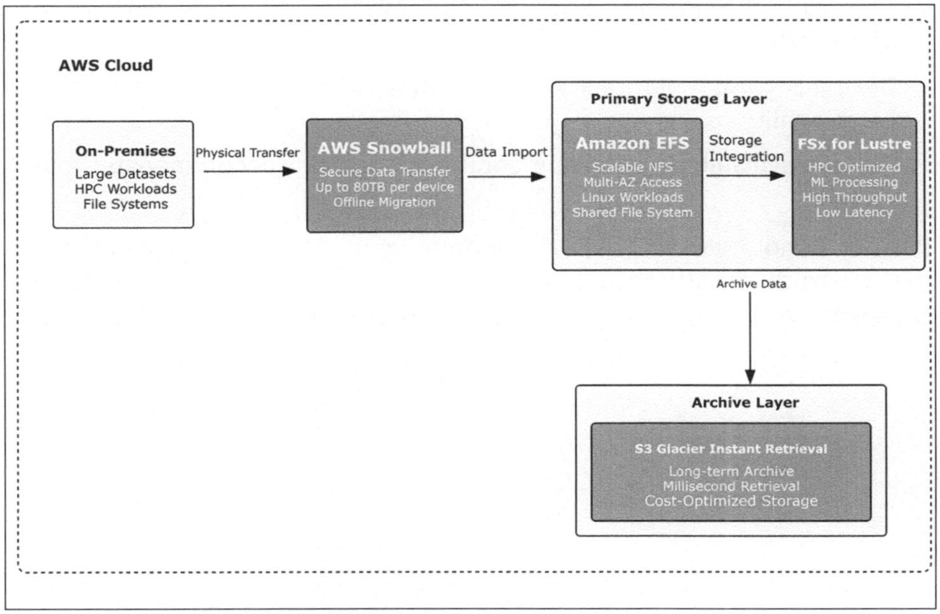

Figure 7.3: *Other Storage Services*

By continually optimizing your data architecture and leveraging advanced services, you can stay ahead of the curve and ensure your data remains a powerful asset in achieving your goals.

Remember, the possibilities are limitless. So, continue your exploration, embrace innovation, and watch your data-driven success soar to new heights!

Conclusion

This chapter has served as your compass, guiding you through the vast and exciting world of AWS data storage solutions. You have explored the unique capabilities of each service, from the object storage powerhouse S3 to the NoSQL champion DynamoDB, the data warehousing behemoth Redshift, and the trusted choice for relational databases, RDS.

Choosing the right storage solution is a crucial step in optimizing your data infrastructure. By understanding your data requirements, analyzing costs, considering hybrid solutions, and planning for future growth, you can make informed decisions and leverage the power of AWS storage services to achieve your data-driven goals. Remember, there is no one-size-fits-all solution; the perfect storage choice depends on your unique needs and circumstances.

Equipped with this knowledge, you are now empowered to:

- Match your data requirements to the most suitable storage options.
- Craft a cost-effective storage strategy that balances performance and affordability.
- Design hybrid solutions by combining different services for enhanced functionality.
- Choose scalable and flexible solutions that can accommodate your future growth.

This journey is not over yet. As you continue your data-driven endeavors, you will discover a wealth of advanced storage services within the AWS ecosystem, each offering specialized functionalities that can further enhance your data infrastructure.

CHAPTER 8
Orchestrating Data Flow

Introduction

Welcome to the conductor's booth of data pipelines! This chapter equips you with the tools and techniques to seamlessly move both batch and real-time data from diverse sources, preparing them for insightful analysis. By the end of this chapter, you will be able to confidently design and build data pipelines for batch and real-time data, leveraging best practices for ingestion, integration, and transformation; master tools such as Kinesis Firehose, SQS/SNS, Lambda, and Glue seamlessly move data from diverse sources, adapting to the specific characteristics of each data flow; and prepare your data for analysis, unlocking the potential for real-time insights and powerful analytics, regardless of the data arrival pattern.

Structure

In this chapter, we will cover the following topics:

- Understanding the Data Symphony
  - Diverse Data Sources
  - Understanding Data Formats
- Introducing the Instruments
  - Kinesis Firehose
  - SQS/SNS
  - AWS Lambda
  - AWS Glue
- Composing the Flow
  - Designing Resilient Pipelines
  - Streamlining Data Processing
  - Orchestrating the Symphony

- Real-World Symphonies
  - Building a Real-Time Analytics Pipeline
  - Integrating Legacy Data Sources

Unleashing the Symphony: Understanding Data Sources and Formats

The first movement of our data symphony begins with understanding the instruments – your data sources. We will explore a vast orchestra of possibilities from the following:

- **Sensor Streams:** Imagine a constant flow of data, like temperature readings from weather stations or website traffic updates. These are real-time data sources, continuously sending information that demands immediate processing.
- **Social Media Feeds:** Tweets, comments, and shares pour in like a never-ending melody. This, too, is real-time data, requiring nimble processing to capture fleeting insights.
- **Traditional Databases:** The tried-and-true data repositories. Think of customer records, financial transactions, or product inventories. These can be either batch or real-time sources, depending on how often they are updated.
- **File Systems:** A treasure trove of documents, logs, and reports waiting to be discovered. These are typically batch data sources, processed periodically in chunks.

Each source has its distinct rhythm. We will train you to distinguish the telltale signs of the following:

- **Data Volume:** Is it a high-frequency, low-volume stream of tweets, or a low-frequency, high-volume batch upload of sales data? Understanding volume helps you choose the right tools and strategies.
- **Arrival Pattern:** Does data arrive continuously, in bursts, or at scheduled intervals? Recognizing the arrival pattern ensures smooth flow and avoids bottlenecks.
- **Structure:** Is it neatly organized data like CSV files, or free-flowing text like social media posts? Identifying data structure determines the processing techniques needed.

Just like musicians need sheet music, data needs formats to be understood. We will demystify common formats, such as:

- **JSON:** A structured format with key-value pairs. It is perfect for web services and APIs and, particularly suitable for real-time data exchange.

- **CSV:** Comma-separated values, simple and widespread, ideal for batch data transfers.
- **Parquet:** Efficient and compressed, optimized for big data analysis, often used in both batch and real-time scenarios.

Not all data follows a rigid structure. We will equip you with the following tools to handle:

- **Text data:** From social media to customer reviews, text analysis techniques unlock hidden insights in unstructured words.
- **Log files:** Unravel the cryptic messages of system logs to understand application behavior and troubleshoot issues.

By mastering both data sources and formats, you will be ready to design data flow strategies. These strategies seamlessly integrate the diverse instruments of your data symphony, paving the way for powerful analysis and insightful discoveries.

Meet the Players: Your Data Flow Instruments

Welcome to the instrument shop of the Data Orchestra! Here, we will meet the tools that power your data flow, ensuring each note reaches its destination with precision and clarity.

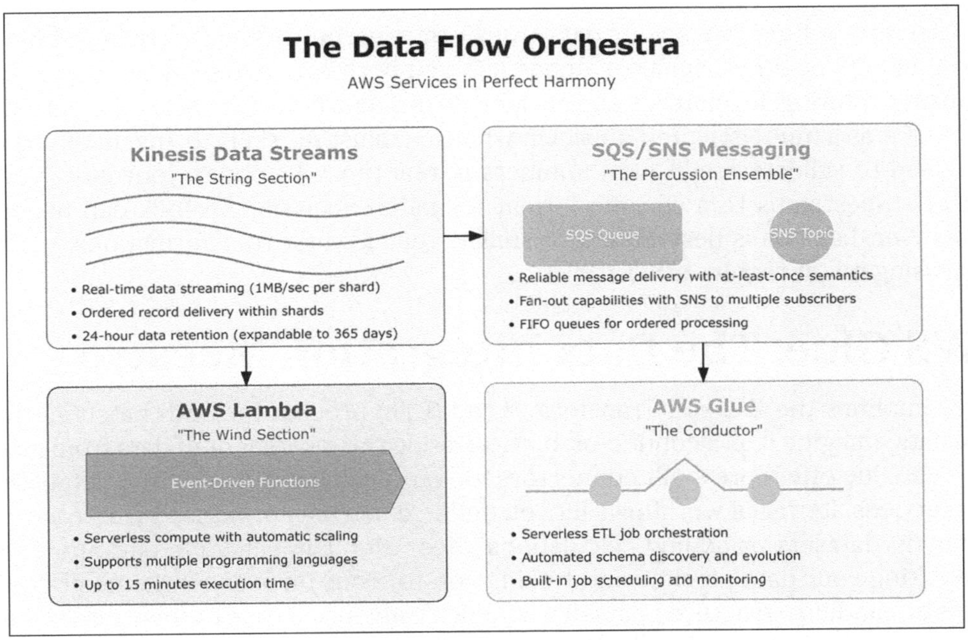

Figure 8.1: *Data Flow Orchestra*

Kinesis Firehose: The Streamlining Screamer

Imagine a fire hose but, for data! This high-velocity channel ingests real-time data streams from millions of sources simultaneously, such as tweets, sensor readings, or website clicks. It seamlessly compresses and transforms your data on the fly, preparing it for smooth downstream delivery. Configure Firehose to send data to various destinations, such as S3 for analysis, Redshift for warehousing, or Lambda for real-time processing. Remember, Firehose thrives on the constant flow of real-time data, so consider its strengths when designing your data pipeline.

SQS/SNS: The Messengers and Alert System

Think of SQS as a reliable backstage queue. It buffers data, both batch and real-time, ensuring smooth delivery even if downstream resources are temporarily unavailable. Imagine a line of musicians waiting to perform; SQS keeps them organized and prevents bottlenecks. Meanwhile, SNS acts as your data concierge, sending alerts or triggering downstream events when new data arrives. Need to kick off a Lambda function when a new batch of sensor data lands? SNS will be your messenger. Remember, SQS and SNS adapt to your data flow rate, handling bursts and steady streams with equal aplomb.

AWS Lambda: The On-Demand Swiss Army Knife

This serverless function is your data transformation powerhouse. Triggered by data arrival in SQS or other signals, Lambda lets you perform on-the-fly actions, such as cleansing, filtering, formatting, and enriching your data before it enters the next stage. Think of it as a multi-talented musician who can adjust his skills to any incoming data set. Need to validate credit card numbers in real time? Lambda's your guy. Want to convert timestamps to a specific format for batch analysis? Lambda can handle it. Remember, Lambda is best suited for smaller, quick-burst transformations; complex processing might require other tools.

AWS Glue: The Data Integration Maestro

Glue simplifies the Extract, Transform, Load (ETL) process for both batch and real-time data. Imagine it as a conductor, orchestrating the movement of data from diverse sources. Glue offers pre-built connectors for various data sources, from databases to web services. Its visual workflows let you define data transformations with ease, such as joining datasets or adding calculations. Plus, Glue can schedule data movement, automating your data pipeline and freeing you to focus on analysis. Remember, Glue excels at handling structured data; for complex transformations or unstructured data, you might need additional tools.

By mastering these instruments, you will be able to design and execute data pipelines that seamlessly move data from its source to its destination, regardless of its arrival pattern or format. Remember, each instrument has its strengths and weaknesses, so choosing the right combination for your data symphony is key to a harmonious flow.

Kinesis Firehose: Your Real-Time Data Ingestion Powerhouse

Imagine a fire hose, but instead of water, it pumps in data at a blazing-fast pace from millions of sources concurrently. That is the magic of Kinesis Firehose, your gateway to capturing and delivering real time data streams for insightful analysis. Buckle up, data enthusiasts, as we delve into its capabilities and configuration for optimal performance.

Key Features:

- **Real-Time Ingestion Champion**: Firehose thrives on continuous data flows, effortlessly handling thousands of records per second. Sensor readings, social media feeds, website clicks – you name it, Firehose gobbles it up in real-time, ensuring you never miss a beat.
- **Scalability that Impresses**: No need to fret about sudden data surges. Firehose automatically scales up and down to accommodate your fluctuating data volume, guaranteeing smooth delivery even during peak periods.
- **Destination Flexibility:** Where does your data journey end? Firehose offers diverse destinations – send it to S3 for analysis, Redshift for warehousing, or any other AWS service or custom endpoint that supports HTTP ingestion. The choice is yours!
- **Basic Transformations Instantly**: While not a full-fledged transformation engine, Firehose provides essential data manipulation tools such as compression, record delimiting, and partitioning. Customize your data for seamless integration with your chosen destination.
- **Cost-Effective Hero:** Pay only for the data you ingest, making Firehose a budget-friendly option for real-time data pipelines.

Configuration Essentials:

- **Delivery Stream Creation**: Define the source of your data stream, be it Kinesis Data Streams, Apache Kafka, or other compatible sources.
- **Transformation Touches**: Apply basic transformations such as compression, record delimiting, and data partitioning to tailor the data to your destination's needs.

- **Destination Defined:** Choose your desired destination – S3, Redshift, Elasticsearch Service, or even a custom endpoint. Firehose delivers!
- **Buffering for Reliability:** Set up buffering to ensure data delivery even if your destination encounters temporary hiccups. Firehose automatically retries failed deliveries, safeguarding your data integrity.
- **Security Always Matters:** Implement IAM roles and encryption to protect your data in transit and at rest. Security is paramount!

Real-World Applications:

- **Real-Time Fraud Detection**: Analyze financial transactions as they occur to identify and prevent fraudulent activities before they cause damage.
- **IoT Analytics Powerhouse**: Collect and analyze sensor data from connected devices in real-time, gaining insights into performance and optimizing operations.
- **Social Media Sentiment Pulse**: Track and analyze public sentiment towards your brand or product based on real-time social media mentions, understanding your audience like never before.

Note:

- *Firehose shines with real-time data streams, not batch processing.*
- *Consider Lambda functions for more complex data transformations alongside Firehose.*
- *Monitor your data flow and adjust configurations for optimal performance and cost-effectiveness.*

To truly master Firehose, dive deeper into the following:

- **Advanced Configuration Options**: Explore buffer sizing, data ordering, and partitioning strategies for tailored performance.
- **Security Best Practices**: Implement granular access control and encryption mechanisms for robust data protection.
- **Integration with Other Services**: Learn how Firehose complements tools such as Lambda, S3, and Redshift for comprehensive data pipelines.
- **Monitoring and Troubleshooting**: Discover techniques to monitor data flow, identify errors, and optimize your Firehose setup.

By harnessing the power of Kinesis Firehose, you unlock the world of real-time data. Gain valuable insights as events unfold, make informed decisions based on the latest information, and revolutionize your data-driven approach. So, unleash the data firehose and watch your analytics soar to new heights!

SQS/SNS: The Unsung Heroes of Your Data Flow Symphony

Imagine an orchestra conductor relying solely on unreliable messengers to deliver sheet music to musicians. Chaos would ensue! In the data world, reliable communication is just as crucial. Enter SQS and SNS, your essential duo for buffering data, triggering actions, and ensuring smooth information flow, regardless of data arrival patterns.

SQS: Your Reliable Data Queue Maestro

In the grand orchestra of data pipelines, Amazon SQS plays a crucial role as the maestro of message queues. It ensures smooth and reliable communication between different components, guaranteeing that data flows seamlessly between services without getting lost or overwhelmed. Let us delve into the magic of SQS and explore how it can elevate your data pipeline to new heights of efficiency and resilience.

Defining SQS:

Think of SQS as a virtual waiting room for your data. It acts as a message queue, temporarily storing data messages of various sizes and formats (text, JSON, and so on) until downstream resources are ready to receive them. This buffering mechanism offers several advantages, such as:

- **Decoupling Components:** SQS decouples data producers (for example, web applications) from consumers (for example, analytics engine), allowing them to operate independently, even with varying processing speeds. Imagine user activity data being sent to SQS without overwhelming your analytics system.
- **Reliability Guarantee**: Data does not disappear! SQS offers at least one delivery, ensuring messages reach their destination even if the receiving system experiences temporary issues. Say goodbye to data loss anxieties.
- **Scalability Magic**: SQS automatically scales up and down based on your message volume, ensuring smooth message delivery during peak periods. No need to worry about infrastructure bottlenecks.
- **Flexibility for All**: SQS caters to diverse use cases. Send short messages for notifications or store larger data payloads for complex processing.

SQS goes beyond basic queuing, offering additional functionalities, such as:

- **FIFO Ordering**: Ensure messages are processed in the exact order they were sent, crucial for financial transactions or log processing.
- **Dead Letter Queues**: Route undeliverable messages to a separate queue for troubleshooting or manual intervention.

- **Visibility Timeout:** Control how long a message remains invisible to other consumers after being received, managing processing timeouts.
- **Message Attributes**: Attach additional metadata to messages for context and richer processing by downstream systems.

Security and Monitoring:

- **Encryption**: Protect your data at rest and in transit with AES-256 encryption.
- **IAM Roles**: Control access to SQS queues and define who can send and receive messages.
- **CloudWatch Metrics**: Monitor queue size, delivery latency, and errors for proactive performance optimization.

Adapting to Your Data Flow:

- **High-Volume Streams**: Use fan-out configurations to distribute messages to multiple downstream consumers for efficient processing.
- **Bursty Data Flows**: Leverage SQS's ability to handle sudden spikes in message arrivals without compromising delivery reliability.

Remember:

- SQS excels at buffering, decoupling, and reliable delivery. Consider Lambda functions for complex data processing triggered by SQS messages.
- Explore complementary tools like SNS for real-time notifications based on message arrival.
- Design your queues with appropriate retention periods and visibility timeouts to optimize performance and cost.

SNS: Your Data Flow Alert System

In the data world, timely notifications and triggers are crucial for efficient data processing. Enter Amazon Simple Notification Service (SNS), your data flow's alert system and trigger maestro, ensuring swift action based on data arrival and events.

Defining SNS:

Think of SNS as your data flow's personal notification system. It acts as a flexible messaging platform, sending real-time notifications based on various triggers to diverse destinations, such as:

- **Email and SMS:** Get instantly notified when new data arrives in queues (such as SQS), allowing for prompt action. Imagine receiving an SMS alert about a critical system error.
- **Lambda Triggers:** Kick-off serverless functions in response to new data or

events, automating downstream processing workflows. Think image resizing triggered by new image uploads.

- **HTTP Endpoints:** Send notifications to any web service that can handle HTTP requests, integrating seamlessly with your existing infrastructure.

SNS adapts to your specific data flow patterns, such as:

- **High-Volume Streams:** Use fan-out configurations to distribute notifications to multiple subscribers efficiently. This ensures timely action even with large data volumes.
- **Real-Time Triggers**: Leverage SNS's low latency messaging for near-instantaneous notifications and trigger actions in real-time. Imagine detecting fraudulent transactions and blocking them immediately.
- **Topic Routing**: Filter notifications based on specific criteria (for example, data type or source) and send them only to relevant subscribers, avoiding information overload.

Beyond Basic Notifications: Advanced Features

SNS offers more than just sending messages, as mentioned below:

- **Subscriptions**: Manage different types of subscriptions (email, SMS, Lambda) with granular control over access and permissions.
- **Platform Endpoints**: Send notifications directly to mobile devices through Apple Push Notification Service (APNS) and Google Cloud Messaging (GCM).
- **Delivery Retry and Redirection**: Ensure notifications reach their destination with retries and fallback mechanisms.
- **Monitoring and Metrics**: Track notification delivery status, latency, and errors for performance optimization.

By mastering SNS, you transform your data pipelines from reactive to proactive. Respond to data events in real time, trigger automated actions, and keep stakeholders informed. So, silence the data communication lag and let the notifications and triggers of your data flow sing in harmony!

Adapting to Your Data Flow Rhythm

Both SQS and SNS adapt to your specific data flow, as mentioned below:

- **For High-Volume Streams**: Use fan-out configurations in SNS to distribute messages to multiple downstream subscribers, ensuring efficient processing of large data volumes.
- **For Bursty Data Flows**: Leverage SQS's ability to handle sudden spikes in message arrivals without compromising delivery reliability.

Beyond the Basics:

- **Security Measures**: Implement IAM roles and encryption to protect your data within SQS and SNS.
- **Monitoring and Metrics**: Track queue sizes, delivery latency, and errors to optimize your configuration.
- **Advanced Features**: Explore SQS message attributes, dead-letter queues, and SNS filtering for granular control.

Remember:

- SQS excels at buffering and decoupling, while SNS focuses on real-time notifications and triggers.
- Consider using them together for comprehensive data flow management.
- Explore complementary tools like Lambda for complex data processing triggered by SNS.

By mastering SQS and SNS, you become the conductor of your data flow symphony, ensuring seamless communication, reliable delivery, and timely action on valuable information. So, silence the data communication chaos and let the music of your data flow resonate!

AWS Lambda: Your Serverless Swiss Army Knife for Data Flow Agility

Imagine needing a tool for every imaginable data transformation within your pipeline. The toolbox would be cumbersome, and managing it, a nightmare. AWS Lambda is your serverless Swiss Army Knife, offering agility and power for on-the-fly data manipulation, catering to both batch and real-time data needs.

Defining Lambda

Think of Lambda as a code execution engine in the cloud. You upload your code (functions) written in various languages, such as Python, Node.js, or Java, and specify triggers. When a trigger fires (for example, new data in SQS), Lambda spins up your code, executes it, and then scales back down, eliminating server management overhead.

Causes to use Lambda for Data Flow:

- **Serverless Magic:** No servers to provision, manage, or scale. Focus on code, and Lambda handles the infrastructure.
- **Trigger-Based Execution**: Respond to various events, including SQS messages, API calls, or scheduled events. Automate data processing based on your needs.

- **Flexible Transformations**: From simple data cleansing to complex calculations and aggregations, Lambda empowers you to manipulate data on the fly.
- **Pay-Per-Use Billing**: Only pay for the compute time your code uses, making it cost-effective for both small and large data volumes.
- **Batch and Real-Time Friendly**: Lambda adapts to your data flow. Process data in batches triggered by SQS or handle real-time data streams seamlessly.

Unleashing Your Data Transformation Power:

- **Data Cleansing and Validation**: Ensure data quality by removing typos, and formatting inconsistencies, and validating against defined rules.
- **Data Enrichment**: Add context to your data by joining records from different sources, calculating derived metrics, or performing geocoding.
- **Data Filtering and Routing**: Send data to different downstream destinations based on specific criteria, ensuring efficient processing.
- **Real-Time Analytics**: Process data streams in real-time for tasks, such as fraud detection, sentiment analysis, or anomaly detection.

Beyond the Basics:

- **Integration with Other Services**: Combine Lambda with SQS, SNS, DynamoDB, and other AWS services for comprehensive data pipelines.
- **Security Best Practices**: Implement IAM roles and encryption to protect data within Lambda functions.
- **Monitoring and Debugging**: Utilize CloudWatch logs and metrics to track function performance and identify issues.

Remember:

- Lambda excels at short-lived, stateless tasks. For complex, long-running processes, consider other options like EC2 instances.
- Choose the right programming language and libraries based on your needs and expertise.
- Design your functions for scalability and efficient resource utilization.

By mastering Lambda, you transform your data pipeline from rigid to agile, responding to changing needs and data patterns with ease. So, unleash the power of this serverless Swiss Army Knife and watch your data flow dance to your commands!

AWS Glue: Conducting Your Data Integration Symphony with Ease

Ever dreamed of being a data integration maestro, effortlessly orchestrating the movement and transformation of information from diverse sources? Look no further than AWS Glue, your conductor's baton for crafting seamless Extract, Transform, Load (ETL) processes, catering to both batch and real-time data needs.

Imagine Glue as your data integration Swiss Army Knife, equipped with the following:

- **A Chorus of Pre-Built Connectors: Connect Seamlessly to Any Data Source**

  Forget complex manual configurations! Glue boasts a vast network of over 80 pre-built connectors, acting as your versatile musicians, each specializing in a different data source, as follows:

  - **Database Maestro:** Connect to relational databases such as MySQL, PostgreSQL, Oracle, and Redshift with ease, extracting data for analysis. Imagine effortlessly retrieving customer data from your CRM system.
  - **File System Harmony**: Integrate with various file systems, including Amazon S3, on-premises storage, and custom endpoints. Think of ingesting sales data from flat files stored in your data lake.
  - **Cloud Storage Integration**: Access data from popular cloud storage services, such as Amazon S3, Azure Blob Storage, and Google Cloud Storage, bringing together information from diverse cloud environments. Imagine combining website logs from different cloud providers for unified analytics.
  - **Custom Endpoint Connection**: Need to connect to a unique data source not covered by pre-built connectors? No problem! Glue's custom endpoint capability allows you to define connections and data formats for tailored integration. Imagine connecting to a specialized sensor data feed for industrial IoT analysis.

This rich library of connectors eliminates the need for manual coding, saving you time and effort while ensuring reliable and secure data access.

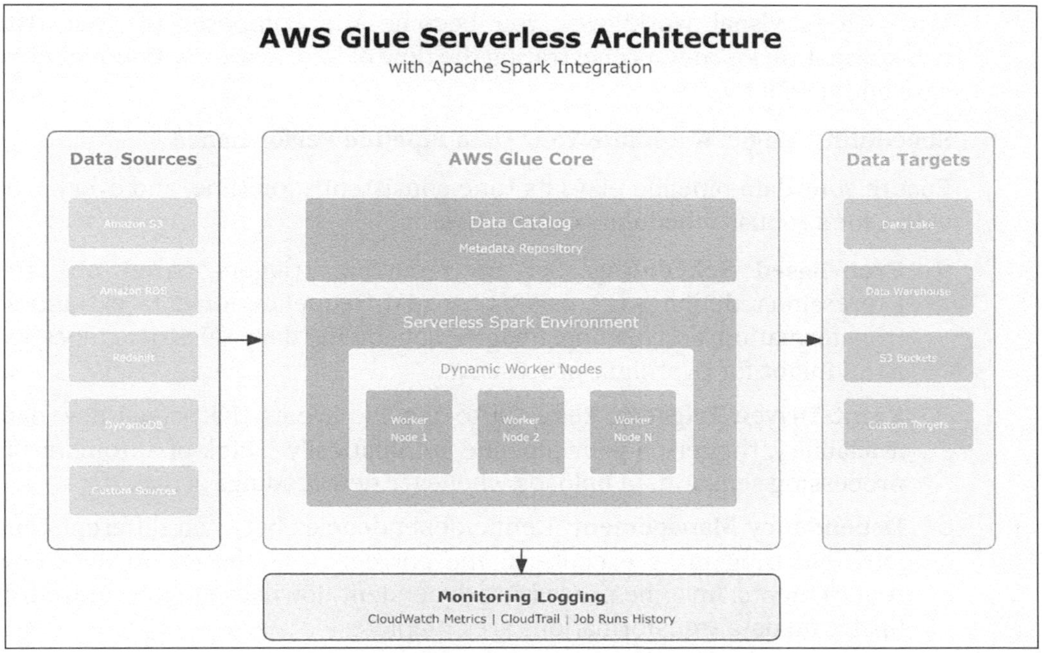

Figure 8.2: AWS *Glue Serverless Architecture*

- **Visual Workflows: Compose Your Data Transformation Symphony**

  Gone are the days of complex coding for data transformations! Glue's intuitive visual interface empowers you to drag and drop your way to success.

  - **Transformation Toolbox**: Access a wide range of built-in operators for data cleansing, filtering, joining, aggregations, and more. Imagine cleansing customer data, filtering out invalid entries, and joining it with purchase records for enriched analysis.
  - **No Coding Required**: The visual interface eliminates the need for writing code, making data transformation accessible to users of all technical skill levels. Think of business analysts easily manipulating data without needing expertise in programming languages.
  - **Custom Code Integration**: For complex transformations beyond built-in operators, Glue seamlessly integrates with custom Python or Scala code. Imagine incorporating advanced logic or machine learning models into your data pipeline.
  - **Visualization and Monitoring**: Visualize your data transformations step-by-step, gain insights into data flow, and monitor job progress for informed decision-making. Think of seeing how each transformation shapes your data and identifying potential bottlenecks.

With Glue's visual workflows, you become the composer of your data transformation journey, orchestrating the flow of information with unmatched ease and flexibility.

- **Scheduling Magic: Automate Your Data Pipeline Performance**

  Ensure your data pipeline plays its tune consistently, on time, and every time with Glue's robust scheduling capabilities.

  - **Cron-Based Scheduling**: Set up recurring triggers based on cron expressions, defining the exact time and frequency for data extraction, transformation, and loading. Imagine scheduling daily sales data ingestion at midnight for overnight processing.
  - **Event-Driven Triggers:** Respond to specific events that signal new data availability, triggering your pipeline automatically. Think of automatically processing sensor data uploads whenever new readings arrive.
  - **Dependency Management**: Define dependencies between different Glue jobs, ensuring tasks execute in the correct order based on data flow requirements. Imagine processing dependent downstream jobs only after upstream data transformations are complete.
  - **Monitoring and Alerts**: Monitor job execution status, track completion times, and receive alerts for errors or failures, maintaining control over your data pipeline's performance. Think of being notified if a job exceeds its expected execution time for proactive intervention.

By leveraging Glue's scheduling features, you transform your data pipeline from manual and reactive to automated and proactive, ensuring timely data availability and insights generation.

Catering to All Data Rhythms

Whether you're dealing with batch data (think daily sales reports) or real-time data streams (for example, social media feeds), Glue adapts to your flow.

Batch Efficiency: Rehearsing for a Flawless Performance

For large datasets like daily sales reports, Glue ensures maximum efficiency and scalability with optimized data partitioning and parallel processing.

- **Data Partitioning**: Imagine dividing your orchestra into sections (partitions) for simultaneous practice. Glue partitions your data into manageable chunks, enabling parallel processing. Each partition can be processed independently, significantly reducing overall processing time. Think of multiple analysts simultaneously analyzing different sales regions.

- **Optimized Storage**: Glue intelligently stores partitioned data in efficient formats such as Apache Parquet, minimizing storage footprint and optimizing access speed. Think of storing sheet music in easily accessible binders for quick retrieval during rehearsals.
- **Job Optimization**: Glue automatically tunes jobs based on data size and available resources, ensuring optimal performance. Imagine adjusting the number of musicians based on the complexity of the piece without compromising quality.

With these features, Glue transforms your batch data processing into a well-rehearsed performance, delivering results swiftly and efficiently.

Real-Time Agility: Improvising with the Flow

For real-time data streams like social media feed from Kinesis Firehose which processes data as it arrives; Glue offers unmatched agility and responsiveness:

- **Real-Time Integration**: Connect directly to real-time data sources such as Kinesis Firehose, ingesting data as it arrives. Imagine your musicians receiving notes and cues in real time, adapting their performance instantly.
- **Continuous Processing**: Unlike batch jobs with defined start and end times, Glue processes real-time data continuously, ensuring you never miss a beat. Think of your orchestra adapting to audience reactions and playing without interruption.
- **Micro-Batching**: For efficient processing of real-time streams, Glue breaks them down into manageable micro-batches, enabling parallel processing and faster insights generation. Imagine dividing incoming music sheets into smaller sections for easier sight-reading by your musicians.
- **Stateful Processing**: Glue can maintain state information across micro-batches, allowing for complex calculations and aggregations on real-time data. Imagine your musicians building upon previous melodies to create a cohesive improvisation.

Glue offers advanced features to fine-tune your data symphony, such as:

- **Custom Code Components**: Extend Glue's capabilities with custom Python or Scala code for complex transformations. It is like adding guest soloists to your orchestra for a unique performance.
- **Data Quality and Monitoring**: Ensure data integrity with built-in data validation and transformation monitoring tools. Keep your musical composition error-free!

- **Cost Optimization**: Leverage serverless capabilities and pay-per-use pricing for cost-effective data integration. No need to rent an entire concert hall when you only need a chamber ensemble.

Note:

- *Glue is best for structured data; for complex unstructured data, consider additional tools.*
- *While Glue offers basic transformations, complex logic might require Lambda functions.*
- *Design your data flows for efficiency and scalability to handle varying data volumes.*

By mastering AWS Glue, you become the conductor of your data integration journey, harmonizing diverse data sources into a cohesive melody. So, raise your baton, let the data flow, and compose beautiful insights for informed decision-making!

Conclusion

Congratulations! You have completed this chapter , along with your journey through the core tools for orchestrating a flawless data flow. You have learned to harness the power of Kinesis Firehose, your real-time data ingestion powerhouse. You have discovered the art of buffering and triggering with the dynamic duo of SQS and SNS. You have unleashed the serverless magic of Lambda for agile data transformations. And finally, you have mastered the data integration maestro, Glue, seamlessly connecting diverse sources and scheduling automated data movement.

Remember, a well-orchestrated data flow isn't a one-time performance; it is a continuous journey. Keep experimenting, monitoring, and optimizing your data pipelines to ensure they adapt to your evolving needs and data patterns. As your data grows and diversifies, remember the tools and techniques in this chapter - they will be your guiding light on the path to data-driven success.

So, step off the conductor's stand, baton held high, and lead your data on a beautiful symphony of insights. The stage is yours, and the music of your data awaits!

As we journey deeper into the world of data pipelines, the next chapter takes us beyond the fundamentals. Dive into advanced techniques for complex transformations, orchestrate intricate flows with mastery, and unlock the hidden insights within your data. Get ready to unleash the full potential of your data pipelines and empower your organization with transformative insights.

Chapter 9
Advanced Data Pipelines and Transformation

Introduction

Having built the solid foundation of your data flow with the tools explored in *Chapter 8, Orchestrating Data Flow*, it is time to embark on a journey to new heights. This chapter will be your guide, unlocking the secrets to orchestrating complex workflows with the finesse of a seasoned conductor. Imagine coordinating multiple data processing steps seamlessly, ensuring every component plays its part flawlessly – that is the power we will tap into with dedicated services such as AWS Data Pipeline and Lambda Step Functions.

But our exploration does not stop there. We will delve deeper, unlocking advanced transformations beyond basic cleansing and filtering. Dive into techniques such as anomaly detection to uncover hidden patterns within your data, and learn the art of feature engineering to craft the perfect ingredients for your machine-learning models.

Finally, we will master the full potential of Glue's capabilities. By writing custom Spark and Python scripts, can handle complex data transformations for batch and real-time data, pushing the boundaries of what is possible. Get ready to unleash the true power within your data pipelines and empower your organization with transformative insights.

By the end of this chapter, you will be equipped to design efficient and scalable data pipelines catering to your specific needs and data volumes; orchestrate complex workflows confidently, ensuring smooth data flow and processing, even for intricate dependencies and conditional logic; and extract deeper insights from your data through advanced techniques, such as anomaly detection and feature engineering.

Take complete control over your data pipelines with powerful orchestration capabilities.

So, put on your data conductor hat, grab your metaphorical baton, and be ready to compose a symphony of advanced data pipelines that unlock valuable insights and propel your business forward!

Structure

In this chapter, the following topics will be covered:

- Building Efficient and Scalable Data Pipelines
  - AWS Data Pipeline
  - Introduction to AWS Step Functions
  - Choosing the Right Service
  - Designing for Efficiency
  - Monitoring and Performance Optimization
- Advanced-Data Transformations
  - Anomaly Detection
  - Feature Engineering
- Mastering Data Pipeline Orchestration
  - Deep Dive into AWS Step Functions
  - Advanced Glue Job Techniques
  - End-to-End Orchestration Strategies

AWS Data Pipeline: Your Orchestrator for Complex Data Workflows

While AWS offers various services for data ingestion, transformation, and analysis, AWS Data Pipeline stands out as a dedicated tool for orchestrating complex data workflows. Think of it as your conductor, overseeing the seamless execution of multiple data processing steps in a defined sequence.

What can you do with AWS Data Pipeline?

- **Build Batch Data Pipelines**: Process large datasets (for example, daily sales reports) periodically, ensuring efficient and reliable data movement and transformation.
- **Define Dependencies**: Chain different data processing activities sequentially, ensuring each step starts only after the previous one finishes successfully.
- **Schedule Pipeline Execution**: Set up recurring schedules (for example, daily, weekly) for automatic data pipeline runs, eliminating manual intervention.

- **Monitor and Manage Pipeline Runs**: Track the progress of each pipeline activity, identify errors, and troubleshoot issues for smooth operation.
- **Integrate with Diverse Services**: Leverage pre-built connectors to access data from various sources such as databases, S3 buckets, and custom endpoints.
- **Transform Data with Custom Code**: Use Python or Scala scripts to perform complex data manipulations beyond built-in functionalities.

Key Features of AWS Data Pipeline:

- **Visual Workflow Designer**: Drag-and-drop interface for building pipeline definitions without coding, even for users with limited technical expertise.
- **Flexible Scheduling**: Schedule pipelines based on cron expressions, event triggers (for example, new data arrival), or manual execution.
- **Fault Tolerance**: Automatically retries failed tasks and handles errors gracefully, ensuring pipeline resiliency.
- **Scalability**: Handles large datasets and scales automatically based on workload demands.
- **Security**: Offers access control and encryption features to protect data privacy and integrity.

Who should use AWS Data Pipeline?

- **Data Engineers and Architects**: Build robust and scalable data pipelines for complex batch data processing needs.
- **Business Analysts**: Leverage the visual interface to create simple pipelines without coding knowledge.
- **Organizations with Large-Scale Data Processing Requirements**: Efficiently manage and orchestrate complex data workflows.

Considerations and Alternatives:

- While powerful, Data Pipeline is in maintenance mode with no new features planned. Consider future-proofing your data pipelines by exploring alternatives, such as:
    - **AWS Glue ETL Jobs**: Serverless data integration service with visual interface and custom code capabilities.
    - **AWS Step Functions**: Orchestrates serverless workflows of Lambda functions for more flexible orchestration.
    - **Custom Coding with Lambda and Other Services**: For maximum control and flexibility, build your orchestration logic using your preferred tools.

Introduction to AWS Step Functions

In the world of data, AWS Step Functions acts as your conductor, orchestrating diverse data processing tasks like a maestro, guaranteeing smooth and reliable data flow.

What is AWS Step Functions?

Think of Step Functions as a serverless workflow orchestration service. It allows you to define and manage the flow of tasks in your data pipeline, eliminating the need for complex code or manual intervention. Each step in your workflow can be as follows:

1. **A Serverless Lambda Function**: Performing specific data transformations or actions.
2. **An AWS Service Invocation**: Using built-in integrations to interact with services such as S3, Redshift, or DynamoDB.
3. **A Wait State**: Pausing the workflow for a specific duration or until a certain condition is met.

Key Features and Benefits:

- **Visual Workflow Designer**: Build workflows using a drag-and-drop interface, making orchestration accessible to users of all technical skill levels.
- **Built-in Error Handling**: Retry failed tasks automatically and handle exceptions gracefully, ensuring workflow resilience.
- **Parallel Execution**: Run multiple tasks simultaneously for faster processing, especially for independent steps.
- **Integrations and Flexibility**: Connect to various AWS services and even custom applications using API calls.
- **Monitoring and Observability**: Track workflow execution status, visualize progress and troubleshoot issues effectively.

Use Cases:

- **Data Pipelines**: Orchestrate complex data ingestion, transformation, and loading processes with various services.
- **Machine Learning Workflows**: Trigger model training, evaluation, and deployment based on specific events or conditions.
- **Microservice Orchestration**: Coordinate interactions between multiple serverless functions for complex applications.
- **Business Process Automation**: Automate tasks across different systems based on rules and events.

Who should use AWS Step Functions?

- **Data Engineers and Architects**: Build data pipelines with robust orchestration and error-handling capabilities.
- **Application Developers**: Create complex serverless applications with intricate workflows.
- **DevOps and Operations Teams**: Automate infrastructure provisioning and deployment processes.
- **Business Analysts and Non-Technical Users**: Leverage the visual interface to automate simple workflows.

However, Step Functions might not be ideal for the following:

- **Very Simple Workflows**: Data Pipeline's visual interface may be easier for basic use cases.
- **Existing Data Pipeline Workflows**: Migration considerations and potential learning curve.

Symphony of Services: AWS Data Pipeline versus Glue Jobs versus Lambda versus Step Functions

When building data pipelines in AWS, selecting the right orchestration service feels like choosing the perfect instrument for your orchestra. Each service has its strengths and weaknesses, and the best choice depends on the specific needs of your data flow symphony. Let us delve into the key characteristics and use cases of AWS Data Pipeline, Glue Jobs, Lambda, and Step Functions.

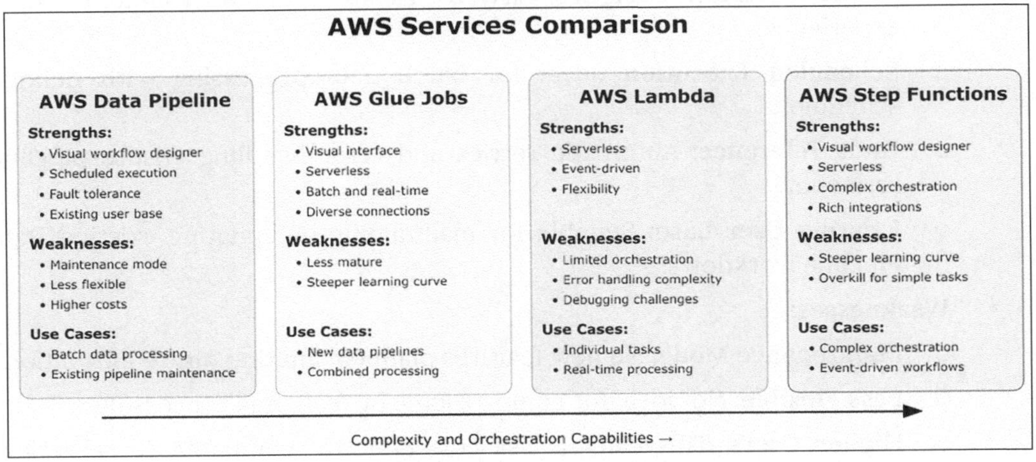

Figure 9.1: *AWS Services Comparison*

AWS Data Pipeline:

- **Provisioning:**
  1. IAM Setup
     a. Create IAM role with **`AWSDataPipelineRole`** policy.
     b. Create EC2 role with **`DataPipelineDefaultRole`** policy.
     c. Attach S3, RDS, or other required service permissions.
  2. Pipeline Configuration
     a. Navigate to the AWS Data Pipeline console.
     b. Click "**`Create Pipeline`**".
     c. Define pipeline name and source.
     d. Choose a schedule (on-demand/scheduled).
     e. Select pipeline definition (console/command line).
  3. Resource Configuration
     a. Configure compute resources (EC2 instances/EMR clusters).
     b. Set up storage locations (S3 buckets/RDS instances).
     c. Define VPC and security groups.
     d. Configure logging options.
- **Strengths:**
  - **Visual Workflow Designer**: Easy to use for users with limited coding experience.
  - **Scheduled Execution**: Ideal for batch data processing with defined schedules.
  - **Fault Tolerance**: Automatic retries and error handling ensure pipeline resiliency.
  - **Existing User Base**: Suitable for maintaining or updating existing Data Pipeline workflows.
- **Weaknesses:**
  - **Maintenance Mode**: No new features planned, limiting future innovation.
  - **Less Flexible**: Not ideal for complex logic or real-time processing.
  - **Higher Costs**: This can be less cost-effective compared to serverless options.

Use Cases:

- Batch data processing with well-defined tasks and schedules (for example, daily sales reports).
- Existing data pipelines built with the Data Pipeline that need ongoing maintenance.

Glue Jobs:

- **Provisioning:**
  1. IAM Configuration
     a. Create IAM role with `AWSGlueServiceRole` policy.
     b. Attach policies for S3, CloudWatch Logs.
     c. Add custom policies for specific data sources.
  2. Network Setup
     a. Configure VPC endpoints for S3 and Glue.
     b. Set up security groups for Glue crawlers.
     c. Enable DNS hostnames and DNS resolution.
  3. Glue Components
     a. Create Glue Database.
     b. Configure Glue Crawler.
     c. Set up Glue Job.
     d. Create necessary connections for data sources.
- **Strengths:**
  - **Visual Interface and Custom Code**: Seamless integration with Glue ETL capabilities for data preparation.
  - **Serverless**: Eliminates infrastructure management and scales automatically.
  - **Batch and Real-Time Capabilities**: Handles both scheduled and event-driven data processing.
  - **Connects to Diverse Data Sources**: Integrates with databases, file systems, and even custom endpoints.
- **Weaknesses:**
  - **Less mature:** Lacks some advanced features compared to Step Functions.
  - **Steeper learning curve:** Requires understanding of both Glue and Spark/Python for custom code.

Use Cases:

- Building new data pipelines with both ETL and orchestration needs.
- Combining batch and real-time data processing within a single service.
- Leveraging Glue's pre-built connectors and data preparation capabilities.

Lambda:

- **Provisioning:**
  1. Basic Setup
     a. Create a Lambda execution role.
     b. Attach basic execution policy:
        ```
        {
          "Version": "2012-10-17",
          "Statement": [{
            "Effect": "Allow",
            "Action": [
              "logs:CreateLogGroup",
              "logs:CreateLogStream",
              "logs:PutLogEvents"
            ],
            "Resource": "arn:aws:logs:*:*:*"
          }]
        }
        ```
     c. Configure VPC access if needed.
  2. Function Configuration
     a. Select runtime environment.
     b. Set memory allocation and timeout.
     c. Configure environment variables.
     d. Set up CloudWatch logging.
  3. Trigger Setup
     a. Configure event sources (API Gateway, S3, and more.).
     b. Set up necessary permissions for triggers.
     c. Configure error handling and retries.
- **Strengths**:
  - **Serverless**: Highly scalable and cost-effective for individual data processing tasks.

  - **Event-Driven**: Reacts to real-time data changes and triggers downstream actions.
  - **Flexibility**: Supports diverse programming languages and integrations.
- **Weaknesses:**
  - **Limited Orchestration**: Not designed for complex workflow management.
  - **Error Handling and State Management**: Requires additional development effort.
  - **Debugging and Monitoring**: Can be challenging for intricate workflows.

Use Cases:

- Individual data processing tasks within a larger orchestration (for example, data transformation within Step Functions).
- Real-time data processing triggered by events (for example, image resizing upon upload).
- Simple data workflows without complex dependencies or error handling.

Step Functions:

- **Provisioning:**
  1. State Machine Setup
     a. Create an IAM role with `AWSStepFunctionsFullAccess`.
     b. Define state machine type (Standard/Express).
     c. Configure logging level.
  2. Workflow Definition

```
{
  "Comment": "Basic Step Function",
  "StartAt": "FirstState",
  "States": {
    "FirstState": {
      "Type": "Task",
      "Resource": "arn:aws:lambda:REGION:ACCOUNT:function:-
FUNCTION_NAME",
      "Next": "FinalState"
    },
    "FinalState": {
      "Type": "Pass",
      "End": true
    }
  }
}
```

3. Integration Configuration
    a. Set up service integrations (Lambda, ECS, and so on).
    b. Configure error handling states.
    c. Set up retry policies.
    d. Define timeout handling.

- **Strengths:**
    - **Visual Workflow Designer**: Accessible for users with varying technical skills.
    - **Serverless**: Scales automatically and eliminates infrastructure management.
    - **Complex Orchestration**: Supports parallel execution, branching, and retries for intricate workflows.
    - **Integrations and Flexibility**: Connects to various AWS services and custom applications.
- **Weaknesses:**
    - **Steeper Learning Curve**: Requires understanding of state machines and workflow design.
    - **Not Ideal for Simple Workflows**: Might be overkill for basic data processing tasks.

Use Cases:

- Orchestrating complex data pipelines with diverse tasks and dependencies.
- Building event-driven workflows that react to data changes and trigger actions.
- Automating business processes across different systems and services.

Choosing the Right Service

Consider the following factors when making your decision:

- **Complexity of Your Workflow**: For simple tasks, Lambda or Glue Jobs might suffice. For intricate orchestration, Step Functions excels.
- **Batch versus Real-Time Processing**: Data Pipeline and Glue Jobs handle batch well, while Step Functions support both.
- **Technical Expertise**: Visual interfaces in Data Pipeline and Glue Jobs ease adoption, while Step Functions require more technical understanding.
- **Existing Infrastructure**: Consider maintaining current Data Pipeline workflows or migrating to newer services.

By understanding the strengths and weaknesses of each service, you can choose the right tool to conduct your data flow symphony. This will ensure smooth, efficient, and scalable data processing for your specific needs.

Designing for Efficiency: Orchestrating Your Data Flow with Optimization in Mind

Building data pipelines isn't just about moving data; it is about doing it efficiently, cost-effectively, and at scale. Like a conductor optimizing their orchestra for a flawless performance, you need to design your data flow with resource management, partitioning, and optimization techniques at the forefront. Let us delve into these key areas:

Partitioning and Optimization Techniques:

- **Data Partitioning**: Imagine dividing your orchestra into sections (partitions) for simultaneous practice. Similarly, partition your data into manageable chunks based on specific criteria (for example, date, region, customer ID). This enables the following:
    - **Parallel Processing**: Multiple tasks can process different partitions simultaneously, reducing overall processing time.
    - **Optimized Storage**: Store partitions in efficient formats such as Parquet, minimizing storage footprint and access speed.
    - **Targeted Filtering**: Quickly narrow down data analysis to specific partitions, improving query performance.
- **Optimized Data Types**: Choose data types carefully. Storing numbers as strings wastes space and slows down processing. Select appropriate data types based on data characteristics and analysis needs.
- **Cost-Effective Algorithms**: Not all algorithms are created equal. Consider the time versus space trade-off for different algorithms, choosing those that balance accuracy with resource efficiency for your specific use case.

Cost-Effective Resource Management:

- **Leverage Spot Instances**: Utilize unused EC2 capacity at a significant discount for batch jobs that have flexible run times.
- **Right-Size Your Resources**: Choose the appropriate instance types and sizes based on your workload demands. Avoid overprovisioning, which leads to unnecessary costs.
- **Auto-Scaling**: Automatically adjust resources based on real-time workload fluctuations, ensuring optimal resource utilization and avoiding idle costs.

- **Serverless Options**: Consider serverless services such as Lambda for tasks that do not require persistent resources, eliminating infrastructure management and scaling concerns.

Handling Diverse Data Volumes:

- **Scaling for Bursts**: Implement auto-scaling mechanisms to handle unexpected spikes in data volume without performance degradation.
- **Cost-Effective Storage**: Select the right storage option based on data access patterns and frequency. Use cost-optimized options such as S3 Glacier for infrequently accessed data.
- **Data Sampling**: For exploratory analysis or large datasets, consider using data sampling techniques to extract representative subsets for analysis, reducing processing time and costs.
- **Incremental Processing**: For continuously updating data, focus on processing only new or changed data instead of reprocessing everything, minimizing resource consumption.

Remember: Efficiency isn't a one-time goal, it is an ongoing journey. Monitoring your pipeline performance, identifying bottlenecks, and implementing cost-optimization strategies are crucial for ensuring your data flow symphony plays effortlessly and cost-effectively.

Additional Tips:

- **Utilize AWS Cost Explorer**: Gain insights into your AWS resource usage and identify areas for cost optimization.
- **Stay Up-to-Date**: Explore new tools and services offered by AWS that can further improve your data pipeline efficiency.
- **Benchmark and Test**: Regularly benchmark your pipeline performance and experiment with different configurations to find the optimal setup.

By incorporating these techniques and considerations into your data pipeline design, you can unleash the power of your data. All this while keeping costs under control, ensuring a harmonious and efficient performance for your data flow symphony.

Monitoring and Performance Optimization: Conducting Your Data Flow Symphony with Insights

Building a data pipeline is just the first act; the real magic happens when you monitor, optimize, and continuously improve its performance. Like a maestro refining their orchestra's sound, you need to track key metrics, troubleshoot issues, and strive for constant betterment. Let us delve into these essential tools and strategies:

Key Metrics to Track:

- **Data Flow Throughput**: Monitor the rate at which data moves through your pipeline, identifying bottlenecks and ensuring smooth flow.
- **Processing Time**: Track the time taken for each stage of data processing, pinpointing slow steps and optimization opportunities.
- **Resource Utilization**: Monitor CPU, memory, and network usage of your resources, ensuring efficient utilization and avoiding over-provisioning.
- **Error Rates**: Track the frequency and types of errors encountered, enabling proactive troubleshooting and data quality improvement.
- **Job Completion Time**: Monitor the duration of your entire pipeline execution, optimizing for overall speed and reliability.

Alerting and Troubleshooting Strategies:

- **Set up Alerts**: Configure alerts for critical metrics exceeding predefined thresholds, allowing for prompt intervention and issue resolution.
- **Log Analysis**: Analyze logs for error messages, patterns, and insights into potential issues.
- **Profiling and Tracing Tools**: Utilize tools such as AWS X-Ray to identify performance bottlenecks and pinpoint specific issues within your pipeline.
- **Testing and Simulations**: Conduct test runs with different data volumes and configurations to understand your pipeline's behavior and identify potential problems.

Continuous Improvement Best Practices:

- **Regular Reviews**: Conduct periodic performance reviews, analyzing metrics and logs to identify areas for improvement.
- **Version Control**: Implement version control for your pipeline code and configurations, enabling safe rollbacks and experimentation.
- **Performance Testing**: Regularly test your pipeline with different data sizes and workloads to ensure optimal performance under varying conditions.
- **Automate Tasks**: Automate repetitive tasks such as monitoring, alerting, and data validation, freeing up your time for strategic optimization.
- **Stay Informed**: Keep up-to-date with new AWS services, tools, and best practices to continuously improve your pipeline's efficiency and capabilities.

Remember: Monitoring and optimization are never-ending processes. Embrace a culture of continuous improvement, utilizing the insights gained from monitoring to refine your data flow symphony for peak performance, reliability, and cost-effectiveness.

Additional Tips:

- **Visualize Your Data**: Use dashboards and visualizations to easily track key metrics and identify trends.
- **Share Insights**: Share performance data and optimization strategies with stakeholders to promote data-driven decision-making.
- **Community Engagement**: Actively participate in the AWS community forums and resources to learn from others and stay updated on best practices.

By embracing these monitoring, optimization, and improvement strategies, you can ensure your data pipeline plays a harmonious and valuable role in your organization's data-driven journey. So, step onto the conductor's stand, pick up your metaphorical baton, and lead your data flow toward a performance of excellence!

Advanced-Data Transformations: Unveiling Hidden Insights and Building Smarter Models

Data pipelines are not just about moving data; they are about transforming it into actionable insights and powerful machine-learning models. This section delves into two crucial areas: Anomaly Detection and Feature Engineering. They will help you uncover hidden patterns, enrich your data, and build smarter models.

Anomaly Detection

Imagine your orchestra conductor noticing a musician playing an unexpected note during a performance. Anomaly detection does the same for your data, identifying unusual patterns and potential issues that deviate from the norm.

Techniques:

1. **Outlier Detection**: Statistical methods pinpoint data points that significantly differ from the expected distribution (for example, a sudden spike in sales).
2. **Clustering**: Group similar data points together and identify anomalies that fall outside of established clusters.
3. **Time Series Analysis**: Detect unusual patterns in time-dependent data, like unexpected drops in website traffic.

Benefits:

- **Fraud Detection**: Identify suspicious activity and potential financial losses.
- **Equipment Failure Prediction**: Proactively maintain equipment based on detected anomalies.
- **Network Intrusion Detection**: Ensure cybersecurity by identifying unusual network activity.

Feature Engineering

Think of your orchestra conductor crafting the perfect sheet music for each musician. Feature engineering similarly involves creating meaningful features from raw data to enhance the performance of your machine learning models.

Techniques:

1. **Data Enrichment**: Combine data from different sources to create new features (for example, combining user demographics with purchase history).
2. **Data Manipulation**: Transform data using techniques such as scaling, normalization, and discretization to improve model performance.
3. **Feature Selection**: Choose the most relevant features from a large set to avoid overfitting and improve model interpretability.
4. **Feature Importance Analysis**: Identify the features that contribute most to your model's predictions, providing valuable insights.

Benefits:

- **Increased Model Accuracy**: Improved features lead to better predictions and decision-making.
- **Reduced Model Complexity**: Fewer features can result in more interpretable and manageable models.
- **Faster Training Times**: Smaller feature sets often train faster, saving time and resources.

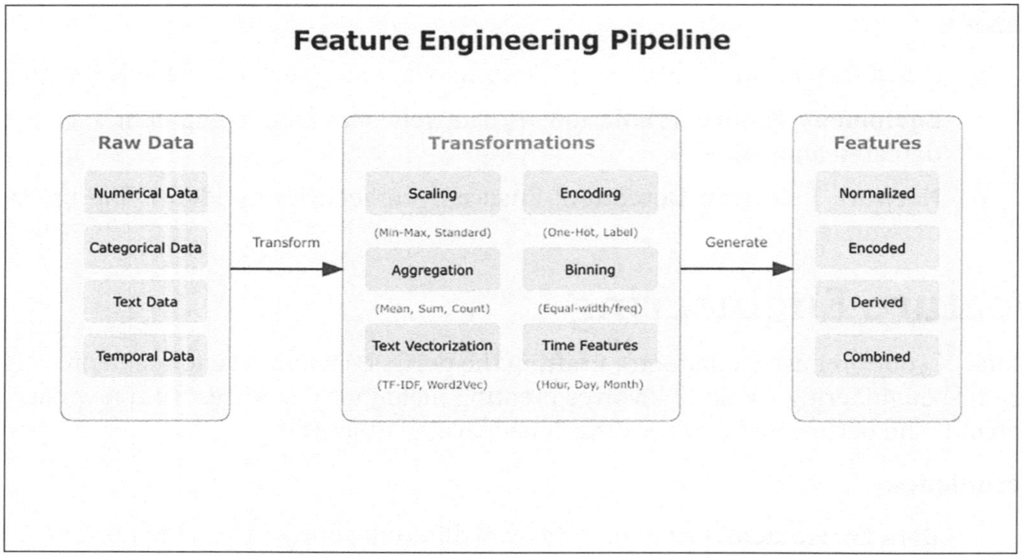

Figure 9.2: *Feature Engineering Pipeline*

Complex Data Cleaning and Validation

Even the most skilled conductor needs musicians playing from clean sheet music. Similarly, ensuring data quality is crucial for downstream analysis and machine learning.

Techniques:

1. **Missing Value Imputation**: Fill in missing data points using techniques such as mean imputation or k-Nearest Neighbors.
2. **Data Consistency Checks**: Identify and correct inconsistencies within your data (for example, invalid email addresses).
3. **Data Normalization**: Ensure data falls within expected ranges to prevent biases in analysis and modeling.
4. **Schema Validation**: Enforce data formatting and type consistency to maintain data integrity.

Benefits:

- **Improved Data Analysis**: Clean data yields more accurate and reliable insights.
- **Enhanced Model Performance**: Cleaner data leads to better training and more accurate predictions.
- **Reduced Errors and Rework**: Ensures downstream processes work with reliable data.

Remember: Advanced data transformations are powerful tools, but understanding their context and applying them with purpose is key. Consider your specific use case, data characteristics, and desired outcomes when choosing and implementing these techniques.

Additional Tips:

- Explore domain-specific techniques for anomaly detection and feature engineering tailored to your industry or application.
- Utilize automated tools and libraries to streamline data cleaning and validation processes.
- Continuously monitor and iterate on your data transformations as your data and understanding evolve.

By mastering these advanced transformations, you can unlock the hidden potential within your data, laying the foundation for superior machine learning models and actionable insights that empower your organization's success.

Deep Dive into Step Functions

AWS Step Functions act as your conductor, allowing you to visually build sequences of these tasks using serverless Lambda functions as the building blocks. This empowers you to create robust, flexible, and efficient data pipelines tailored to your needs.

Chaining Lambda Functions

Imagine your orchestra playing a piece with multiple movements. Each movement might require different instruments and playing styles. Similarly, your data pipeline might involve diverse tasks. Step Functions allow you to take the following actions:

- **Define a Sequence**: Arrange your Lambda functions in the order they should be executed, ensuring each function receives the correct output from the previous one.
- **Pass Data between Functions**: Specify the output data from one function as the input for the next, enabling seamless data flow through your pipeline.
- **Handle Errors**: Configure error handling mechanisms for individual functions or the entire workflow, ensuring your data pipeline gracefully handles unexpected situations.

Conditional Branching

Think of a conductor responding to changes in the music by directing the different sections to play diverse parts. Step Functions empower you to make similar decisions within your data pipeline using the following decision states:

- **Define Branching Criteria**: Set conditions based on data values, events, or function outputs to determine which path your workflow should take.
- **Branching Based on Data**: For example, route data processing based on customer segment (Gold, Silver, Bronze) using different Lambda functions for each segment.
- **Event-Driven Branching**: Trigger specific workflows based on real-time events (for example, a new image upload) and direct data processing accordingly.

Wait States

Imagine your conductor pausing the orchestra briefly before a dramatic crescendo. Step Functions offer wait states similar functionality, as follows:

- **Pause for a Duration**: Introduce defined wait times between tasks, allowing for batch processing or time-sensitive actions (for example, waiting for a scheduled event).
- **Wait for a Condition**: Pause until a specific condition is met, enabling data-driven waiting behavior (for example, wait for a file upload before processing).
- **Combine with Branching**: Use wait states within branching logic to create complex workflows with conditional pauses.

Benefits of Visual Workflows:

- **Accessibility**: The drag-and-drop interface makes orchestration accessible to users with varying technical skills.
- **Visibility and Debugging**: Easily visualize the flow of your data pipeline and identify bottlenecks or errors.
- **Flexibility**: Combine various Lambda functions, branching, and wait states to create complex and versatile workflows.

Remember: Building visual workflows with Step Functions is just the beginning. Mastering these functionalities and combining them with other advanced techniques unlocks the true power of data pipeline orchestration. It empowers you to conduct your data flow symphony with efficiency, clarity, and control.

Advanced Glue Job Techniques: Unveiling the Power of Custom Transformations

While AWS Step Functions excels at orchestration, the magic of true data transformation happens within AWS Glue Jobs. This service empowers you to unleash the potential of custom Spark and Python scripts, integrate with diverse tools, and optimize performance for complex data processing needs. Let us delve into these advanced techniques:

Custom Spark and Python Scripts

Think of these scripts as your bespoke tools for data manipulation. Imagine needing to sculpt intricate shapes – basic tools just will not do. Glue Jobs lets you do the following:

- **Spark for Large-Scale Processing**: Handle massive datasets efficiently using the power of Spark's distributed computing framework.
- **Python for Flexibility**: Leverage the vast Python ecosystem with diverse libraries for tailored data transformations and analysis.
- **Beyond Built-in Functionalities**: Go beyond basic data cleansing and transformations to handle complex logic, aggregations, and custom algorithms.

Integrating with External Libraries and Tools

Imagine expanding your orchestra's repertoire by inviting guest musicians with unique instruments. Glue Jobs lets you integrate with the following:

- **External Libraries**: Expand your data processing capabilities by incorporating specialized libraries such as Pandas for data manipulation or scikit-learn for machine learning tasks.
- **Custom Tools**: Integrate your existing data processing tools written in different languages (for example, Java, R) to leverage your established workflows.
- **Open-Source Frameworks**: Tap into the power of open-source tools such as TensorFlow or PyTorch for advanced data analysis and modeling within your Glue Jobs.

Optimizing Glue Job Performance

Imagine refining your orchestra's sound by optimizing instrument selection and seating arrangements. Glue Jobs offers the following ways to fine-tune performance:

- **Resource Allocation: Striking the Right Balance**

  Imagine selecting the perfect instruments for your orchestra – too few and the sound suffers, too many and you create unnecessary clutter. Similarly, resource allocation in Glue Jobs involves:

  - **Memory**: Allocate sufficient memory based on your data size and transformations, avoiding out-of-memory errors and slowdowns. Tools such as AWS Glue Data Catalog can provide insights into data size and memory requirements.
  - **CPU**: Choose the right CPU type and number of cores based on your workload's compute intensity. Consider using AWS Cost Explorer to monitor resource utilization and identify areas for optimization.

- **Executors**: These "*conductors*" manage tasks within your Spark application. Adjust the number of executors based on your data parallelism and desired granularity for efficient task distribution.

Remember, resource allocation is a balancing act. Choose the right resources based on your specific workload and data characteristics to avoid overprovisioning and unnecessary costs.

- **Partitioning Strategies: Divide and Conquer for Speed**

  Imagine dividing your orchestra into smaller sections for simultaneous rehearsals. Partitioning your data in Glue Jobs follows the same principle, as follows:

  - **Divide and Conquer**: Split your data into smaller, manageable partitions based on specific criteria (for example, date, region, customer ID). This enables parallel processing, significantly speeding up transformations compared to processing the entire dataset at once.
  - **Dynamic Partitioning**: Leverage dynamic partitioning to automatically choose partitioning columns based on schema or data characteristics, simplifying workload management.
  - **Choosing the Right Key**: Select the partitioning key wisely, considering both data distribution and the transformations being performed. This ensures efficient data access and avoids unnecessary shuffles within your Spark application.

By effectively partitioning your data, you unlock the power of parallel processing, transforming your data in record time.

- **Serialization Formats: Selecting the Right Data Language**

  Imagine choosing the most efficient script for your actors based on the play's requirements. Serialization formats stated below in Glue Jobs act similarly:

  - **Parquet**: A columnar format offering fast reads, efficient compression, and support for complex data types. Ideal for large datasets and analytical workloads.
  - **ORC**: Another columnar format with good compression and performance, offering a balance between Parquet's efficiency and JSON's flexibility.
  - **Avro**: A flexible, schema-based format suitable for semi-structured data and integration with different tools. Consider using Avro if you need schema evolution or interoperability.

By choosing the right serialization format based on your data characteristics and access patterns, you optimize data reading and writing, ensuring a smooth flow within your Glue Job.

- **Tuning Spark Configurations: Tweaking the Engine for Peak Performance**

  Imagine fine-tuning individual instruments within your orchestra for optimal sound quality. Spark configurations offer similar customization:

  - **Broadcast Variables**: Share small, frequently accessed data across tasks without unnecessary shuffling, improving performance for repetitive operations.
  - **Caching**: Temporarily store intermediate results in memory for faster access within your job, especially for iterative transformations.
  - **Tuning Memory Settings**: Adjust JVM memory settings (heap size, off-heap memory) based on your workload memory requirements for efficient resource utilization.

Note: *These configurations are specific to your use case and require experimentation. Utilize tools such as Spark UI and AWS X-Ray to monitor performance and identify areas for further optimization.*

Remember: Optimization is an ongoing process. Monitor your Glue job performance, identify bottlenecks, and experiment with different configurations to ensure optimal efficiency for your specific workloads.

Additional Tips:

- **Utilize AWS Glue Data Catalog**: Store and manage your metadata schema for seamless access and consistency within your Glue Jobs.
- **Explore Managed Libraries**: Consider AWS-managed libraries such as Amazon SageMaker Spark Runtime for simplified integration with machine learning frameworks.
- **Stay Updated**: Keep up with the latest Glue Job features, libraries, and optimization best practices for continuous improvement.

By mastering these advanced techniques, you can transform Glue Jobs from basic data processing tools into powerful engines for complex transformations. This will empower you to unlock the true potential of your data and unleash insights that drive your organization forward.

End-to-End Orchestration Strategies: Conducting Your Data Flow Symphony with Harmony and Security

Building data pipelines isn't just about processing data; it is about creating a seamless, efficient, and secure flow from ingestion to insights. This is where End-to-End Orchestration Strategies come in, allowing you to combine different AWS services like a maestro combining the talents of diverse musicians. Let us delve into the key aspects of crafting a harmonious and secure data flow:

Combining Different Services for Seamless Data Flow

Imagine your orchestra collaborating with a choir and dance troupe for a grand performance. Similarly, your data pipeline might involve various AWS services playing specific roles:

- **Data Ingestion**: Use services such as Kinesis Firehose for real-time data streams or S3 for batch uploads.
- **Data Processing**: Leverage Lambda functions for simple transformations or Glue Jobs for complex custom scripts.
- **Data Analytics**: Analyze processed data with RedShift for large datasets or Athena for interactive querying.
- **Orchestration**: Conduct the entire flow with Step Functions, ensuring tasks run in the right order and handle errors gracefully.

Remember to choose the right service based on its strengths and your specific needs. Think of it as selecting the best instrument for each part of your musical composition.

Managing Dependencies and Data Lineage

Imagine tracing the journey of a musician's melody throughout the piece. Similarly, managing dependencies and data lineage is crucial.

- **Dependencies**: Define relationships between tasks and data flows, ensuring proper execution order and data availability.
- **Data Lineage**: Track the origin, transformations, and flow of data throughout your pipeline for auditability, regulatory compliance, and debugging.

Utilizing tools such as AWS Glue Data Catalog can help manage metadata and lineage, offering visibility and control over your data flow.

Ensuring Data Security and Governance

Imagine protecting your orchestra's performance with meticulous security measures. Data security and governance are equally crucial.

- **IAM Roles**: Grant least privilege access to services and resources involved in your pipeline, following the principle of least privilege.

- **Encryption**: Encrypt data at rest and in transit using services such as AWS KMS to protect sensitive information.
- **CloudTrail and CloudWatch**: Monitor activity and logs for security events, anomalies, and troubleshooting purposes.
- **Compliance**: Adhere to relevant industry regulations and internal security policies by implementing appropriate controls and auditing mechanisms.

Remember: Security is an ongoing process. Regularly review your security posture, update configurations, and stay informed about emerging threats.

Additional Tips:

- Utilize AWS X-Ray for detailed tracing and visualization of your entire data flow, providing insights into performance and potential bottlenecks.
- Explore serverless workflow patterns such as fan-out, fan-in, and retries for efficient orchestration strategies.
- Monitor and optimize: Continuously monitor your data pipeline performance, identify optimization opportunities, and experiment with different configurations.
- Stay updated: Keep up-to-date with the latest advancements in AWS services, orchestration best practices, and security protocols.

Combine different services with strategic orchestration, managing dependencies, and data lineage, and prioritizing security and governance. This way, you can transform your data pipelines from isolated instruments into a well-rehearsed orchestra playing a harmonious and secure data flow symphony. It will empower your organization with valuable insights and informed decision-making. Remember, the conductor's role is never truly finished – strive for continuous improvement and enjoy the symphony of data-driven success!

The Final Curtain: Data Pipelines as Symphonies of Insight

We have embarked on a journey through the intricate world of data pipelines, exploring the tools, techniques, and strategies to orchestrate your data flow like a maestro conducting a symphony. From the individual notes of Lambda functions to the powerful chords of Glue Jobs, we have learned to combine diverse services into a seamless flow, ensuring efficiency, security, and governance.

Remember, building data pipelines is not just about moving data; it is about unlocking the hidden potential within to drive informed decisions, fuel innovation, and empower your organization. By embracing continuous learning, experimentation, and optimization, you can transform your data pipelines from mere data movers into instruments of discovery and insight.

So, step onto the conductor's stand, raise your metaphorical baton, and lead your data flow symphony toward a crescendo of success! Remember, the music is always evolving, and the audience awaits the next captivating performance. Keep refining your techniques, embrace new instruments, and most importantly, enjoy the exhilarating journey of transforming data into the melodies that guide your organization's future.

Conclusion

This chapter has been your backstage pass to the world of advanced data pipelines and transformations. You have explored the tools and techniques needed to orchestrate complex workflows, unlock hidden insights, and push the boundaries of what is possible. Remember, data orchestration is an ongoing symphony, requiring continued exploration and refinement. Dive deeper into specific services, embrace emerging technologies, and join the vibrant data community – with each discovery, you will compose even more powerful and impactful data pipelines.

Next, we shift focus to a different corner of the data landscape: data warehouses. In *Chapter 10, Data Warehousing Demystified*, you will unlock the power of structured data analysis by understanding the key differences between data warehouses and data lakes. Get ready to demystify data warehousing and add another powerful tool to your data analysis repertoire!

CHAPTER 10
Data Warehousing Demystified

Introduction

Congratulations! You have mastered the art of data orchestration, transforming your data pipelines into a well-oiled symphony. But the raw notes, however expertly arranged, remain silent until interpreted. In this chapter, we unlock a powerful tool capable of translating those notes into a chorus of insights: the data warehouse.

Unlike the sprawling, ever-evolving data lakes you encountered earlier, data warehouses offer a structured haven for your well-defined, historical data. Imagine a meticulously organized library, each book categorized, indexed, and ready to be devoured for knowledge. Redshift, your data librarian, stands ready to assist, guiding you through this realm of information and empowering you to extract specific insights with ease.

Prepare to step beyond data in motion and delve into the depths of data at rest. This chapter marks a pivotal shift in your journey, equipping you with the tools and knowledge to extract meaningful stories from your historical data, stories that can inform decisions, fuel innovation, and propel your organization forward. So, open the doors to your data warehouse, embrace the organized knowledge within, and embark on a path to richer, deeper insights than ever before.

Structure

In this chapter, we will cover the following topics:

Part 1: Data Warehouses and Data Lakes

- Understanding Data Warehouses
    - Definition and Key Characteristics of Data Warehouses
    - Benefits of Using Data Warehouses for Structured Data Analysis
    - Limitations of Data Warehouses

- Contrasting Data Warehouses with Data Lakes
    - Key Differences Between Data Warehouses and Data Lakes in Terms of:
        - Structure
        - Purpose
        - Use Cases
        - Scalability
        - Cost
    - Choosing the Right Tool for Your Needs

Part 2: Building and Querying Your Redshift Data Warehouse

- Building Your Data Warehouse
    - Setting up Redshift for Your Specific Needs
    - Designing your Data Warehouse Schema
    - Loading Data into Your Redshift Data Warehouse
- Mastering SQL for Data Exploration
    - Writing Basic SQL Queries to Retrieve Data from Redshift
    - Filtering and Aggregating Data for Specific Insights
    - Utilizing Advanced SQL Features for Complex Queries

Part 3: Advanced Techniques and Best Practices

- Optimizing Your Data Warehouse
    - Strategies for Improving Data Warehouse Performance and Efficiency
    - Cost Optimization in Redshift
    - Security and Governance Considerations for Your Data Warehouse
- Advanced Analytics with Redshift
    - Leveraging Redshift for More Complex Analytical Tasks
    - Integrating Redshift with Other Data Analytics Tools

Part 1: Data Warehouses and Data Lakes

Understanding Data Warehouses

Data warehouses, often referred to as **enterprise data warehouses (EDWs)**, are more than just repositories for historical data. They are meticulously organized havens specifically designed for analyzing **structured data**. Think of them as well-curated libraries, where information is categorized, indexed, and readily accessible for exploration and analysis. Here is a deep dive into their definition, key characteristics, benefits, and limitations:

Key Characteristics:

- **Centralized Repository:** Data warehouses gather data from various sources, such as databases, applications, and logs, integrating it into a single, consistent location. This centralized approach ensures everyone works with the same data, eliminating inconsistencies and facilitating unified analysis.
- **Subject-Oriented Organization:** Data isn't just dumped in piles; it is organized around specific subjects (for example, customers, products, or sales). This subject-oriented structure allows analysts to focus on specific areas of interest and gain deeper insights without getting lost in irrelevant information.
- **Schema-Based Structure:** Unlike the free-flowing nature of data lakes, data warehouses follow a defined schema. Data is organized into tables and columns, with clear relationships between them. This structure enables efficient querying, retrieval, and analysis, similar to how an index makes navigating a library much easier.
- **Historical Focus:** While real-time data processing has its place, data warehouses shine in analyzing historical trends and patterns. They are ideal for understanding how your business has evolved, identifying long-term trends, and predicting future behavior based on past experiences.

Benefits of Using Data Warehouses for Structured Data Analysis:

- **Fast and Efficient Analysis:** Optimized storage and indexing mechanisms ensure queries run quickly, even with large datasets. This empowers analysts to explore various hypotheses and extract valuable insights without waiting hours for results.
- **Consistent and Reliable Data:** The centralized nature and defined schema ensure data consistency and reliability. Everyone works with the same information, eliminating discrepancies and leading to more trustworthy conclusions.
- **Subject-Area Focus:** Subject-oriented organization makes it easier to find relevant data and gain deeper insights into specific areas of your business. You can analyze customer behavior, product performance, or campaign effectiveness without getting sidetracked by irrelevant information.
- **Trend Analysis and Forecasting:** Historical data stored in data warehouses provides a rich foundation for identifying trends and patterns over time. By understanding these trends, you can make informed predictions about future outcomes and proactively address potential challenges.
- **Improved Decision-Making:** Faster analysis, consistent data, and deeper insights ultimately lead to better decision-making. Data warehouses empower

you to make informed choices based on factual evidence and historical trends, not just gut feeling.

Demystifying Data Warehouses and Data Lakes

When it comes to data storage and analysis, choosing the right tool becomes crucial. In this battle of havens, **data warehouses**, and **data lakes** each offer unique strengths and weaknesses, depending on your specific needs.

Data Warehouses: The Structured Sanctuary

Think of data warehouses as meticulously organized libraries. Inside, you will find **structured data**, neatly arranged in tables and columns with defined relationships. This structure grants several advantages:

- **Fast querying:** Finding specific information is like searching a well-indexed catalog, making data warehouses ideal for **historical analysis** and identifying trends over time.
- **Efficient analysis:** Optimized storage and indexing mechanisms ensure queries run quickly, even on large datasets, empowering analysts to delve deeper into historical insights.
- **Subject-oriented:** Data is organized around specific themes (for example, sales and customers), offering a cohesive view of a particular domain.

However, like any library, data warehouses also have limitations:

- **Less flexible:** Changing the structure (schema) requires careful planning and can lead to downtime, making them less adaptable to rapidly evolving data.
- **Higher cost:** Structured storage, specialized hardware, and optimized performance come at a premium.
- **Limited to structured data:** They thrive on well-defined information, struggling with diverse formats, such as images or sensor data.

Data Lakes: The Unstructured Oasis

Imagine a vast, open landscape unlike any library. Data lakes offer a **flexible** refuge for **diverse data**, welcoming structured, semi-structured, and even unstructured formats like images or text. This flexibility brings the following benefits:

- **Exploration and Experimentation:** Ideal for exploring new data sources and uncovering hidden patterns, especially with machine learning and data science techniques.

- **Scalability:** Easily adapting to accommodate large volumes and diverse data types, making them suitable for rapidly changing environments.
- **Cost-Effective:** Typically, less expensive than data warehouses due to simpler storage requirements.

However, data lakes also have their limitations:

- **Slower Analysis:** Lack of structure requires additional processing and transformation before analysis, making querying less efficient.
- **More Effort Required:** Finding specific information is like searching an unorganized archive, demanding more effort from analysts.
- **Security Concerns:** Managing security and governance across diverse data types can be challenging.

Choosing Your Haven:

Feature	**Data Warehouse**	**Data Lake**
Structure	Schema-based (tables, columns)	Flexible, unstructured
Purpose	Historical analysis, identifying trends	Exploration, experimentation, discovery
Use Cases	Reporting, dashboards, business intelligence	Machine learning, data science, advanced analytics
Scalability	Limited	Highly scalable
Cost	Higher (structured storage, hardware)	Lower (simpler storage)
Data Types	Primarily structured (for example, numbers, text)	All data types (structured, semi-structured, unstructured)
Querying	Fast and efficient	Requires additional processing and transformation

Table 10.1: *Data Warehouse versus Data Lake*

The ideal haven depends on your specific needs:

- **Structured, Historical Analysis with Fast Querying: Data warehouse** is your sanctuary.
- **Exploration, Experimentation, and Diverse Data: Data lake** is your open oasis.
- **Hybrid Needs:** Consider **lakehouse** (structured data lake) or **data mesh** architectures for a blend of both worlds.

Remember, understanding your data characteristics, analysis goals, and budget is key to choosing the right tool and unlocking the true potential of your data journey.

Part 2: Building and Querying Your Redshift Data Warehouse

Now that you have grasped the power of data warehouses as havens for structured data, it is time to unlock their potential. In this section, we will transform your theoretical understanding into practical action. Get ready to **build and query your very own Redshift data warehouse**, transforming your historical data into an **analytical oasis**.

We will embark on a step-by-step journey, starting with:

1. **Laying the Foundation:** We will explore how to set up your Redshift instance based on your specific needs and budget.
2. **Designing the Blueprint:** Learn about data warehouse schema design, focusing on efficient organization for your Redshift haven.
3. **Filling Your Oasis:** We will delve into the process of loading data into your Redshift warehouse, ensuring smooth and efficient transfer.
4. **Unlocking Your Oasis:** Master the art of querying with **SQL**, the lingua franca of data warehouses, empowering you to extract specific insights and answer your burning questions.

Building Your Redshift Data Warehouse: From Blueprint to Oasis

This section delves into three crucial steps: setting up Redshift, designing your schema, and loading data.

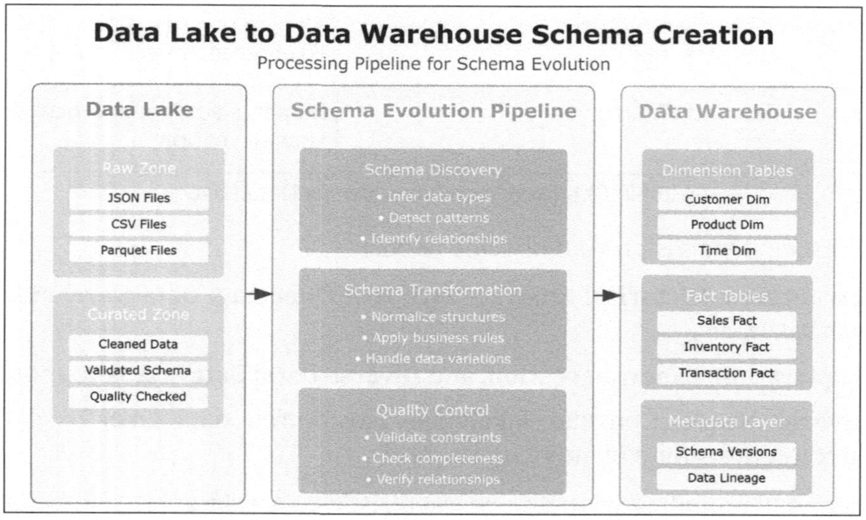

Figure 10.1: *Data Lake to Data Warehouse Schema Creation*

Setting Up Redshift for Your Specific Needs: A Comprehensive Guide

Imagine you're building a physical data center. You would not just pick any building, right? You would consider your needs – how much space you need to store servers, the processing power required for your workloads, and, of course, your budget. Selecting an instance for your Redshift data warehouse follows a similar logic. Besides, building your Redshift data warehouse requires more than just choosing an instance type. This section delves deeper into the configuration options and strategies that unlock Redshift's full potential, tailored to your specific needs.

Decoding the Redshift Instance Landscape:

Amazon Redshift offers a diverse range of instance types, each catering to different needs and budgets. These instances vary in:

- **Node Type:** This refers to the hardware configuration of the individual processing units within your Redshift cluster. Different node types offer varying levels of processing power (CPU, RAM), storage capacity, and network bandwidth.
- **Cluster Size:** This represents the total number of nodes in your Redshift cluster. More nodes translate to increased processing power and parallel execution capabilities, ideal for handling large datasets or complex queries concurrently.

Factors to Consider for Making the Perfect Match:

When selecting your Redshift instance, carefully consider these crucial factors:

- **Data Volume:** How much data do you plan to store in your data warehouse? Opt for an instance with sufficient storage capacity to accommodate your existing and projected data growth.
- **Expected Query Workload:** How complex and frequent are your anticipated queries? Demanding queries require instances with higher processing power (CPU, RAM) and potentially, a larger cluster size for parallel processing.
- **Budget:** Redshift instances come at different price points based on their capabilities. Balancing your needs with your available budget is crucial.

Instance Selection: Power, Storage, and Budget in Harmony

We have already explored how to choose an instance type based on data volume, workload, and budget. However, remember that even within node types, Redshift offers various configurations, such as:

- **Memory-Optimized versus Compute-Optimized:** Choose memory-optimized nodes (RA3, DC2) for faster query performance, especially for analytical workloads that involve complex joins and aggregations. Opt for compute-optimized nodes (DC1, R4) for cost-efficiency when focusing on loading and storing large datasets.
- **Storage Options:** Select the right storage type based on your access frequency and performance needs. Standard storage (gp2) is cost-effective for less frequently accessed data, while SSD storage (io1) offers higher performance for frequently accessed and queried data.

Configuration Options: Beyond the Instance Type

Once you have chosen your instance type, configure Redshift to align with your specific requirements.

- **Cluster Size:** Start small and scale up as your needs evolve. Redshift allows you to add or remove nodes within a cluster, offering flexibility to adjust processing power dynamically.
- **Security Settings:** Configure security groups and IAM roles to restrict access to your Redshift cluster and data, ensuring robust security measures are in place.
- **Maintenance Window:** Schedule regular maintenance windows for Redshift to perform updates and apply patches, minimizing downtime and ensuring optimal performance.
- **Cluster Parameter Groups:** Utilize cluster parameter groups to manage various settings, such as query execution, resource utilization, and logging behavior, allowing you to fine-tune Redshift's operation for your specific use case.

Cost Optimization: Leveraging Strategies and Tools

Building a cost-effective data warehouse is crucial. Here are some strategies to consider:

- **Redshift Spectrum:** Utilize Redshift Spectrum, a serverless query engine, to run ad-hoc queries directly on data in S3 without loading it into your warehouse. This can be significantly cheaper for exploratory analysis on large datasets.
- **Reserved Instances and Savings Plans:** Commit to using specific instance types for a defined period through reserved instances or savings plans. This can lead to significant cost savings compared to on-demand pricing.
- **Data Skipping and Compression:** Leverage techniques such as data skipping

and compression to reduce the amount of data stored in your warehouse, minimizing storage costs.

- **Optimize Queries:** Write efficient SQL queries to minimize resource utilization and query execution time, leading to lower costs.

Integration with Other Services: Building a Seamless Pipeline

Redshift does not exist in isolation. Leverage other AWS services to create a robust and efficient data engineering pipeline, starting with:

- **Amazon Glue:** Utilize Glue Jobs to orchestrate the Extract, Transform, Load (ETL) process. Glue can seamlessly extract data from various sources, transform it into the desired format, and load it efficiently into your Redshift warehouse.
- **Amazon S3:** Utilize S3 as a central data lake to store both structured and unstructured data. Redshift Spectrum allows you to query data directly from S3 for cost-effective analysis without loading it into the warehouse.
- **Amazon QuickSight:** Integrate Redshift with QuickSight for interactive data visualization. This allows users to explore insights and create compelling dashboards directly from your data warehouse.

By understanding and utilizing these configuration options, cost optimization strategies, and integration possibilities, you can set up a Redshift data warehouse. That will perfectly suit your specific needs, balancing performance, security, and cost-effectiveness for your analytical journey. Remember, this is an ongoing process – monitor, adapt, and refine your setup as your needs and the data landscape evolve.

Data Warehouse Schema Design: Building a Foundation for Analysis

The **schema** of your data warehouse is like the blueprint of a house. It defines the structure and organization of your data, dictating how efficiently you can access and analyze it. This section delves into essential aspects of designing your Redshift data warehouse schema for optimal performance and analytical capabilities.

Understanding Data Model Types

Data warehouse schemas are not built haphazardly. They follow specific **data model types** that optimize data organization and query performance. Here are two widely used models:

- **Star Schema:** Imagine a star with a central "*fact table*" surrounded by smaller "*dimension tables.*" The fact table stores the core metrics of your analysis (for example, sales transactions), while dimension tables contain descriptive attributes (for example, product information and customer details). This structure allows for efficient querying of specific metrics within a specific context.

- **Snowflake Schema:** Similar to the star schema, but with additional levels of dimension tables. This further normalizes the data, reducing redundancy and improving data integrity. However, it can lead to more complex queries compared to the star schema.

Choosing the Right Model:

- **Star Schema:** Ideal for most analytical workloads due to its simplicity and efficient querying.
- **Snowflake Schema:** Consider this model for scenarios where data integrity is a top priority, or you have complex relationships between dimensions.

Data Modeling Tools

Creating and managing data warehouse schemas can be complex. Luckily, tools such as the **Amazon Schema Conversion Tool (SCT)** can simplify the process.

- **Translate Existing Models:** Convert your existing data models from various sources into formats compatible with Redshift. This saves time and ensures consistency.
- **Optimize for Redshift:** SCT can recommend schema optimizations specific to Redshift performance, improving your data warehouse's efficiency.

Denormalization for Performance

Normalization is a process of organizing data to minimize redundancy. While this ensures data integrity, it can sometimes impact query performance. **Denormalization** involves strategically introducing controlled redundancy to improve query speed.

Consider Denormalization in the following scenarios:

- **Frequently Queried Data Points:** Duplicate frequently queried data points across relevant tables to avoid complex joins, potentially improving query performance.
- **Small Dimension Tables:** If a dimension table is small and frequently joined with the fact table, consider incorporating it directly into the fact table to avoid complex joins.

Remember:

Denormalization has trade-offs. While it can improve performance, it increases data redundancy and complexity, making updates and maintaining data integrity more challenging. Weigh the benefits carefully before denormalizing your schema.

Data Partitioning

Imagine searching for a specific book in a library without any organization. It would be time-consuming! Similarly, searching through large datasets in your data warehouse can be slow. **Data partitioning** comes to the rescue with the following:

- **Divide and Conquer:** Partition your data based on specific criteria such as time (for example, year or month), region, or product category. This allows Redshift to quickly identify and access relevant data segments instead of scanning the entire dataset.
- **Improved Query Performance:** Partitioning significantly improves query performance, especially for large datasets, and facilitates efficient data management when working with specific segments.

Choosing the Right Partitioning Key:

- **Select a column or set of columns frequently used in WHERE clauses of your queries.** This ensures queries can leverage partitions effectively.
- **Balance the number of partitions.** Too many partitions can lead to overhead, while too few might not offer significant performance improvement.

Designing your Redshift data warehouse schema requires careful consideration of these elements. Utilize data model types, leverage tools such as SCT, strategically consider denormalization, and implement data partitioning to build a foundation for efficient data access and insightful analysis.

Getting Your Data In: Strategies for Loading Your Redshift Data Warehouse

Once you have built the foundation of your data warehouse, it is time to populate it with the lifeblood – your data! This section explores various methods and strategies for loading your data efficiently into your Redshift data warehouse.

Extract, Transform, Load (ETL) with Glue

Imagine you're moving into a new house. You would not just dump all your belongings in at once, right? You would probably sort, clean, and organize them before placing them in their designated spots. **ETL** (Extract, Transform, Load) follows a similar approach for data warehouses.

- **Extract:** Utilize Glue Jobs to **extract** data from various sources, such as databases, applications, or log files. Glue supports a wide range of connectors, making it easy to access data from diverse locations.

- **Transform:** Often, data needs cleaning, formatting, and transformation before it can be loaded into your warehouse. Glue Jobs allows you to perform these **transformations** within the same job, ensuring data consistency and quality before loading.
- **Load:** Finally, the transformed data is **loaded** into your Redshift data warehouse using efficient methods optimized for large datasets.

Benefits of Using Glue for ETL:

- **Orchestration and Automation:** Glue Jobs helps orchestrate the entire ETL process, automating data extraction, transformation, and loading, saving you time and effort.
- **Scalability and Flexibility:** Glue can handle large datasets and complex transformations, scaling seamlessly as your data volume and processing needs grow.
- **Cost-Effectiveness:** Compared to building and maintaining custom ETL solutions, Glue offers a cost-effective and managed service.

Copy Commands: A Simpler Approach for Specific Scenarios

While Glue offers a robust ETL solution, Redshift also provides native options for simpler scenarios, such as:

- **Copy Commands:** Utilize these commands to **load data directly from S3 buckets** into your Redshift data warehouse. This method is ideal for smaller datasets or frequently updated tables where complex transformations might not be necessary.
- **Supported Formats:** Redshift supports various file formats, such as CSV, JSON, and Parquet, allowing for flexibility in data storage and loading options.

Remember:

When using copy commands, ensure your data is already formatted and cleaned appropriately before loading.

Incremental Loading: Efficient Updates for Evolving Data

Imagine constantly moving furniture around your house to keep things fresh. With large datasets, constantly reloading everything in your data warehouse can be inefficient. **Incremental loading** offers the following solutions:

- **Focus on Changes:** Instead of reloading the entire dataset, identify and load only **new or changed data** since the last update. This significantly reduces processing time and resource utilization, making it ideal for frequently changing data sources.
- **Change Data Capture (CDC):** Utilize technologies like CDC to capture and track changes in your source data, allowing you to efficiently identify and load only the relevant updates into Redshift.

Monitoring and Optimization: Ensuring Smooth Data Flow

Just like monitoring your home's plumbing for leaks, regularly **monitoring your data loading process** is crucial for efficiency and performance.

- **Identify and Address Errors:** Utilize Redshift logs and monitoring tools to identify potential errors or bottlenecks during the data loading process.
- **Optimize Loading Jobs:** Analyze performance metrics and experiment with different loading strategies (for example, adjusting sort keys and compression settings) to optimize your data loading jobs for efficiency and performance.
- **Utilize Redshift Tools:** Redshift provides various tools, such as UNLOAD and STAGING tables to help manage and optimize your data-loading process.

By leveraging the right approach – whether it is Glue jobs, copy commands, or incremental loading – and actively monitoring your process, you can ensure your data flows smoothly into your Redshift data warehouse, keeping your analytical oasis well-fed with the latest information.

Remember, building a data warehouse is an iterative process. Start simple, experiment with different approaches, and continuously refine your design and data-loading practices based on your specific needs and performance requirements.

Mastering SQL for Data Exploration: Advanced Features for Complex Queries

We have explored the fundamental building blocks of SQL, allowing you to retrieve and filter data from your Redshift data warehouse. Now, let us delve deeper into **advanced SQL features** that unlock the true power of data exploration and analysis:

`JOINs`: Uniting Data from Different Tables

Imagine you have separate tables for "*customers*" and "*orders*." How can you find out which products were ordered by specific customers? **`JOINs`** come to the rescue! They allow you to combine data from multiple tables based on a shared attribute, enabling you to analyze relationships and answer complex questions.

- **Types of JOINs**:
  - **Inner JOIN:** Returns rows where the join condition is met in both tables. For example, **SELECT c.name, o.product_id FROM customers c INNER JOIN orders o ON c.id = o.customer_id** retrieves customer names and product IDs for matching customer ID entries in both tables.
  - **Left JOIN:** Returns all rows from the left table, along with matching rows from the right table, even if there is no match. For example, **SELECT c.name, o.product_id FROM customers c LEFT JOIN orders o ON c.id = o.customer_id** retrieves all customer names and any matching product IDs, even for customers who have not placed orders.
  - **Right JOIN:** Similar to left join, but prioritizes the right table.
  - **Full JOIN:** Returns all rows from both tables, regardless of whether there is a match in the other table.

Window Functions: Calculations within Data "*Windows*"

Imagine you want to calculate the cumulative sales for each month throughout the year. Window functions operate on "*windows*" of data within a single table, allowing you to perform calculations such as running totals, rank, or percentiles.

- **Examples:**
  - **SELECT date, SUM(sales) OVER (PARTITION BY year ORDER BY date) AS total_sales** calculates the cumulative sales for each date within each year.
  - **SELECT *, RANK() OVER (ORDER BY quantity DESC) AS product_rank** assigns a rank to each product based on sales quantity, with the highest seller being ranked 1.

Common Table Expressions (CTEs): Reusable Building Blocks

Imagine you need to filter data based on a complex condition used multiple times within your query. **CTEs** offer a solution.

```
WITH filtered_sales AS (
  SELECT * FROM sales WHERE year = 2023
)
SELECT product_name, SUM(quantity)
FROM filtered_sales
GROUP BY product_category;
```

This example defines a CTE named "`filtered_sales`" that filters the "`sales`" table for the year 2023. Uses the filtered data within the main query to analyze product categories without repeating the filter condition.

User-Defined Functions (UDFs): Extending SQL Functionality

If you find yourself repeating complex logic across multiple queries, consider **UDFs**. You can create custom functions using languages, such as Python or SQL itself, extending the capabilities of your Redshift environment for specific needs.

Remember:

Mastering these advanced features takes time and practice. Start by experimenting with basic examples, gradually building your understanding and complexity. Utilize online resources, tutorials, and practice exercises to become proficient in utilizing these advanced features and unlock the full potential of data exploration and analysis with your Redshift data warehouse.

Part 3: Advanced Techniques and Best Practices Taking Your Redshift Data Warehouse to the Next Level

Having built a solid foundation, let us explore advanced techniques and best practices to optimize, secure, and leverage your Redshift data warehouse for even greater analytical capabilities.

Optimizing Your Redshift Data Warehouse: Diving Deeper

Building a data warehouse is just the beginning. The real power lies in **optimizing** it for efficient performance and cost-effectiveness. Here is a detailed look at three key strategies:

Monitoring and Performance Analysis: Unmasking Bottlenecks

Imagine your data warehouse is a car. You would not just drive it without checking the engine, right? Similarly, **monitoring your Redshift data warehouse** is crucial to identify bottlenecks and optimize performance.

- **Amazon CloudWatch:** This powerful tool is your pit crew, providing insights into your data warehouse's health and performance. Utilize CloudWatch to do the following:
  - **Monitor Key Metrics:** Track essential metrics, such as query execution time, CPU utilization, and I/O operations.
  - **Identify Bottlenecks:** Analyze spikes in execution time or high resource utilization to pinpoint areas needing improvement.
  - **Set Alarms:** Configure alerts to notify you when specific metrics exceed predefined thresholds, allowing you to take proactive action and address potential issues.
- **Query Execution Plans: Understanding the Inner Workings**

  Beyond monitoring overall metrics, analyze **query execution plans**. These plans, generated by Redshift, reveal how your queries are translated into physical operations. Analyzing them can be like opening the hood of your car and understanding how its components work together.
- **Understanding the Plan:** Each plan outlines the steps Redshift takes to execute your query. Look for elements such as:
  - **Table Scans versus. Index Scans:** Ideally, your queries should utilize indexes for efficient data retrieval. If they involve full table scans, consider adding appropriate indexes.
  - **Join Orders:** The order in which tables are joined can significantly impact performance. Analyze the join order and experiment with different options to find the most efficient execution strategy.
  - **Filter Usage:** Ensure your filters effectively narrow down the data early in the query execution process, reducing the amount of data Redshift needs to process.

By combining CloudWatch monitoring and analyzing query execution plans, you can gain valuable insights into your data warehouse's performance, identify bottlenecks, and optimize your queries for faster and more efficient execution.

Denormalization: A Double-Edged Sword for Performance

Remember normalization, the process of organizing data to minimize redundancy? While generally preferred, there are situations where **denormalization** can be considered for **performance optimization**.

- **The Trade-off:** Denormalization involves strategically introducing controlled redundancy. This can improve query performance for frequently joined tables or frequently queried columns. However, it comes at a cost as stated below:

- **Increased Data Redundancy:** This can lead to higher storage costs and require additional effort to maintain data consistency across tables.
- **Increased Complexity:** Managing multiple versions of the same data can introduce complexity and increase the risk of inconsistencies.

- **Consider Denormalization in the following scenarios:**

  Carefully consider denormalization only in specific scenarios where the potential performance benefits outweigh the drawbacks. Some situations where denormalization might be beneficial include:

  - **Frequently Joined Tables**: Duplicating a frequently joined column from one table to another can significantly improve query performance by avoiding complex joins.
  - **Frequently Queried Columns**: Including rarely updated columns from other tables in the main fact table can speed up queries that frequently use these columns.

Remember:

Denormalization should be a strategic decision, not a default approach. Before denormalizing, thoroughly analyze the potential benefits and drawbacks, and weigh them against alternative optimization strategies.

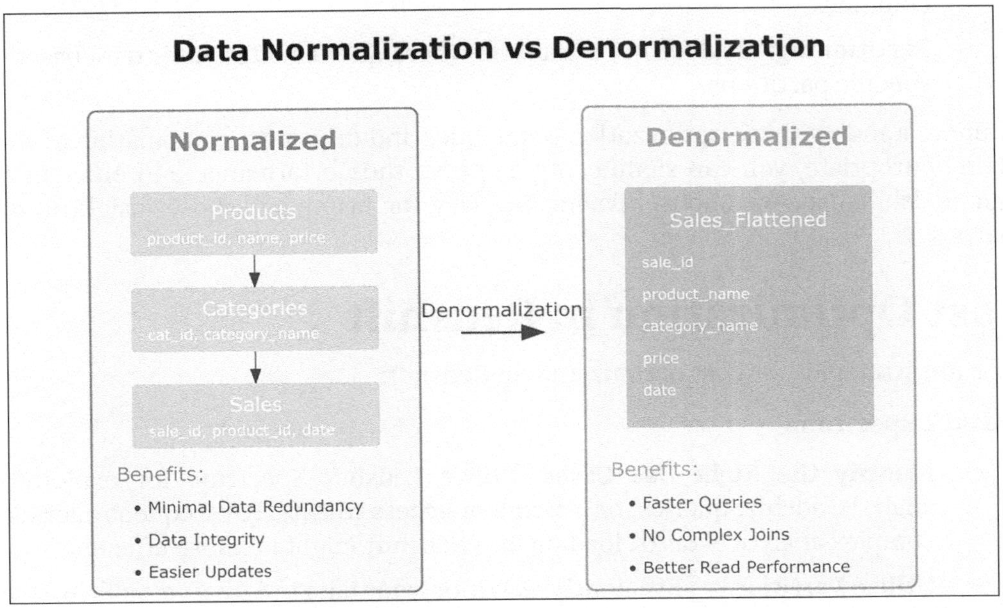

Figure 10.2: *Data Normalization versus Denormalization*

Clustering and Partitioning: Organizing for Efficiency

Imagine searching for a specific book in a library without any organization. It would be time-consuming! Similarly, searching through large datasets in Redshift can be slow without proper organization. **Clustering and partitioning** can significantly improve this.

- **Clustering:** Group related data together based on frequently joined columns. This allows Redshift to physically store related data on the same disk, minimizing the need to access different physical locations during joins, leading to faster query execution.
- **Partitioning:** Divide your data into smaller segments based on specific criteria like time (for example, year or month), region, or product category. This allows Redshift to quickly identify and access relevant data segments instead of scanning the entire dataset, significantly improving query performance for large datasets.

Choosing the Right Strategy:

The effectiveness of clustering and partitioning depends on your specific workload and query patterns.

- **Clustering:** Most beneficial for data that is frequently joined based on specific columns.
- **Partitioning:** Ideal for large datasets where queries often filter data based on specific partitions.

By understanding these optimization techniques and utilizing a combination of them when appropriate, you can significantly improve the performance and efficiency of your Redshift data warehouse, paving the way for faster and more insightful data analysis.

Cost Optimization in Redshift

Here are strategies for cost optimization in Redshift:

Redshift Spectrum:

- **Identify the Right Use Cases:** Utilize Redshift Spectrum for exploratory analysis, ad-hoc queries, or infrequent access to data. For frequent queries or complex analytical tasks, loading into Redshift might be more efficient.
- **Utilize Partitioning Efficiently:** Partition your data in S3 based on factors you frequently query. This allows Redshift Spectrum to only scan relevant data partitions, reducing costs.

- **Monitor Spectrum Usage:** Keep track of your Spectrum usage and identify potential cost spikes. Consider alternative approaches for frequently accessed data to optimize cost-effectiveness.

Reserved Instances and Savings Plans:

- **Forecast Your Needs:** Analyze your expected data volume and query workloads to predict instance usage patterns.
- **Choose the Right Commitment Terms:** Consider one-year or three-year commitment terms for reserved instances or savings plans depending on your budget and risk tolerance. Longer commitments offer greater discounts but less flexibility.
- **Monitor Utilization and Adjust:** Regularly review your instance usage and adjust your reserved instances or savings plans as your needs evolve. Unused reserved instances can be refunded while increasing utilization can unlock further discounts.

Data Skipping and Compression:

- **Identify Unused Columns and Data:** Regularly analyze your data to identify columns rarely used in queries or data that can be archived. Removing unnecessary data reduces storage costs.
- **Leverage Partitioning and Sorting:** Partition your data strategically and sort it based on frequently used columns. This allows Redshift to skip irrelevant data segments, improving query performance and potentially reducing storage requirements.
- **Choose the Right Compression Codec:** Experiment with different compression codecs, such as LZO or GZIP based on your data characteristics. While some codecs offer better compression ratios, they may impact query performance.

Optimize Queries:

- **Understand Query Execution Plans:** Use Redshift's EXPLAIN command to understand how your queries are executed. Identify bottlenecks and optimize queries to minimize resource utilization.
- **Utilize Appropriate Data Types:** Choose data types that accurately represent your data without unnecessary precision. Storing data in smaller data types minimizes storage space and potentially improves query performance.
- **Denormalize Strategically:** In specific situations, denormalizing your data schema can simplify queries and improve performance. However, weigh the benefits against potential data redundancy and increased storage requirements.

Bonus Tip:

- **Utilize Amazon Cost Explorer:** Regularly monitor your Redshift costs using

Amazon Cost Explorer. This tool provides insights into your spending patterns and identifies potential cost optimization opportunities.

Remember:

Cost optimization is an ongoing process. Experiment, monitor, and adapt your strategies as your data warehouse evolves and your needs change. By leveraging these tips and tricks, you can build a cost-effective Redshift data warehouse that empowers your data-driven decision-making without breaking the bank.

Security and Governance Considerations: Safeguarding Your Data Warehouse

Your data warehouse holds valuable information, and ensuring its security and proper governance is paramount. Here is an in-depth exploration of three crucial strategies:

1. **Secure Network Access: Building a Fortress**

   Imagine your data warehouse is a physical building. You would not just leave the doors wide open, right? Similarly, **secure network access** is essential to protect your data from unauthorized access.

   - **Security Groups:** These act like digital security guards, allowing you to define which network traffic can reach your Redshift cluster. Restrict access only to authorized IP addresses or Amazon Virtual Private Clouds (VPCs) using security groups.
   - **IAM Roles:** Within your Redshift cluster, utilize Identity and Access Management (IAM) roles to define **granular access control**. Assign specific permissions to users and groups, allowing them to only access the data and resources they need to perform their tasks. This ensures that even authorized users have limited access, minimizing the risk of accidental or malicious data exposure.

2. **Data Encryption: Double-Layered Protection**

   Imagine your data is a treasure chest. You would not just leave it unlocked, would you? **Data encryption** adds the following two layers of security to your data warehouse:

   - **Data Encryption at Rest:** This encrypts your data while it is stored in S3, protecting it even if someone manages to access your storage. Redshift utilizes industry-standard encryption algorithms like AES-256 to ensure robust data protection.
   - **Data Encryption in Transit:** This encrypts data while it is being transmitted between your applications and Redshift, safeguarding it from potential

interception during network communication. This additional layer of protection adds further peace of mind.

3. **Regular Backups: A Safety Net for Your Data**

   Imagine your house is prone to occasional power outages. You might have a backup generator to ensure essential systems remain operational. Similarly, **regular backups** act as a safety net for your data warehouse.

   - **Schedule Backups:** Automate regular backups of your data warehouse to a secure location, like another S3 bucket or a different AWS region. This allows you to recover your data in case of accidental deletion, system failure, or even potential ransomware attacks.
   - **Test Your Backups:** Do not just set it and forget it! Regularly test your backups to ensure they are functional and allow you to successfully restore your data in case of a disaster.

Remember:

Security and governance are ongoing processes. Regularly review and update your security practices, conduct vulnerability assessments, and stay informed about evolving threats. By implementing these strategies, you can build a secure and well-governed data warehouse, fostering trust and confidence in your data-driven decision-making.

Advanced Analytics with Redshift: Unlocking Deeper Insights

Redshift transcends its core functionality of efficient data storage and retrieval, offering powerful capabilities for **advanced analytics**. Let us explore how to leverage Redshift for more complex analytical tasks and integrate it with other tools for a comprehensive data analysis ecosystem.

Leveraging Redshift for Advanced Analytics:

- **Machine Learning (ML) Integration:** Redshift seamlessly integrates with **Amazon SageMaker**, a managed service for building, training, and deploying machine learning models. This allows you to:
  - **Train ML Models Directly within Your Data Warehouse:** Leverage the processing power of Redshift to train models on your data, eliminating the need to move data outside the warehouse.
  - **Score New Data Using Trained Models:** Once trained, utilize your models within Redshift to score new data, allowing you to make predictions or generate insights based on your data.

- **Time Series Analysis:** Redshift provides native support for **time series data**, allowing you to analyze trends and patterns over time. Utilize built-in functions to:
  - **Aggregate and Windowing Functions:** Calculate statistics such as moving averages, standard deviations, and year-over-year comparisons for specific time windows in your data.
  - **Time-Based Partitioning:** Partition your data by time (for example, year, month, day) to efficiently analyze historical trends and forecast future values.

Redshift Integration with Other Data Analytics Tools: A Deep Dive

Integrating Redshift with other data analytics tools within the AWS ecosystem unlocks a vast potential for data exploration, visualization, and analysis. Let us delve deeper into the details of integrating Redshift with the following:

Amazon QuickSight: Interactive Data Visualization and Exploration

Key Benefits:

- **Empowering Users:** QuickSight empowers **non-technical users** to explore Redshift data through user-friendly dashboards and visualizations. Users can filter, drill down, and create different chart types, enabling them to **understand insights independently**, and fostering broader data adoption within your organization.
- **Collaboration and Sharing:** QuickSight allows **seamless sharing** of dashboards and visualizations, fostering data-driven decision-making **across teams and departments**. This facilitates collaboration and knowledge sharing, promoting a data-driven culture.
- **Reduced Workload on Redshift:** QuickSight offloads the burden of building visualizations from Redshift. Complex visualizations can be resource-intensive on Redshift, freeing up resources for **faster data processing and analysis**.

Integration Process:

1. **Establish Connection:** Connect QuickSight to your Redshift data warehouse using its **connection settings**. This allows QuickSight to access data directly from Redshift.

2. **Data Source Selection:** Choose the specific Redshift **dataset** you want to analyze within QuickSight. This dataset represents a specific table or view within your Redshift cluster.

3. **Building Visualizations:** Utilize QuickSight's visual editor to drag and drop data fields, create charts, and build interactive dashboards. QuickSight offers a variety of chart types, including bar charts, line charts, pie charts, and maps, allowing you to tailor visualizations to specific insights.

Amazon Athena: Cost-Effective Exploration of S3 Data

Key Benefits:

- **Cost-Effectiveness:** Athena is a **serverless** service, meaning you only pay for the queries you run. This makes it ideal for **exploring large datasets** in S3 or performing **ad-hoc queries** on data **before loading it into Redshift**. This helps keep costs low for initial data analysis and exploration.
- **Standard SQL Support:** Athena utilizes **standard SQL syntax**, allowing you to use your existing SQL skills to query data in S3. This eliminates the need to learn a new language and enables analysts and data scientists to **quickly access and analyze data**.
- **Complementing Redshift:** While not a replacement for Redshift, Athena serves as a valuable tool for initial data exploration. After utilizing Athena for preliminary analysis, you can selectively **load specific datasets into Redshift** for more complex analysis and efficient querying, optimizing your data analysis workflow.

Integration Process:

1. **Configure Athena:** Ensure your S3 data bucket has the appropriate **access control settings** to allow Athena to access the data.
2. **Write SQL Queries:** Utilize standard SQL syntax to write queries that retrieve data from the specific S3 bucket where your data resides.
3. **Analyze Results:** Athena displays the query results in a tabular format. You can then download the results or analyze them directly within the Athena console.

Data Lake Integration: Unleashing the Power of Both Worlds

Key Benefits:

- **Holistic Data View:** Integrating Redshift with your S3 data lake allows you to gain a **comprehensive view** of your organization's data. This encompasses both **structured data** in Redshift and **unstructured data,** such as logs, images, and audio files in the data lake. This empowers you to analyze relationships and patterns across diverse data types, leading to deeper insights.
- **Advanced Analytics Potential:** Data lake integration unlocks the potential for advanced analytics scenarios that leverage **structured and unstructured data together**. Tools like Amazon SageMaker can be utilized to build machine

learning models that can learn from both data sources, enabling you to extract valuable insights for predictive analytics and other complex analysis tasks.

Integration Considerations:

- **Data Transformation:** Ensure consistent data formats and schema across Redshift and the data lake to facilitate seamless analysis. You might need tools such as AWS Glue or data pipelines to transform and prepare data for consistent use.
- **Data Quality Checks:** Implement data quality checks to ensure data consistency and accuracy across both data sources. This is crucial for ensuring the reliability and validity of your analysis.
- **Security and Governance:** Establish appropriate security controls and governance policies to manage access and ensure data security across the data lake and Redshift.

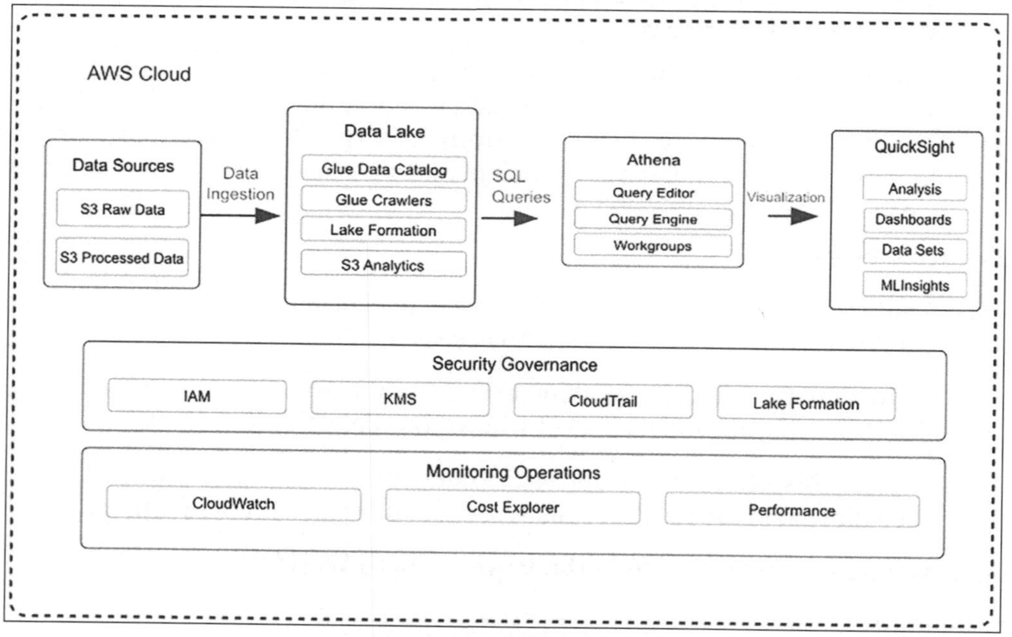

***Figure 10.3:** High-level flowchart*

Remember: Choosing the right data analytics tool depends on your specific needs and data analysis goals. QuickSight empowers interactive exploration, Athena offers cost-effective discovery, and data lake integration unlocks the potential of diverse data analysis. By understanding their capabilities and integration methods with Redshift, you can build a robust and efficient data analytics ecosystem for your organization.

Conclusion

In this chapter, we delved into the world of **data warehouses**, unlocking their potential for structured data analysis. We distinguished them from data lakes, explored their construction through ETL processes, and mastered the art of querying with SQL to extract valuable insights. Through practical steps and thought-provoking questions, we solidified our understanding of how data warehouses can empower organizations with historical data analysis and informed decision-making.

However, the insights hidden within data often remain silent until translated into a compelling narrative. In the next chapter, *Chapter 11, Visualizing the Unseen*, we will embark on a journey to **master data visualization**. We will explore essential tools and techniques to breathe life into your data, transforming it into engaging stories that resonate with stakeholders. We will also dive into connecting Redshift with popular BI tools, such as Tableau and Power BI, unlocking the power of both batch and real-time data exploration. Get ready to transform your data into a captivating visual language, effectively communicating insights and inspiring action!

CHAPTER 11
Visualizing the Unseen

Introduction

Imagine a treasure trove of information, meticulously organized and ready for exploration. We have spent the past chapter unlocking the secrets of your data warehouse, a powerful tool that has helped you unearth valuable insights hidden within its structured walls. However, raw data, like a collection of unpolished gemstones, holds the potential to shine even brighter.

In this chapter, we embark on a transformative journey. We will **transform** your data from its raw state into **captivating narratives**, crafting **compelling stories** that resonate with your stakeholders. We will delve into the world of **data visualization**, a powerful art form that breathes life into numbers and statistics, allowing you to **communicate insights effectively** and **inspire action**.

Building upon your newfound mastery of data warehousing from the previous chapter, we will venture beyond batch operations. We will explore how to **connect Redshift to industry-leading BI tools** such as Tableau and Power BI. This potent combination unlocks the power of **interactive data exploration**, enabling you to not only analyze historical data but also **gain real-time insights** from the ever-evolving stream of information.

Get ready to **transform from a data analyst into a data storyteller**. We will equip you with the tools and techniques to **visualize the unseen**, transforming the silent whispers of data into clear and compelling narratives that captivate your audience and illuminate the path toward informed decisions. Join us as we delve into the captivating world of data visualization and unlock the **full potential of your data to tell its story.**

Structure

In this chapter, we will cover the following topics:

Part 1. The Power of Data Visualization

- From Data to Narrative
- Benefits of Data Visualization
  - Enhance Understanding and Communication of Insights
  - Identify Trends and Patterns Effectively
  - Engage and Inspire Stakeholders with Compelling Narratives

Part 2. Exploring Data Visualization Tools and Techniques

- Popular Data Visualization Tools
  - Tableau
  - Power BI
  - Other Options
- Essential Visualization Techniques
  - Bar Charts
  - Line Charts
  - Pie Charts
  - Maps
  - Scatter Plots
  - Additional Techniques
- Designing Effective Visualizations
  - Choosing the Right Chart Type for Your Data and Audience
  - Utilizing Clear and Concise Labels and Titles
  - Applying Color, Size, and Other Visual Elements Effectively

Part 3. Connecting Redshift to BI Tools: Interactive Data Exploration

- The Power of BI Tools
  - Interactive Dashboards and Reports
  - Real-Time Data Exploration
  - Enhanced Collaboration and Information Sharing
- Connecting Redshift to Tableau and Power BI
  - Overview of the Integration Process

  - Benefits and Considerations
- Exploring Both Batch and Real-Time Data Sets
  - Integrating Real-Time Data Sources
  - Gaining Insights from the Ever-Evolving Data Stream

The Power of Data Visualization: From Data to Narrative

We will look into transforming raw data into compelling stories with effective visualization techniques—unlock insights and drive decisions with clarity and impact.

Unlocking the Potential of Data Storytelling

Data, in its raw form, can be overwhelming and often fails to capture the full picture. It is like a collection of scattered pieces of a puzzle; it holds valuable information, but without context, it is difficult to grasp the complete story. **Data visualization** acts as the bridge, transforming these fragments into a **cohesive narrative** that resonates with your audience.

Benefits of Data Visualization

Enhance understanding and communication of insights:

- **Clarity and Simplicity:** Visualizations translate complex data into **easily digestible formats**, such as charts, graphs, and maps. This eliminates the need for viewers to decipher intricate tables and spreadsheets, allowing them to **grasp the information readily**.
- **Pattern and Trend Identification:** Visual elements such as color, size, and position **highlight patterns and trends** that might go unnoticed in raw data. For example, a line chart showing sales trends over time can instantly reveal seasonal fluctuations, whereas a table listing monthly sales figures might not.
- **Universal Appeal:** Visualizations transcend language barriers, simplifying communication across diverse audiences. A well-designed chart can convey information effectively to everyone, regardless of their linguistic background.

Identify trends and patterns effectively:

- **Highlighting Correlations:** Visualizations can reveal **hidden relationships** between different data points. For instance, a scatter plot depicting customer age and purchase amount can highlight potential correlations, allowing you to tailor marketing strategies based on specific age groups.
- **Identifying Outliers:** Data visualization can effectively **identify anomalies and**

outliers in your data. This allows you to investigate potential errors or discover unique segments within your data that might warrant further exploration.

- **Forecasting Future Trends:** By analyzing historical data trends visually, you can **predict future patterns and behaviors** with greater accuracy. This empowers you to make informed decisions and proactively plan for potential outcomes.

Engage and inspire stakeholders with compelling narratives:

- **Captivate Your Audience:** People are naturally drawn to visuals. Compelling data visualizations **capture attention** and hold interest, making it easier to engage your audience in the story your data tells.
- **Evoking Emotions and Stimulating Action:** Well-designed visualizations can **evoke sentiments** such as curiosity, excitement, or concern, depending on the story they convey. This emotional connection can **motivate stakeholders to take action** based on the insights presented.
- **Supporting Decision-Making:** By presenting data clearly and concisely, visualizations empower stakeholders to **understand complex situations** and **make informed decisions** with greater confidence.

In conclusion, data visualization is a powerful tool that goes beyond simply presenting data. It unlocks the potential of data storytelling, allowing you to **transform insights into compelling narratives** that enhance understanding, identify patterns, engage stakeholders, and ultimately, **drive informed decisions and positive outcomes.**

Exploring Data Visualization Tools and Techniques: Popular Options

In this section, we are going to discover the essential tools and techniques that bring data to life. Making complex information accessible and actionable.

Popular Data Visualization Tools

The data visualization landscape offers a variety of tools, each catering to different needs and skill levels. Here, we explore some of the most popular options:

Tableau:

- **Features:** Tableau is widely recognized for its user-friendly interface, powerful drag-and-drop functionality, and extensive library of built-in charts and graphs. It offers advanced capabilities such as data blending, calculations, and interactive dashboards.
- **Strengths:** Tableau excels in creating **visually appealing and interactive**

dashboards with a focus on **intuitive usability**. Its drag-and-drop functionalities allow even non-technical users to create effective visualizations.

- **Considerations:** Tableau has a **paid licensing structure** that can be costly for individual users or smaller organizations.

Power BI:

- **Features:** Power BI is a powerful tool from Microsoft that seamlessly integrates with other Microsoft products such as Excel and Azure. It offers a comprehensive set of features, including data exploration tools, visual authoring, and report building.
- **Strengths:** Power BI shines in its **tight integration with the Microsoft ecosystem** and its **robust features for data analysis and reporting**. This makes it a preferred choice for organizations already heavily invested in Microsoft products.
- **Considerations:** Power BI **may have a steeper learning curve** compared to Tableau for users unfamiliar with the Microsoft ecosystem. Its free version has limitations, and advanced features require paid subscriptions.

Other Options:

The data visualization landscape is constantly evolving, offering a multitude of choices beyond the two giants mentioned above. Here is a brief mention of some noteworthy options:

- **Amazon QuickSight:** A cloud-based BI service from AWS, offering a cost-effective option for visualizing data stored in Redshift and other AWS services.
- **Google Data Studio:** A free tool from Google, ideal for creating basic visualizations and easily integrating with other Google products.
- **Open-Source Tools:** Options such as Matplotlib and Plotly offer powerful functionalities for experienced users seeking greater customization and control over their visualizations.

Choosing the Right Tool:

Selecting the ideal data visualization tool depends on several factors, including:

- **Budget:** Consider the licensing costs associated with different tools.
- **Skill Level:** Choose a tool that aligns with your comfort and expertise level.
- **Integration Needs:** If you use specific platforms or services, consider tools that offer seamless integration.
- **Functionality Requirements:** Evaluate the specific features and functionalities offered by each tool to ensure it meets your visualization needs.

By exploring these popular options and understanding their strengths and considerations, you can make an informed choice and leverage the power of data visualization tools to bring your data to life.

Essential Visualization Techniques: Unveiling the Power of Data through Visuals

Data visualization thrives on a variety of techniques, each with its strengths and applications. Mastering these essential techniques empowers you to effectively communicate your message and unlock valuable insights from your data.

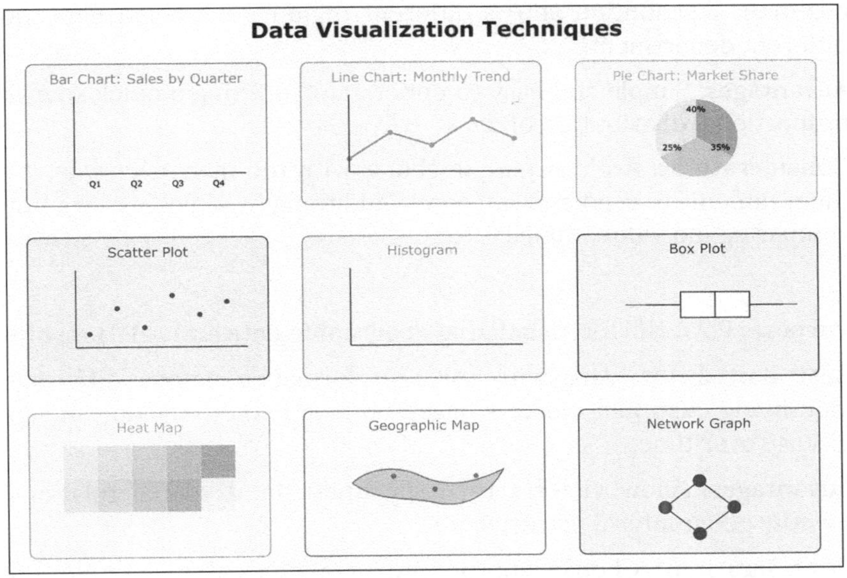

Figure 11.1: *Data Visualization Techniques*

Bar Charts:

- **Purpose:** Ideal for **comparing categories and quantities** across different data points.
- **Best Suited for:** Comparing sales figures across different product categories, customer demographics such as age groups, or website traffic sources.
- **Advantages:** Easy to understand and interpret, allowing for quick comparisons between categories.
- **Considerations:** Avoid using bar charts with too many categories, as it can clutter the visualization and make comparisons difficult.

Line Charts:

- **Purpose:** Effective for **visualizing trends and changes over time**.

- **Best Suited for:** Tracking stock prices over time, customer satisfaction scores across quarters, or website traffic trends over a specific period.
- **Advantages:** Highlight trends with clarity and identify patterns in data points over time.
- **Considerations:** Ensure the time axis is clearly labeled and evenly scaled to avoid misinterpretations.

Pie Charts:

- **Purpose:** Best suited for **displaying the proportions of a whole**.
- **Best Suited for:** Illustrating the market share of different competitors, customer distribution across different regions, or budget allocation across different departments.
- **Advantages:** Simple and easy to understand, offering a quick snapshot of the proportional distribution of data.
- **Considerations:** Avoid using pie charts with too many slices, as it can make them difficult to read and interpret. Additionally, pie charts are not ideal for comparing individual values.

Maps:

- **Purpose:** Powerful for **visualizing geographic data and relationships**.
- **Best Suited for:** Analyzing sales performance across different regions, identifying customer clusters based on location, or tracking the spread of a disease over time.
- **Advantages:** Allow viewers to easily understand spatial relationships and identify geographical patterns.
- **Considerations:** Choose appropriate map types (for example, choropleth, heatmap) depending on your data and ensure clear labeling of locations and legends for interpretation.

Scatter Plots:

- **Purpose:** Useful for **identifying correlations between two variables**.
- **Best Suited for:** Exploring the relationship between customer age and purchase amount, employee experience and job satisfaction, or product price and sales volume.
- **Advantages:** Reveal potential relationships and identify outliers in your data.
- **Considerations:** Label your axes clearly and avoid overcrowding the plot with too many data points, as it can hinder interpretation.

Histograms:

- **Purpose: Visualize the distribution of data points within a continuous range**.

This helps you understand how data is spread out and identify potential patterns such as skewness or outliers.

- **Best Suited for:** Analyzing continuous data such as customer age, income levels, or product weights.
- **Advantages:** Provide a clear understanding of how data is concentrated or dispersed within a specific range.
- **Considerations:** Ensure the bin sizes (intervals) are chosen appropriately to avoid misrepresenting the data distribution.

Box Plots:

- **Purpose: Compare the distribution of data across different groups**. They offer a concise way to visualize the median, quartiles, and outliers within each group.
- **Best Suited for:** Comparing sales figures across different regions, customer satisfaction scores from various departments, or exam scores across different age groups.
- **Advantages:** Allow for quick comparisons of central tendencies and variations in data distribution between different groups.
- **Considerations:** Avoid using box plots with too many groups, as it can make the visualization cluttered and difficult to interpret.

Heatmaps:

- **Purpose: Display data as color variations on a grid**, highlighting areas of high and low values. This helps identify patterns and trends across different dimensions.
- **Best Suited for:** Analyzing website traffic patterns across different sections and pages, visualizing stock prices over time, or showcasing customer sentiment across various product categories.
- **Advantages:** Offer a visually intuitive way to identify clusters, trends, and anomalies in data with two dimensions.
- **Considerations:** Choose appropriate color gradients to effectively represent the value variations and ensure clear labeling of the grid axes for interpretation.

Network Diagrams:

- **Purpose: Represent relationships between entities in a network structure**. They help visualize complex relationships and connections between different data points.
- **Best Suited for:** Analyzing social networks, organizational structures, supply chain connections, or relationships between different proteins in a biological network.

- **Advantages:** Provide a clear visual representation of connections and interactions between different entities within a complex system.
- **Considerations:** Ensure the layout of the network diagram is clear and avoid overwhelming the viewer with too many connections. Utilize different visual elements such as node size and color to highlight specific entities or relationships within the network.

Additional Techniques:

Beyond these core options, numerous other visualization techniques cater to specific data types and communication goals. These include:

- **Treemaps:** Represent hierarchical data structures visually.
- **Waterfall charts:** Showcase how different factors contribute to a final value.
- **Sankey diagrams:** Visualize flows and connections between different stages in a process.

Choosing the Right Technique:

The success of your data visualization hinges on selecting the technique that best aligns with your data and intended message. Consider the following factors:

- **Data Type:** Choose a technique that effectively represents the type of data you are using (for example, numerical, categorical, geographical).
- **The Goal of Visualization:** Determine whether you aim to compare categories, analyze trends, identify relationships, or showcase geographical patterns.
- **Audience:** Consider the level of technical expertise of your audience and choose a technique that is clear and easy to understand.

By mastering these essential techniques and exploring additional options, you will be well-equipped to translate your data into compelling narratives, fostering data-driven insights and informed decision-making.

Designing Effective Visualizations: Transforming Data into Captivating Narratives

Crafting compelling data visualizations goes beyond simply choosing a chart and presenting the information. It requires careful consideration of design principles that ensure your data tells a clear and impactful story. Here, we delve into the key elements of **designing effective visualizations**:

Choosing the right chart type for your data and audience:

- **Matching Data Type and Chart Functionality:** Align the chart type with the nature of your data. For instance, bar charts are ideal for comparing categories, while line charts excel at showcasing trends over time. Choose a chart that accurately represents the relationships and patterns within your data.

- **Considering Audience Understanding:** Tailor the chosen chart type to the level of technical expertise your audience possesses. Simpler charts such as bar charts and pie charts cater to a wider audience, while complex charts such as scatter plots or network diagrams might require more background knowledge for effective interpretation.

Utilizing clear and concise labels and titles:

- **Comprehensive Labeling:** Ensure all axes, data points, and legends are clearly labeled with appropriate units and descriptions. This avoids confusion and allows viewers to understand the information presented instantly.
- **Meaningful Titles:** Craft concise and informative titles that accurately reflect the data and the message you aim to communicate. A well-crafted title sets the context and guides viewers toward understanding the key takeaway of the visualization.

Applying color, size, and other visual elements effectively:

- **Color Selection:** Choose color palettes thoughtfully. Utilize colors that are visually appealing, accessible for color-blind viewers, and effectively represent the data. Avoid using too many colors, as it can overwhelm the viewer and distract from the message.
- **Strategic Use of Size:** Utilize variations in size to highlight specific data points or emphasize comparisons. For instance, larger bars in a bar chart could represent higher values, while smaller points in a scatter plot could represent outliers.
- **Leveraging Additional Elements:** Explore the use of shapes, patterns, and annotations to add further clarity and emphasize specific elements within your visualization. However, use these elements sparingly to avoid cluttering the visual, and hindering readability.

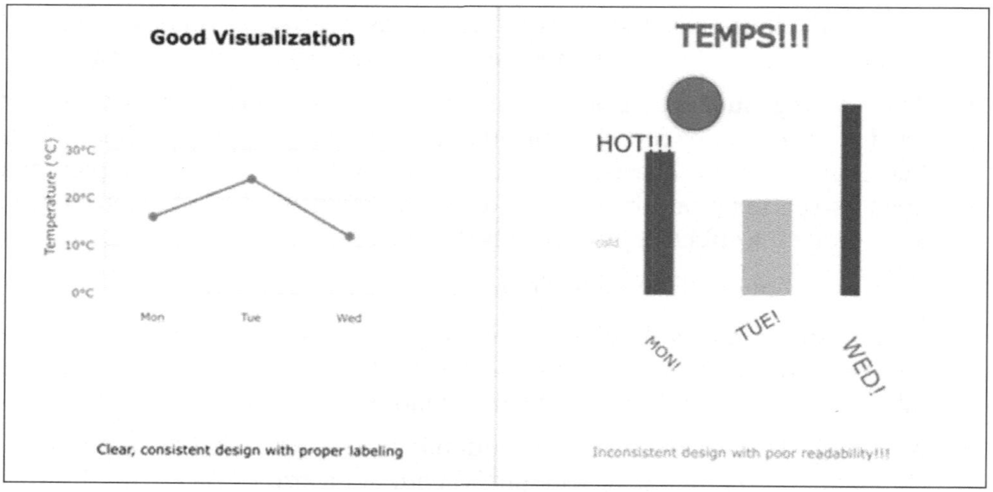

Figure 11.2: *Good versus Bad Visualization Comparison*

Remember:

- **Prioritize Clarity and Simplicity:** Avoid overwhelming viewers with excessive information or overly complex designs. Aim to present the data clearly and concisely that facilitates understanding and engagement.
- **Focus on the Message:** Keep the intended message at the forefront of your design choices. Ensure all visual elements contribute to communicating your message effectively and avoid including elements that distract or detract from the story you want to tell.

By mastering these design principles and tailoring your approach to your specific data and audience, you can craft impactful data visualizations that resonate with your viewers, transform data into captivating narratives, and drive informed decision-making.

Connecting Redshift to BI Tools: Interactive Data Exploration

We are going to explore how Redshift can be integrated with other Visualization tools.

Unlocking the Power of Interactive Insights

While traditional data visualization tools offer valuable insights, **Business Intelligence (BI) tools** such as Tableau and Power BI elevate the experience to a whole new level. By connecting your Redshift data warehouse with these tools, you can harness the power of **interactive data exploration**, transforming static visualizations into dynamic dashboards and reports that empower deeper understanding and informed decision-making.

The Power of BI Tools

Let us understand the power of BI tools.

Interactive Dashboards and Reports:

Move beyond static visuals: BI tools allow you to create **dynamic dashboards** that update automatically as your data changes. These dashboards can include a combination of charts, graphs, and other visual elements, providing a **comprehensive overview** of key performance indicators (KPIs) and critical metrics. However, unlike static visualizations, BI tools allow viewers to take the following actions:

- **Interact with the Data Directly:** Filter dashboards and reports to specific timeframes, product categories, or other dimensions, fostering a **deeper exploration** of the information and uncovering hidden insights.
- **Drill Down and Explore Details:** Navigate through different levels of detail within the data, gaining a granular understanding of specific trends or patterns within various segments.

Real-Time Data Exploration:

- **Beyond Batch Data:** BI tools can integrate with **real-time data sources**, breathing life into your analyses. Imagine being able to visualize and analyze data **as it is generated**, such as:
    - **IoT Sensor Readings:** Monitor the performance of equipment in real-time, allowing for proactive maintenance and optimization.
    - **Streaming Social Media Data:** Identify sentiment trends and brand mentions as they occur, informing marketing strategies and customer service efforts.
- **Increased Agility and Responsiveness:** By receiving insights in real-time, you can **identify potential issues or opportunities** early on, enabling you to **make data-driven decisions** with greater agility and effectiveness.

Enhanced Collaboration and Information Sharing:

- **Seamless Communication and Collaboration:** BI tools facilitate the easy **sharing of dashboards and reports** within your organization. Imagine a scenario where:
    - **Sales Teams** can access real-time sales figures and customer insights, allowing them to tailor their approach accordingly.
    - **Marketing Teams** can monitor campaign performance and adjust strategies based on real-time feedback and engagement metrics.

- **Democratizing Access to Data:** BI tools present data in a user-friendly format, allowing users with varying levels of technical expertise to **interact with and understand data** through intuitive dashboards and reports. This promotes **wider adoption of data insights** within your organization, fostering a data-driven culture where everyone can contribute to informed decision-making.

Connecting Redshift to Tableau and Power BI

Overview of the Integration Process:

Connecting Redshift to BI tools such as Tableau and Power BI is a relatively straightforward process. Both tools offer **official connectors**, readily available instructions, and various online resources to guide you through the setup. These connectors establish a **secure connection** between your data warehouse and the chosen BI tool, allowing you to **seamlessly access and visualize your data** stored in Redshift directly within the BI platform.

Benefits and Considerations:

- **Benefits:** Connecting Redshift to BI tools offers numerous benefits, including:
    - **Enhanced Data Exploration and Analysis Capabilities:** Unlock the full potential of your data through interactive dashboards, filtering, and drill-down functionalities.
    - **Increased Agility and Responsiveness:** Make data-driven decisions faster with real-time insights from constantly evolving data streams.
    - **Improved Collaboration and Information Sharing:** Foster a data-driven culture by empowering everyone to access and understand critical information through interactive dashboards and reports.
- **Considerations:** When selecting a BI tool, consider the following factors:
    - **Cost:** While both offer free versions with limited features, paid editions unlock advanced functionalities at various cost points.
    - **Ease of Use:** Evaluate the user interface and learning curve for both tools, considering the technical expertise within your organization.
    - **Feature Set:** Ensure the chosen BI tool possesses the functionalities and integrations needed to meet your specific data analysis and visualization requirements.

Exploring Both Batch and Real-Time Data Sets

While this chapter primarily focuses on the integration of Redshift with BI tools for **batch data analysis** (pre-existing data stored in the warehouse), the potential of incorporating **real-time data sources** should not be overlooked. BI tools offer functionalities to connect to various **real-time data sources**, such as:

- **Amazon Kinesis**: A scalable and real-time data streaming service for processing large volumes of data streams, allowing you to analyze data as it is generated, like website traffic or social media activity.
- **Amazon SQS**: A highly available message queuing service for receiving and sending messages. This can be particularly useful for integrating real-time data from external applications or services that communicate through.

A Glimpse into the Future of Data Visualization and Storytelling: Embracing New Frontiers

The future of data visualization and storytelling holds immense promise, brimming with exciting possibilities that promise to revolutionize how we interact with and extract meaning from data. Here is a glimpse into some of the captivating trends shaping this landscape:

Enhanced interactivity and user experience:

- **Beyond Passive Consumption:** Data visualizations will move beyond static representations, evolving into **interactive experiences** that respond to user input and allow dynamic exploration. Imagine dashboards and reports that adapt to your inquiries, offering deeper insights in real time.
- **Augmented Reality and Virtual Reality (AR/VR) Integration:** By incorporating AR/VR technologies, data visualization can be transformed into **immersive experiences** that allow users to **step inside the data**. Imagine viewing sales trends unfolding within a virtual 3D store environment or exploring customer demographics across a geographically interactive world map.

Artificial Intelligence (AI) and Machine Learning (ML) powered insights:

- **Automated Data Analysis and Storytelling:** Leveraging AI and ML algorithms, data visualization tools will offer **automated recommendations** for chart types, color schemes, and layouts based on the specific data and intended message. This will streamline the creation process and ensure visualizations are tailored for maximum impact.
- **Intelligent Narrative Generation:** AI can go beyond data visualization alone, assisting in **crafting compelling narratives** that accompany the visuals. Imagine AI-powered tools generating automated reports that highlight key insights and trends, freeing human analysts to focus on higher-level interpretations and strategic decision-making.

Democratization of data storytelling:

- **User-Friendly and Accessible Tools:** Data visualization tools will become **more intuitive and user-friendly**, allowing individuals with varying levels of technical expertise to create impactful visual stories. This will empower a wider range of people to leverage the power of data communication, fostering a data-driven culture across diverse fields.
- **Voice-Activated and Natural Language Interactions:** The future holds the potential for **voice-activated data exploration** and **natural language interactions** with visualizations. Imagine querying your data through voice commands and receiving insights presented in a clear and concise narrative format, eliminating the need for complex chart interpretations.

Ethical considerations and responsible storytelling:

- **Addressing Bias and Fairness:** As AI and ML become more prominent in data visualization, it is crucial to address potential biases and ensure algorithms are trained on **diverse and ethically sourced data**. Responsible data storytelling will remain paramount, requiring careful consideration of how data is represented and interpreted to avoid perpetuating biases or misinforming audiences.
- **Focus on Human-Centered Design:** At the heart of these advancements lie the **human users** who will interact with and interpret the information. The future of data visualization prioritizes **human-centered design** principles, ensuring the information is presented in a way that is clear, understandable, and ultimately beneficial to its audience.

Summary: Visualizing the Unseen - A Quick-Review Guide

Key Takeaways:

- **Data Storytelling:** Transform raw data into engaging narratives through data visualization.
- **Benefits:** Enhance understanding, improve communication, and engage stakeholders.
- **Essential Techniques:** Master core visuals such as bar charts, line charts, pie charts, maps, and scatter plots.
- **Choosing the Right Chart:** Align the chart type with your data and intended message.
- **Design Principles:** Clear labels, titles, and effective use of color, size, and other elements.
- **BI Tools:** Unlock interactive exploration with dynamic dashboards and real-time insights.

- **Connecting Redshift to BI Tools:** Utilize official connectors for secure and seamless data access.
- **Exploring Real-Time Data:** Integrate streaming sources, such as Kinesis or SQS for deeper insights.

Thought-Provoking Questions:

- How can you leverage data visualization to better communicate insights to your stakeholders?
- Beyond the techniques discussed, what other creative approaches can you consider for data storytelling?
- When choosing a BI tool, what factors would be most important for your specific needs?
- How might incorporating real-time data sources benefit your decision-making processes?

By engaging with these questions and revisiting the key takeaways, you can solidify your understanding of data visualization principles and leverage their power to transform data into actionable insights and compelling narratives.

Conclusion

In this chapter, we embarked on a journey to visualize the unseen, transforming raw data into compelling narratives that empower effective communication and engage stakeholders. We explored essential data visualization tools and techniques, allowing you to craft clear and concise representations of complex information.

Furthermore, we delved into the power of connecting Redshift to BI tools, unlocking a world of interactive exploration and real-time insights. This empowers you to not only analyze historical data but also harness the ever-evolving stream of information, driving agile decision-making and fostering a data-driven culture.

However, the story does not end here. While this chapter laid the foundation, the next chapter, beckons you to venture further. We will delve into the realm of data mining, machine learning, and real-time analytics, equipping you with advanced tools to uncover hidden patterns and make informed decisions based on both historical and streaming data. Prepare to go beyond the basics and unlock the full potential of your data to gain a deeper understanding of the world around you.

Are you ready to embark on this exciting journey? Turn the page and let us delve deeper into the fascinating world of advanced analytics!

CHAPTER 12
AWS Machine Learning: Classic AI to Generative AI

Introduction

In recent years, Machine Learning (ML) has moved from a niche field to a cornerstone of data-driven decision-making across industries. AWS has been at the forefront of this transformation, offering a suite of managed services and tools that simplify the machine learning lifecycle, from data preparation to model deployment. By providing scalable infrastructure, powerful algorithms, and integrated solutions, AWS enables data engineers and data scientists to build and deploy machine learning applications at scale, whether they are working with structured data, text, images, or audio.

This chapter explores how to leverage AWS for diverse machine learning applications, including traditional AI models, Natural Language Processing (NLP), and cutting-edge Generative AI (GenAI) models. We begin with an overview of foundational AWS services for machine learning, such as Amazon SageMaker, that support the entire ML workflow. Then, we delve into specific types of ML applications, including classic machine learning workflows, NLP for text and speech, and the exciting possibilities of GenAI for text and image generation. Throughout, we emphasize best practices for model training, deployment, monitoring, and security, empowering readers to design intelligent, resilient, and cost-effective machine learning systems on AWS.

By the end of this chapter, you will have a solid understanding of AWS's machine learning ecosystem and how to build sophisticated, production-ready ML pipelines that can unlock actionable insights, enhance user experiences, and drive innovation across domains.

Structure

In this chapter, we will cover the following topics:

- Foundations of Machine Learning on AWS
    - AWS ML Infrastructure
    - Amazon SageMaker Overview
    - Model Training and Optimization
- Classic Machine Learning Workflows on AWS
    - Data Preparation and Feature Engineering
    - Training, Validation, and Evaluation
    - Deploying and Scaling Models
- Natural Language Processing (NLP) with AWS
    - Text Analysis with Amazon Comprehend
    - Speech Recognition and Synthesis
    - Custom NLP Models on SageMaker
- Generative AI (GenAI) on AWS
    - Overview of GenAI Capabilities
    - Amazon Bedrock for GenAI
    - Custom Generative Models with SageMaker
- Best Practices for Monitoring, Security, and Cost Management
    - Monitoring and Model Drift Detection
    - Security in ML Workflows
    - Optimizing Costs

Foundations of Machine Learning on AWS

AWS provides a powerful ecosystem for machine learning, making it accessible and scalable for businesses of all sizes. At the heart of this ecosystem is Amazon SageMaker, a fully managed service that simplifies each step of the ML workflow, from data preparation and model building to deployment and monitoring. SageMaker's capabilities reduce the need for manual setup, helping data engineers and data scientists focus on refining model accuracy and optimizing performance.

AWS's infrastructure for machine learning includes specialized EC2 instance types (such as GPU-optimized instances) that support intensive ML training workloads, enabling data engineers to run large-scale training jobs efficiently. For those who want to experiment quickly, AWS offers Deep Learning AMIs pre-installed with popular ML frameworks, such as TensorFlow, PyTorch, and MXNet, providing flexibility for custom development.

Amazon SageMaker: An End-to-End Solution for ML

Amazon SageMaker stands out as the cornerstone of ML on AWS, designed to support end-to-end workflows. It includes:

- **Data Preparation and Labeling:**
  - SageMaker integrates with AWS Glue and AWS Data Wrangler to handle data extraction, cleaning, and transformation, streamlining the preparation process. Additionally, SageMaker Ground Truth provides a managed data labeling service that combines automated and manual labeling, making it easier to create high-quality labeled datasets.
  - **Use Case**: A manufacturing company uses SageMaker Ground Truth to label images of defective products, creating a training dataset for an anomaly detection model.
- **Training and Tuning:**
  - SageMaker provides built-in algorithms optimized for AWS infrastructure, ranging from linear regression to advanced deep learning models. For custom models, SageMaker also supports popular frameworks (for example, TensorFlow and PyTorch) and distributed training. Automatic model tuning, or hyperparameter optimization, allows data engineers to refine model parameters for optimal accuracy.
  - **Use Case**: An e-commerce company trains a recommendation model using SageMaker's XGBoost algorithm, leveraging automatic hyperparameter tuning to improve its precision.
- **Deployment and Inference:**
  - SageMaker simplifies model deployment by offering options for both real-time and batch inference. Models can be deployed to scalable endpoints for real-time applications or used in batch jobs for processing large datasets periodically.
  - **Use Case**: A healthcare provider deploys a patient risk prediction model in SageMaker, using a real-time endpoint to predict patient outcomes as new data is entered.
- **Monitoring and Model Management:**
  - With SageMaker Model Monitor, organizations can automatically track

deployed models, detecting model drift and ensuring accuracy over time. SageMaker also provides tools for A/B testing and monitoring, ensuring that models remain reliable in production.

- **Use Case**: A financial institution monitors its fraud detection model with Model Monitor, setting up alerts for accuracy changes, which signal the need for retraining.

Model Training and Optimization with SageMaker

Training high-performing models requires substantial data and computational power. SageMaker supports both single-machine and distributed training, allowing data engineers to scale up as needed. For large datasets, distributed training divides workloads across multiple instances, shortening training times and enabling the use of complex models.

To further optimize model performance, SageMaker offers Automatic Model Tuning, which performs hyperparameter optimization by testing different configurations to find the most accurate model. This automation not only improves accuracy but also saves time, as manual tuning is often a tedious process.

- **Example:** A fintech startup uses SageMaker's distributed training capability to train a deep learning model on vast transaction data, optimizing hyperparameters with automatic model tuning for improved fraud detection.

Key Benefits and Considerations for Using SageMaker in ML Workflows:

- **Scalability:** SageMaker's managed infrastructure handles the scaling of training jobs, allowing teams to build and deploy models that can process large datasets and serve predictions at high volumes.
- **Flexibility:** SageMaker supports a wide range of algorithms, frameworks, and deployment options, making it versatile enough to fit various ML applications and industry needs.
- **Cost Efficiency:** AWS offers Spot Instances and SageMaker Savings Plans to reduce the cost of training and deploying models, making it a cost-effective choice for production workloads.
- **Considerations:** While SageMaker simplifies the ML workflow, engineers should still consider costs associated with instance types and manage data storage carefully to avoid unexpected charges.

Example Case Study

Building an ML Pipeline with SageMaker for Customer Churn Prediction

Scenario: A telecom provider wants to predict customer churn based on usage data and demographics, enabling targeted retention efforts.

- **Data Preparation with AWS Glue:** The provider uses AWS Glue to extract, clean, and format customer data from different sources, storing it in S3 for easy access.
- **Labeling and Feature Engineering in SageMaker:** SageMaker Data Wrangler performs data transformations, creating features such as monthly call duration, average data usage, and recent service interactions.
- **Model Training and Tuning:** SageMaker trains a churn prediction model using the XGBoost algorithm, with automatic tuning to maximize predictive accuracy.
- **Deployment and Monitoring:** The model is deployed to a real-time endpoint in SageMaker. Model Monitor tracks the model's performance and sends alerts if there is a drop in accuracy, prompting retraining with fresh data.

Amazon SageMaker and the broader AWS ML infrastructure provide a robust foundation for machine learning, supporting everything from data preparation and training to deployment and monitoring. By leveraging these tools, data engineers can create ML pipelines that are efficient, scalable, and adaptable, laying the groundwork for sophisticated machine learning applications across industries.

Classic Machine Learning Workflows on AWS

Classic machine learning workflows encompass the end-to-end process of data collection, feature engineering, model training, and deployment. These workflows focus on structured pipelines to develop predictive models efficiently and iteratively.

Data Preparation and Feature Engineering

The first stage in any machine learning workflow is preparing the data, which involves cleaning, transforming, and organizing raw data into a suitable format for model training. In AWS, AWS Glue and AWS Data Wrangler are commonly used for this purpose. AWS Glue serves as a fully managed ETL service that simplifies data extraction and transformation from various sources, while Data Wrangler provides a point-and-click interface within SageMaker for data preparation and feature engineering.

Key steps in data preparation include:

- **Data Cleaning:** Removing duplicates, handling missing values, and correcting inconsistencies.
- **Feature Engineering:** Creating meaningful variables from raw data that improve model accuracy.

- **Data Transformation:** Normalizing, encoding categorical variables, and scaling data to prepare it for algorithms that require specific input formats.

  Example: In a customer segmentation project, Glue is used to clean customer transaction data and generate features like average purchase amount and frequency, which are then loaded into S3 for training.

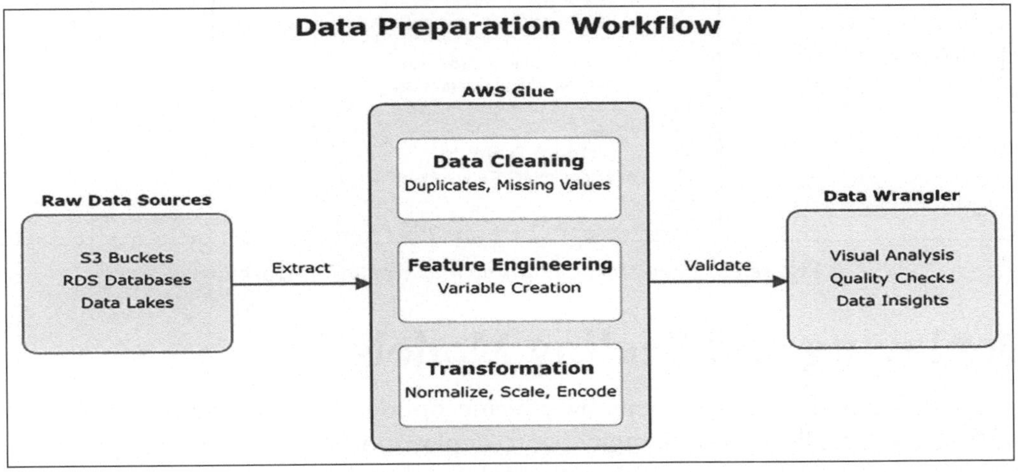

Figure 12.1: *Data Preparation Workflow*

Training, Validation, and Evaluation

Once the data is prepared, the next stage involves training, validating, and evaluating machine learning models. Amazon SageMaker offers built-in algorithms, including linear regression, k-means clustering, and XGBoost, optimized for AWS's infrastructure. SageMaker also supports custom models using frameworks, such as TensorFlow and PyTorch, allowing data engineers to bring their scripts.

Key steps in this stage:

1. **Model Training**: Training involves feeding labeled data to an algorithm to learn patterns and relationships.
2. **Cross-Validation**: Techniques like k-fold cross-validation help assess model performance and prevent overfitting by training multiple times on different data subsets.
3. **Model Evaluation**: Performance metrics such as accuracy, precision, recall, and F1-score are used to evaluate model quality.

   Example: A retail company uses SageMaker to train an XGBoost model for product recommendations. K-fold cross-validation is performed to ensure the model generalizes well on new customer data.

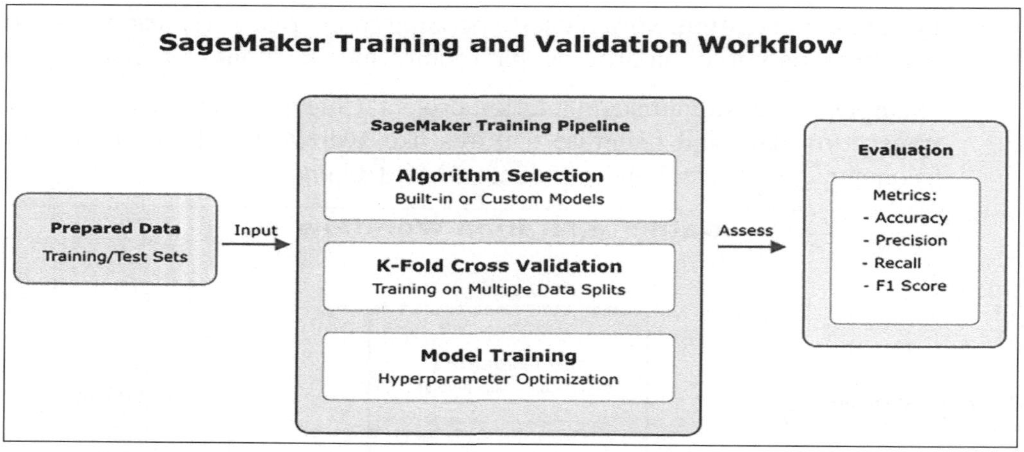

Figure 12.2: *SageMaker Training and Validation Workflow*

Deploying and Scaling Models

SageMaker simplifies deployment by offering options for real-time endpoints and batch inference, allowing data engineers to deploy models that serve live predictions or process data in batches. With auto-scaling capabilities, SageMaker can handle varying loads, automatically adjusting instance counts based on traffic volume. This flexibility ensures that models remain responsive, regardless of workload.

- **Real-Time Endpoints**: For applications requiring immediate predictions, models are deployed to scalable endpoints that provide real-time inference.
- **Batch Inference**: For large datasets or less time-sensitive tasks, batch inference allows models to generate predictions in batches, which are stored for later use.

  Example: A financial service deploys a credit scoring model as a real-time endpoint to assess loan applications instantly, while also using batch inference to re-evaluate existing customer profiles quarterly.

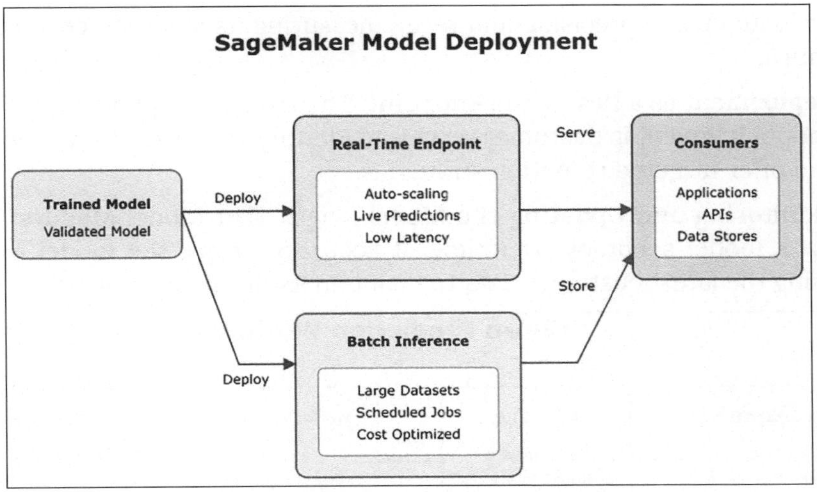

Figure 12.3: *SageMaker Model Deployment*

Best Practices for Classic Machine Learning Workflows

Here are the best practices for classic ML workflows:

- **Automate Data Pipelines:** Using AWS Glue and Data Wrangler helps automate repetitive data preparation tasks, ensuring data quality and consistency.
- **Choose the Right Algorithm:** SageMaker provides a range of algorithms suited for classification, regression, clustering, and anomaly detection. Selecting the appropriate algorithm for the problem is key to effective modeling.
- **Monitor Model Performance**: Once deployed, models should be continuously monitored to track changes in performance and detect drift in data patterns. SageMaker Model Monitor can help by sending alerts when accuracy drops below a threshold.

Example Case Study

Classic ML Workflow for Customer Churn Prediction

Scenario: A subscription-based streaming service wants to predict customer churn based on usage patterns, account history, and demographics.

- **Data Preparation with Glue:** The company uses AWS Glue to extract and clean customer usage data from their data warehouse. Features such as total hours streamed, number of logins, and average session length are engineered.
- **Model Training and Validation in SageMaker**: An XGBoost algorithm is chosen for training, with k-fold cross-validation to ensure robustness. The model is

evaluated using precision and recall measuring its ability to correctly predict churn.

- **Deployment as a Real-Time Endpoint**: The model is deployed to a SageMaker endpoint, enabling customer service to identify at-risk customers in real-time and offer targeted retention strategies.
- **Monitoring and Updating the Model**: SageMaker Model Monitor is used to track model accuracy over time. If accuracy drops, the model is retrained using the latest customer data to maintain its predictive power.

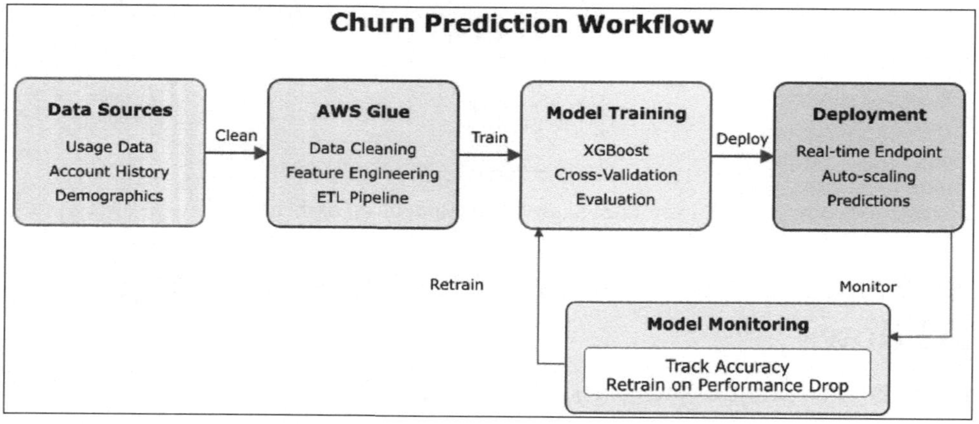

Figure 12.4: *Customer Churn Prediction Workflow*

Summary of Classic ML Workflows on AWS

Classic machine learning workflows in AWS combine data preparation, training, deployment, and monitoring into a streamlined pipeline. By leveraging AWS services, such as Glue, SageMaker, and Model Monitor, data engineers can efficiently build, deploy, and maintain high-performing ML models. This foundation is essential for moving into more specialized applications, including natural language processing and generative AI, which we will explore in the following sections.

This section outlines a complete ML pipeline on AWS, setting the stage for specialized machine learning tasks in NLP and GenAI, where more complex data types and algorithms come into play. Let us proceed to explore AWS's NLP capabilities in the next section.

Natural Language Processing (NLP) with AWS

Natural Language Processing (NLP) enables machines to understand, interpret, and respond to human language, opening applications such as sentiment analysis, entity recognition, and language translation. AWS provides a range of managed services and tools that make it easier to build NLP capabilities, including **Amazon Comprehend** for text analysis, **Amazon Transcribe** for speech-to-text, and **Amazon Polly** for text-to-speech. Additionally, **Amazon SageMaker** supports the development of custom NLP models using popular frameworks, allowing data engineers to build and deploy advanced NLP solutions.

This section covers the AWS services available for NLP, highlighting how each service can be used individually or integrated into custom workflows to enhance business applications with language understanding capabilities.

Text Analysis with Amazon Comprehend

Amazon Comprehend is a fully managed NLP service that provides a range of pre-trained models for text analysis, including:

- **Sentiment Analysis:** Determines the overall sentiment of text—positive, negative, neutral, or mixed.
- **Entity Recognition:** Identifies entities such as people, places, dates, and organizations within the text.
- **Language Detection**: Automatically detects the language of the input text, supporting multilingual processing.
- **Key Phrase Extraction**: Extracts important phrases or topics from text, aiding in summarization and categorization.

  Example: A retail company uses Comprehend to analyze customer feedback, identifying sentiment trends and key themes. This allows the company to address customer concerns proactively.

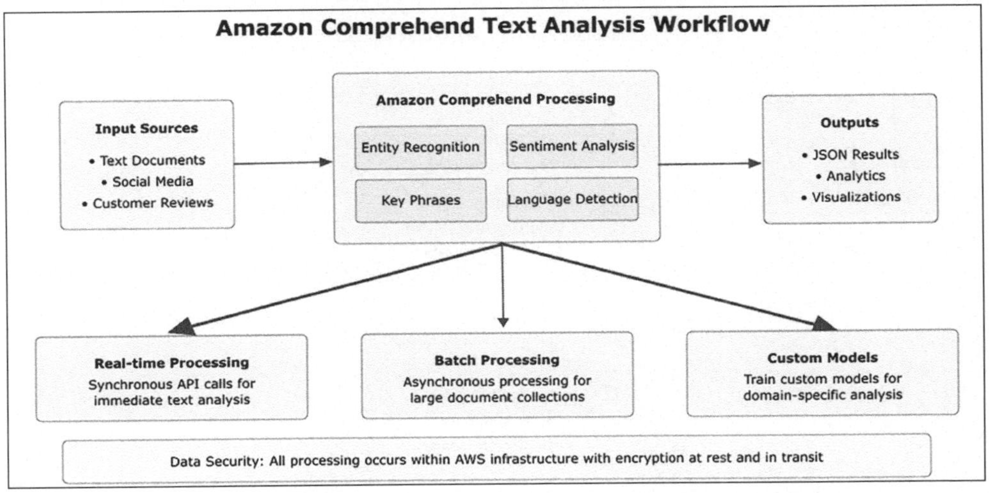

Figure 12.5: *Amazon Comprehend Text Analysis Workflow*

Speech Recognition and Synthesis: Amazon Transcribe and Polly

In addition to text analysis, AWS provides services for handling audio data, enabling transcription and voice synthesis.

- **Amazon Transcribe:**
  - Transcribe is AWS's speech-to-text service that converts audio files into text. It supports real-time and batch transcription and can recognize multiple languages and speaker roles.
  - **Use Case**: A call center uses Transcribe to convert customer calls into text, allowing the team to analyze common queries and identify service improvement opportunities.
- **Amazon Polly:**
  - Polly is a text-to-speech service that generates natural-sounding speech from text, supporting a variety of voices and languages. It enables applications to speak to users, adding a human-like interaction layer.
  - **Use Case**: An e-learning platform uses Polly to generate audio lessons, allowing students to listen to content in their preferred language and accent.

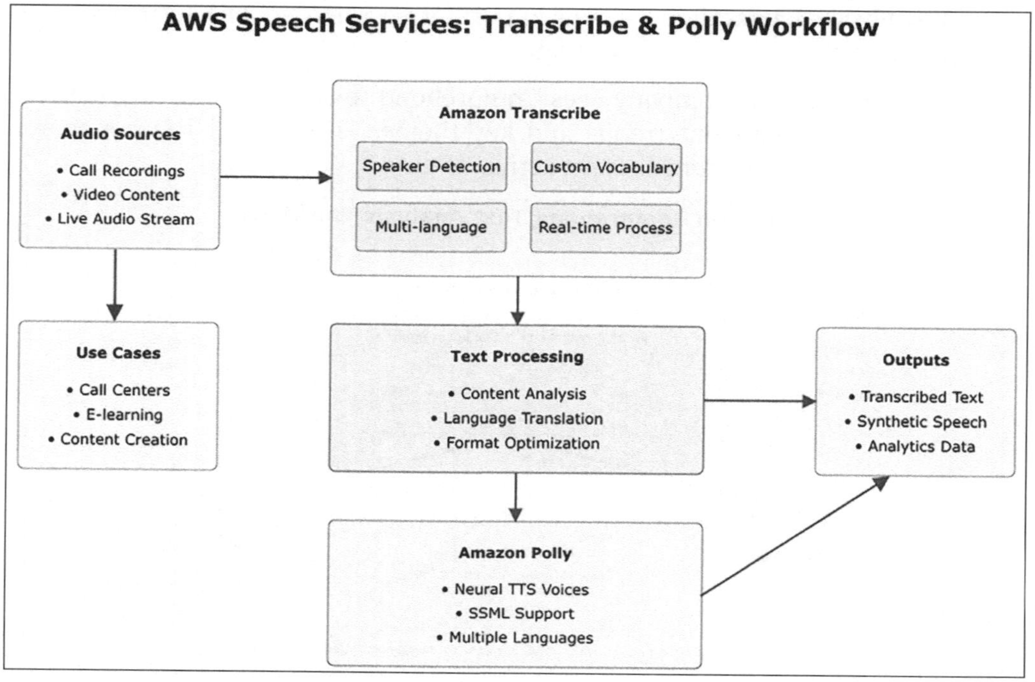

Figure 12.6: *AWS Speech Services: Transcribe and Polly Workflow*

Building Custom NLP Models on Amazon SageMaker

For organizations that need specialized NLP capabilities, SageMaker allows users to train and deploy custom NLP models using popular frameworks such as Hugging Face Transformers, TensorFlow, and PyTorch. By fine-tuning pre-trained models or building custom ones from scratch, engineers can create NLP solutions tailored to specific industry needs, such as legal document analysis or clinical text mining.

Steps for building custom NLP models:

- **Data Preparation and Tokenization:**
    - Tokenization is a key step in NLP, where text is broken down into smaller units (tokens) that can be processed by the model. SageMaker Data Wrangler and built-in preprocessing functions support tokenization and text transformation.

  Example: For an insurance company developing an NLP model to analyze claims, the text is tokenized to identify relevant keywords such as "*accident*," "*claim*," and "*injury*."

- **Model Training and Fine-Tuning:**
    - Fine-tuning pre-trained models (for example, BERT, GPT) allows engineers to adapt them to domain-specific tasks. SageMaker supports distributed training, which is beneficial for large datasets and deep-learning NLP models.

  Example: A healthcare provider fine-tunes a BERT model on clinical data to extract patient symptoms and conditions from medical notes, enabling more efficient data entry.

- **Deploying and Testing NLP Models:**
    - Once trained, the NLP model is deployed to a SageMaker endpoint for real-time inference or batch processing. Engineers can test the model's performance on sample data to ensure it meets accuracy and latency requirements.

  Example: A legal firm deploys an NLP model to extract key information from contracts, reducing manual review time and improving accuracy.

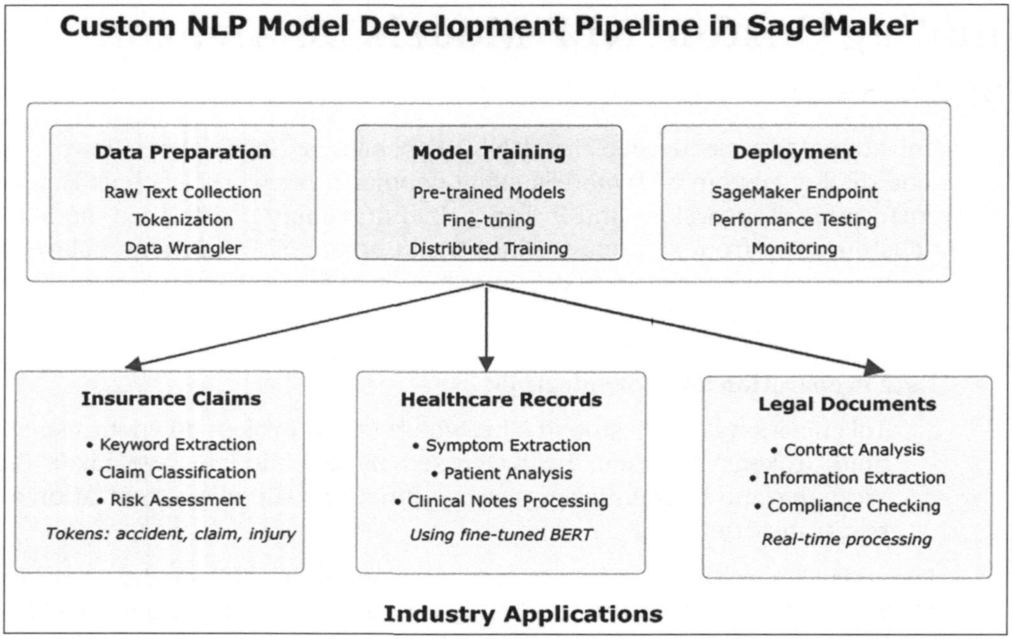

Figure 12.7: *Custom NLP Model Development Pipeline in SageMaker*

Practical Applications of NLP on AWS

Here are the applications of NLP:

- **Sentiment Analysis for Customer Feedback:**
  - Comprehend can analyze customer reviews or social media comments to identify common themes and sentiment trends, enabling businesses to enhance customer satisfaction.

  Example: A hotel chain uses Comprehend to analyze social media posts, identifying complaints and positive feedback for continuous improvement.
- **Chatbots and Virtual Assistants:**
  - Combining Transcribe, Polly, and custom NLP models enables the creation of conversational agents that can interact with users via text and voice, providing a seamless customer experience.

  Example: An insurance company builds a virtual assistant using Polly and Comprehend to guide customers through the claims process.
- **Document Classification and Analysis:**
  - SageMaker supports custom NLP models for document classification, entity extraction, and text summarization, enabling efficient handling of large volumes of documents.

Example: A law firm uses a SageMaker NLP model to classify legal documents by type, automatically tagging contracts, agreements, and court orders.

Best Practices for NLP on AWS:

- **Use Pre-Trained Models for Faster Results:** Leverage AWS's pre-trained models in Comprehend for common NLP tasks, such as sentiment analysis, entity extraction, and language detection, to save time.
- **Fine-Tune Models with Domain-Specific Data:** For industry-specific NLP tasks, fine-tuning pre-trained models on domain-specific data improves accuracy and relevance.
- **Optimize Model Performance**: Monitor deployed NLP models with SageMaker Model Monitor to track performance, especially when handling new types of data or processing high volumes.
- **Combine Services for Multimodal Solutions**: Integrate text, audio, and custom NLP capabilities (for example, Transcribe, Polly, SageMaker) to create comprehensive solutions for applications such as virtual assistants and interactive customer service.

Example Case Study

NLP Pipeline for Customer Sentiment Analysis

Scenario: A global e-commerce platform wants to monitor and respond to customer sentiment across various channels, including reviews, social media, and support tickets.

- **Data Collection**: Customer comments are collected from social media, support tickets, and reviews and stored in Amazon S3.
- **Sentiment Analysis with Amazon Comprehend**: Comprehend analyzes the sentiment of each comment, categorizing it as positive, negative, or neutral. Key phrases and entities are also extracted.
- **Real-Time Alerts with Lambda and SNS**: AWS Lambda triggers alerts via SNS when negative sentiment is detected, allowing the customer support team to respond quickly.
- **Dashboard Visualization**: The analysis results are sent to Amazon QuickSight, where sentiment trends are visualized for marketing and customer support teams.

This NLP pipeline enables the e-commerce platform to gain immediate insights into customer sentiment, allowing proactive responses to issues and enhancing customer experience.

Natural Language Processing on AWS offers powerful tools to build language-aware applications that enhance customer experiences, automate processes, and generate actionable insights. By leveraging Amazon Comprehend, Transcribe, Polly, and SageMaker, data engineers can create robust NLP workflows that handle both structured and unstructured data. This foundation in NLP will be essential as we move forward into the realm of generative AI in the next section, where we explore AWS's capabilities for creating and managing generative models.

Generative AI (GenAI) on AWS

Generative AI (GenAI) represents an advanced frontier in machine learning, where models are designed to create new content—such as text, images, or even audio—that mimics human-like creativity and intelligence. AWS provides a range of tools that make it easier to integrate GenAI into production workflows, including **Amazon Bedrock** for accessing and deploying pre-trained generative models and **Amazon SageMaker** for building custom generative models. GenAI offers powerful capabilities across industries, supporting applications from automated content creation to personalized recommendations and creative design.

This section covers the AWS tools and workflows for working with GenAI, offering insights into how to fine-tune and deploy generative models and best practices for integrating these models into scalable architectures.

Overview of GenAI Capabilities on AWS

Generative AI models can produce new, unique outputs based on patterns learned from vast datasets. Key applications include:

- **Text Generation:** Models generate human-like text for applications such as chatbots, content creation, and summarization.
- **Image and Video Synthesis**: GenAI can create realistic or stylized images and videos, useful for design, entertainment, and marketing.
- **Audio and Speech Generation**: Models generate audio and music or convert text to natural-sounding speech, supporting virtual assistants and multimedia applications.

  Example: An e-commerce site uses text generation to create personalized product descriptions for its catalog, enhancing customer engagement and reducing content production costs.

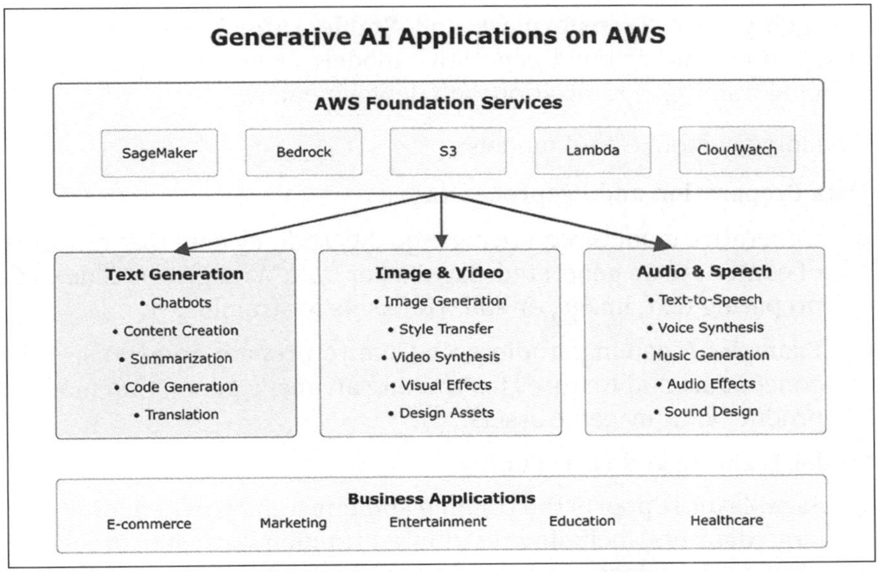

Figure 12.8: *Generative AI Applications on AWS*

Amazon Bedrock for GenAI

Amazon Bedrock is AWS's fully managed service for GenAI, providing access to powerful Foundational Models (FMs) from leading providers, including models for text, image, and code generation. Bedrock simplifies the deployment of GenAI models by offering API-based access to these models, with options for customization and fine-tuning to fit specific business requirements.

- **Text Models**: Bedrock provides language models capable of generating coherent text for applications such as automated customer support, content generation, and summarization.
- **Image Models**: Bedrock includes image generation models that can create visual content based on textual prompts, supporting creative design workflows.
- **Customization and Fine-Tuning**: Bedrock allows users to fine-tune foundational models with proprietary data, making them more relevant to specific business needs.

  Use Case: A marketing agency uses Bedrock to generate social media content and visual assets, tailoring text and images to specific brand voices and audiences.

Building Custom Generative Models with Amazon SageMaker

For organizations with unique requirements or domain-specific data, SageMaker enables the creation of custom generative models. By leveraging popular frameworks such as **Hugging Face Transformers** and **Stable Diffusion** on SageMaker, data engineers can fine-tune or build generative models from scratch, controlling every aspect of model training, optimization, and deployment.

Steps for building custom GenAI models:

- **Data Preparation and Preprocessing:**
    - Generative models require high-quality training data that reflects the type of content to be generated. SageMaker Data Wrangler or Glue can assist in preparing text, image, or audio datasets for training.
    - **Example**: A gaming studio uses Glue to prepare an extensive dataset of concept art and textures for training an image generation model that can produce new in-game assets.
- **Model Training and Fine-Tuning:**
    - SageMaker supports the training and fine-tuning of generative models on large datasets, including distributed training for faster processing. Fine-tuning pre-trained models can save time and improve results by adapting models to specific applications.
    - **Example**: A legal firm fine-tunes a language model on legal documents to create a GenAI system capable of drafting contract clauses based on input prompts.
- **Deployment and Inference:**
    - Once trained, generative models can be deployed to SageMaker endpoints for real-time or batch inference. SageMaker endpoints allow for scalable deployment, enabling applications to request on-demand content generation.
    - **Example**: A news organization deploys a SageMaker text generation model to a real-time endpoint, automatically generating summaries for breaking news stories as they are published.

Practical Applications of GenAI on AWS

- **Content Creation and Personalization:**
    - Text and image generation models enable businesses to create personalized content at scale, catering to customer preferences and improving engagement.
    - **Example**: An online retailer uses GenAI to generate personalized email subject lines and product recommendations based on individual shopping habits.

- **Automated Chatbots and Virtual Assistants:**
  - Generative language models support advanced chatbots and virtual assistants, allowing them to generate nuanced and personalized responses for customer support or e-commerce.
  - **Example**: A bank deploys a chatbot powered by a text generation model that can handle complex customer inquiries, offering detailed and accurate responses.
- **Creative Design and Prototyping:**
  - Image generation models help designers create concept art, prototypes, and visual assets more efficiently, supporting industries such as gaming, marketing, and fashion.
  - **Example**: A fashion brand uses an image generation model to create virtual prototypes of new clothing designs, speeding up the design process.

Best Practices for Deploying GenAI on AWS

- **Fine-Tune Models for Relevance:** Customizing models with domain-specific data ensures that generated content aligns with business needs, improving accuracy and relevance.
- **Monitor and Control Model Outputs**: Generative models can produce unexpected or inappropriate outputs. Implement monitoring and quality control to ensure content meets standards.
- **Optimize Cost with Spot Instances**: Training generative models can be resource-intensive. Use SageMaker Spot Instances to reduce training costs, especially for large models.
- **Leverage Pre-Trained Models When Possible**: Pre-trained models in Bedrock can be highly effective for many applications, saving time and computational resources compared to training from scratch.

Example Case Study

Generative AI for Automated News Summarization

Scenario: A media company needs to automatically generate summaries for news articles, providing brief, engaging content for its mobile app.

- **Data Preparation with Glue**: The company collects thousands of articles and uses Glue to preprocess the text data, preparing it for model training.
- **Model Training in SageMaker**: Using SageMaker, the company fine-tunes a pre-trained language model to generate concise summaries of news content. The model learns to capture essential details and convey them with clarity.

- **Deployment as a Real-Time Endpoint**: The model is deployed to a SageMaker endpoint, allowing the mobile app to request summaries for new articles in real time.
- **Monitoring and Refinement**: SageMaker Model Monitor tracks the model's performance, and retraining is scheduled periodically to adapt to new trends and topics.

This setup allows the media company to automatically generate high-quality summaries, enhancing the reading experience on mobile and ensuring content is timely and relevant.

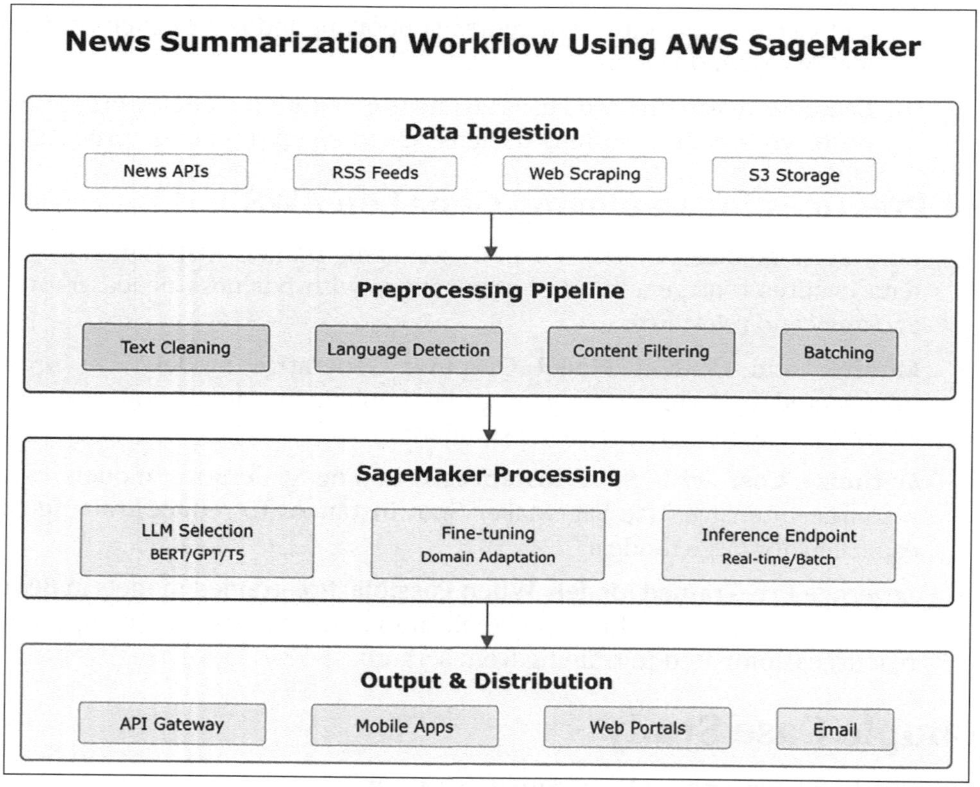

Figure 12.9: *News Summarization Workflow using AWS SageMaker*

Generative AI on AWS opens exciting opportunities to automate content creation, enhance personalization, and empower creative applications. By leveraging Amazon Bedrock for foundational models and SageMaker for custom generative workflows, data engineers can build scalable, production-ready GenAI solutions. This foundation in generative AI will be valuable for further exploring AWS's advanced machine learning capabilities in the next section. Where, we cover best practices for monitoring, security, and cost optimization in ML workflows.

Best Practices for Monitoring, Security, and Cost Management in Machine Learning on AWS

Deploying machine learning models in production requires ongoing monitoring, security enforcement, and cost management to ensure that applications remain reliable, secure, and cost-effective. AWS provides robust tools for tracking model performance, securing data and resources, and managing expenses, allowing data engineers to maintain ML workflows efficiently over time. This section explores AWS's best practices and services that help ensure production-grade ML pipelines are stable, secure, and economically viable.

Monitoring and Model Drift Detection

Once a model is deployed, it is crucial to monitor its performance to detect potential issues such as model drift, where a model's accuracy degrades due to changes in data patterns. **Amazon SageMaker Model Monitor** provides automated tools for monitoring model predictions, detecting anomalies, and alerting engineers when performance drops below acceptable thresholds.

- **Setting Up Baselines and Metrics:**
    - Model Monitor can establish baselines for key metrics, such as accuracy, precision, and recall. These baselines allow the service to track deviations and detect model drift.
    - **Example**: A fraud detection model's baseline accuracy is set at 95%. Model Monitor alerts the team if accuracy falls below 90%, indicating the need for retraining.
- **Real-Time and Batch Monitoring:**
    - Real-time monitoring is ideal for applications requiring immediate insights, while batch monitoring periodically checks large datasets, ideal for models with slower data cycles.
    - **Example**: A retail recommendation system monitors its accuracy daily in batch mode, comparing predictions with actual customer behaviors to maintain recommendation relevance.
- **Automated Retraining and Pipelines:**
    - In case of model drift, SageMaker Pipelines can automate the retraining process, triggering workflows that ingest fresh data, retrain the model, and deploy the updated model.
    - **Example**: A healthcare provider automates model retraining every quarter

using SageMaker Pipelines, ensuring patient risk prediction models are accurate.

- **Model Drift Detection:**
    - SageMaker Model Monitor detects both data and concept drift through statistical analysis of feature distributions and model outputs, helping identify when model performance degrades.
    - **Example**: A credit scoring model uses KL divergence to detect shifts in customer income distributions, triggering alerts when feature drift exceeds predefined thresholds.
- **Smart Retraining Decisions:**
    - Automated decision frameworks evaluate drift severity, retraining costs, and performance impact to determine optimal retraining timing. This prevents unnecessary retraining while ensuring model reliability.
    - **Example**: An insurance pricing model initiates retraining only when both features, drift exceeds 20% AND performance drops by 10%, optimizing resource utilization.

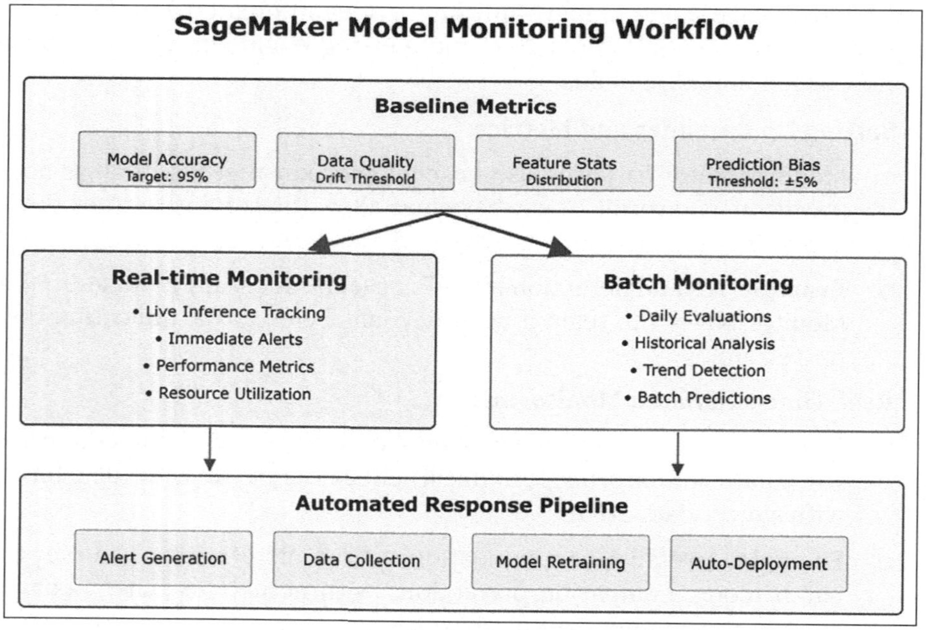

***Figure 12.10**: SageMaker Model Monitoring Workflow*

Security in Machine Learning Workflows

Ensuring data security and model integrity is vital in ML workflows, especially when handling sensitive data. AWS offers comprehensive security tools and services to protect machine learning applications, including **AWS Identity and Access Management (IAM)**, **AWS Key Management Service (KMS)**, and **AWS CloudTrail**.

- **Access Control with IAM:**
    - Use IAM to assign role-based access controls, limiting permissions based on user roles, and ensuring that only authorized personnel can access specific ML resources.
    - **Example**: A financial institution assigns IAM roles to data engineers and data scientists, restricting access to customer data based on need-to-know permissions.
- **Data Encryption with KMS:**
    - AWS KMS enables encryption of data at rest and in transit, protecting sensitive data such as PII or financial records used in training datasets.
    - **Example**: A healthcare company encrypts patient data stored in S3 using KMS, ensuring data confidentiality during model training.
- **Audit Logging with CloudTrail:**
    - CloudTrail logs all access and usage of AWS resources, providing a complete audit trail that helps teams detect and respond to any suspicious activity.
    - **Example**: An e-commerce company uses CloudTrail to log access to its SageMaker models, helping it comply with data governance policies and security audits.

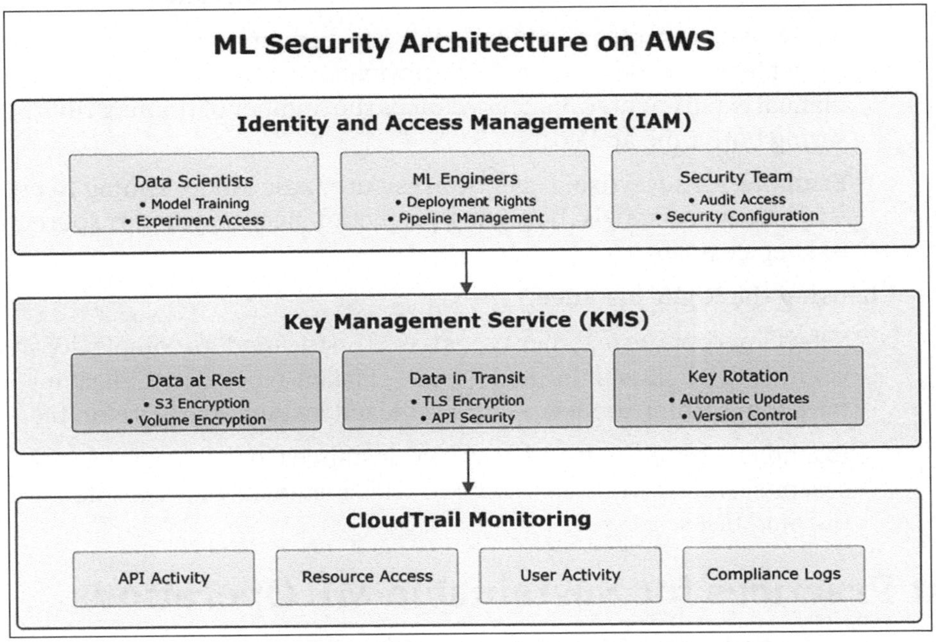

Figure 12.11: *ML Security Architecture on AWS*

Optimizing Costs in Machine Learning on AWS

Efficient cost management is essential for running ML workflows sustainably, especially as data volumes and model complexity grow. AWS provides cost-saving features, such as **Spot Instances**, **Savings Plans**, and **Automatic Model Tuning** to help teams optimize their ML expenses.

- **Using Spot Instances for Training:**
    - Spot Instances allow organizations to run training jobs at a significantly reduced cost by using excess EC2 capacity. Spot Instances are ideal for non-urgent or batch training jobs.
    - **Example**: A media company runs nightly training jobs on Spot Instances, reducing the overall training cost of its recommendation model by up to 70%.
- **Applying Savings Plans for Consistent Workloads:**
    - Savings Plans offer reduced prices for a one- or three-year commitment on EC2 instances, benefiting models that require continuous or frequent retraining.
    - **Example**: An IoT platform with a steady workload applies a one-year Savings Plan to its SageMaker instances, saving on model deployment costs.
- **Automatic Model Tuning to Balance Cost and Performance:**
    - SageMaker's Automatic Model Tuning feature optimizes hyperparameters to achieve the best possible performance without requiring repeated, manual experimentation. This reduces the number of training runs needed, saving both time and costs.
    - **Example**: An advertising agency uses Automatic Model Tuning to optimize ad placement models, balancing prediction accuracy and resource usage to keep costs low.
- **Choosing the Right Instance Types:**
    - Select appropriate instance types based on the model's complexity and data volume. For lightweight models, use smaller, more economical instances; for deep learning models, GPU-optimized instances are preferable.
    - Example: A retail company uses CPU instances for basic models predicting seasonal trends while switching to GPU instances only for intensive deep learning tasks.

Best Practices for Sustainable ML Operations

Here are some best practices for sustainable MLOps:

- **Monitor Usage and Set Budgets**: Use AWS Cost Explorer and Budgets to track ML costs, set alerts, and identify potential savings across different stages of the ML pipeline.
- **Optimize Storage with Lifecycle Policies**: Implement S3 lifecycle policies to automatically archive or delete old data, reducing storage costs over time.
- **Use Scheduled Training and Inference**: For batch inference or scheduled training, set up jobs to run during off-peak hours when spot prices are lower, or resources are less likely to be in demand.
- **Enable Auto-Scaling for Endpoints**: Use SageMaker's auto-scaling for deployed models, ensuring that inference endpoints scale up to meet demand and down during off-peak hours.

Below is an Example Case Study showing the application of these principles.

Example Case Study

Cost-Effective, Secure ML Workflow for E-Commerce Demand Forecasting

Scenario: An e-commerce company wants to forecast product demand securely and cost-effectively, ensuring that its model remains accurate without inflating expenses.

- **Data Encryption and Access Control:** The company uses KMS to encrypt customer data and IAM roles to control access, ensuring compliance with data privacy regulations.
- **Cost-Effective Training with Spot Instances**: Training jobs for demand forecasting run nightly on Spot Instances, saving 60% on compute costs.
- **Model Monitoring and Drift Detection**: SageMaker Model Monitor tracks model accuracy, triggering retraining when accuracy falls, ensuring predictions remain relevant to current trends.
- **Automatic Scaling and Optimization**: Real-time demand forecasts are provided through a scalable SageMaker endpoint, automatically adjusting the instance count based on traffic volume to control costs.

With robust monitoring, strong security practices, and smart cost management, AWS provides data engineers with the tools to maintain high-performing, secure, and efficient machine learning workflows. These practices allow organizations to deploy and scale ML applications confidently, enabling teams to focus on innovation while keeping operations sustainable and compliant. This comprehensive approach to ML operations rounds out the capabilities needed for deploying advanced machine learning systems on AWS, empowering data engineers to build resilient and impactful models that drive business success.

Conclusion

Machine learning on AWS offers a robust ecosystem that supports the full lifecycle of ML workflows, enabling data engineers and data scientists to build, deploy, and manage a wide variety of machine learning models. From classic machine learning applications, such as customer segmentation and demand forecasting to advanced NLP and generative AI models, AWS provides the tools to integrate intelligent, scalable solutions into production environments.

This chapter has covered the foundational aspects of machine learning on AWS, including data preparation, model training, deployment, and monitoring. We explored specialized services, such as Amazon Comprehend, Transcribe, Polly, and Bedrock, each tailored to specific types of ML applications, as well as SageMaker's powerful capabilities for custom model development and deployment. Emphasis on best practices for monitoring, security, and cost management rounds out the guidance for maintaining resilient and efficient ML workflows.

By leveraging these AWS services and following best practices, data engineers are equipped to create production-ready ML systems that not only drive actionable insights but also scale with business needs. Machine learning on AWS empowers organizations to transform data into powerful predictions and intelligent solutions, laying the groundwork for innovative, data-driven applications that will continue to evolve with advancements in AI and cloud technology.

CHAPTER 13
Advanced Data Engineering with AWS

Introduction

As data continues to fuel business innovation and operational intelligence, the future of data engineering will be defined by its ability to adapt to new demands and technologies. Architecting resilient, scalable, and efficient systems is more important than ever, as organizations navigate an era of rapid change characterized by the expansion of real-time analytics, machine learning, and serverless computing. Data engineers must now balance traditional data architecture principles with evolving best practices to ensure their solutions are future-ready.

In this final chapter, we explore emerging trends in data engineering, focusing on serverless architectures, real-time data processing, and the growing emphasis on data governance and security. These advancements present new opportunities to simplify infrastructure, increase agility, and enhance data accessibility while emphasizing responsible data handling. By understanding and implementing these trends, data engineers can build architectures that are both powerful and adaptable, prepared to meet the demands of tomorrow's data-driven applications. We conclude with reflections on the journey of mastering data engineering fundamentals and preparing for the road ahead.

Structure

In this chapter, we will cover the following topics:

- The Evolution of Serverless Architectures
    - Benefits and Trade-offs
    - Serverless Data Engineering

- Real-Time Data Processing and Streaming Analytics
  - Demand for Real-Time Analytics
  - Streaming Technologies and Tools
- Data Governance and Security in Modern Architectures
  - The Need for Data Governance
  - Security Best Practices

The Evolution of Serverless Architectures

The rise of **serverless architectures** has transformed the way organizations approach data engineering, offering a model where infrastructure management is abstracted away, allowing developers to focus on writing code rather than managing servers. Serverless enables automatic scaling, pay-as-you-go billing, and reduced operational overhead, making it an attractive choice for dynamic workloads and applications that experience fluctuating demand. In data engineering, serverless architectures streamline data pipelines, ETL processes, and analytics, offering both scalability and cost efficiency.

Serverless has evolved to encompass a range of services, from data ingestion to orchestration and processing. For data engineers, this shift opens the door to building highly agile, cost-effective solutions that adapt quickly to changes in data volume and usage patterns.

Benefits and Trade-offs of Serverless for Data Engineering

Serverless architectures offer unique benefits but come with specific trade-offs that engineers should consider when architecting solutions, including:

- **Scalability:** Serverless services automatically scale to handle spikes in demand without manual intervention, allowing data workflows to handle unexpected load increases seamlessly.
- **Cost Efficiency**: With a pay-per-use model, serverless reduces costs associated with idle infrastructure, making it highly economical for intermittent or event-driven workloads.
- **Reduced Operational Complexity**: Serverless abstracts away infrastructure management tasks, reducing the need for extensive DevOps resources and enabling engineers to focus on building data logic.
- **Trade-offs**: While serverless offers flexibility, limitations include potential latency from cold starts, vendor lock-in concerns, and less control over the

underlying infrastructure, which may not be ideal for low-latency, high-performance applications.

Key AWS Serverless Tools for Data Engineering

AWS offers a suite of serverless tools that support various stages of the data lifecycle, from ingestion to storage, processing, and orchestration, starting with:

- **AWS Lambda:**
  - Lambda allows engineers to run code in response to events without provisioning or managing servers. It is ideal for lightweight data transformations, event-driven processing, and extending ETL pipelines.
  - **Use Case**: A Lambda function can be triggered to clean and filter data from a streaming source, preparing it for ingestion into a data lake or warehouse.
- **AWS Step Functions:**
  - Step Functions enable the orchestration of complex workflows by chaining together multiple serverless functions, making it a powerful tool for building automated, fault-tolerant data pipelines.
  - **Use Case**: Step Functions can manage an ETL pipeline that pulls data from multiple sources, applies transformations, and loads it into Amazon Redshift or S3, handling errors and retries automatically.
- **Amazon EventBridge:**
  - EventBridge simplifies event-driven architectures by allowing services to communicate through events. It acts as a central event bus, ideal for connecting data sources to processing workflows in real time.
  - **Use Case**: EventBridge can route data from a source system, such as a CRM to an analytics service, triggering Lambda functions to process the data upon receiving specific events.
- **AWS Glue:**
  - Glue is a serverless ETL service that enables data preparation and transformation. With Glue, engineers can build, schedule, and manage ETL jobs without managing servers.
  - **Use Case**: AWS Glue can transform raw data from Amazon S3 and load it into an Amazon Redshift data warehouse, with built-in scalability and automated schema discovery.

Selecting Serverless for Data Engineering

Serverless is an ideal solution for certain data engineering scenarios, including:

- **Event-Driven Workflows:** For applications that need to respond to real-time data events (for example, IoT data processing), serverless architectures provide efficient, automated handling of incoming data without maintaining continuous infrastructure.

- **Intermittent or Unpredictable Workloads**: Workloads that experience unpredictable demand or long idle periods benefit from serverless, which scales down to zero when not in use.
- **Data Ingestion and Transformation Pipelines**: For ETL processes where raw data requires rapid transformation, serverless enables scalable, on-demand processing, making it well-suited to handle fluctuating data volumes.
- **Rapid Prototyping and Experimentation**: Serverless allows teams to test new ideas quickly without committing significant infrastructure resources, ideal for data teams experimenting with new models or workflows.

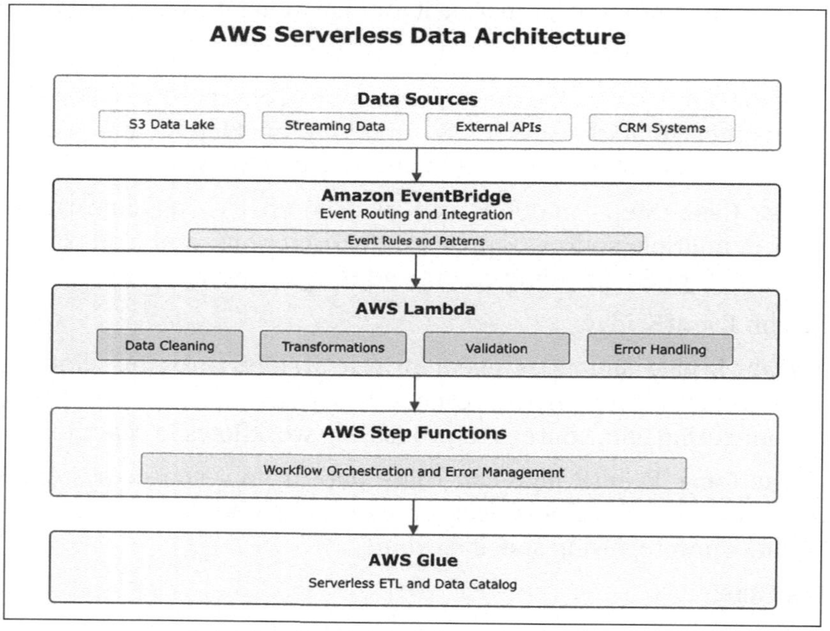

Figure 13.1: *AWS Serverless Data Architecture*

Best Practices for Building Serverless Data Architectures

Following are some of the best practices that can be leveraged while building Serverless Data Architectures:

- **Optimize for Cold Starts:** Reduce latency in serverless applications by reusing connections or using provisioned concurrency for Lambda functions in latency-sensitive applications.

- **Decouple Workflows with Event-Driven Architecture:** Use services such as EventBridge to create loosely coupled workflows that can scale independently, enhancing flexibility and resilience.
- **Leverage Automation and Monitoring:** Use CloudWatch for logging, monitoring, and setting alerts on serverless components to ensure visibility into pipeline performance.
- **Cost Optimization:** Regularly review usage patterns and costs for serverless services, tuning configurations to maximize efficiency, especially as workloads evolve.
- **Design for Fault Tolerance:** Use retries and fallbacks in Step Functions and Lambda error handling to ensure resilience in the face of transient issues, maintaining reliable data processing pipelines.

Example Case Study

Serverless Architecture for Real-Time Social Media Analytics

Scenario: A social media analytics platform ingests and processes real-time data from social networks to provide insights on trending topics and user sentiment. The platform relies on serverless services for scalability, efficiency, and rapid response times.

- **Data Ingestion with EventBridge:** Events from social media APIs are published to EventBridge, which routes the data to Lambda functions for initial processing and filtering.
- **Real-Time Processing with AWS Lambda:** Lambda functions clean and tag data, preparing it for sentiment analysis. Additional Lambda functions handle different stages of data processing, such as keyword extraction and language detection.
- **Orchestration with AWS Step Functions:** Step Functions coordinate multiple processing tasks, ensuring that data moves through each stage reliably and handling errors if a task fails.
- **Storage and Reporting**: Processed data is stored in Amazon S3 and analyzed further in Amazon Redshift. Visualizations are generated with Amazon QuickSight for client-facing dashboards.

This serverless architecture allows the social media analytics platform to process large volumes of data in real time without over-provisioning, scaling seamlessly based on demand, and minimizing operational overhead.

By embracing serverless architectures, data engineers can achieve a new level of flexibility and efficiency, offloading infrastructure management while focusing on scalable, responsive solutions. As serverless tools and best practices continue to evolve, this architecture paradigm will play an increasingly pivotal role in shaping the future of data engineering.

Real-Time Data Processing and Streaming Analytics

As businesses strive to gain instant insights and make data-driven decisions, real-time data processing has become a critical capability in data engineering. Real-time analytics enables organizations to respond to events as they occur, supporting applications such as fraud detection, recommendation engines, and IoT monitoring. In contrast to batch processing, which analyzes data in large, predefined chunks, real-time processing analyzes data continuously as it arrives, ensuring that decisions are made based on the latest information.

Streaming analytics platforms are essential to real-time data processing, as they can handle vast amounts of data with low latency, ensuring that organizations capture and process data flows quickly and efficiently. These platforms allow data engineers to design solutions that seamlessly integrate live data into analytics pipelines, providing timely insights that drive business value.

Benefits and Challenges of Real-Time Data Processing

Following are the benefits and challenges of real-time data processing:

- **Benefits:**
  - **Immediate Insights:** Real-time analytics enables organizations to make fast, data-driven decisions in response to current conditions, improving agility.
  - **Enhanced Customer Experience:** Applications such as personalized recommendations, dynamic pricing, and instant fraud detection create a more responsive and tailored user experience.
  - **Operational Efficiency**: Real-time monitoring and alerting allow for proactive issue resolution, reducing downtime and improving overall operational efficiency.
- **Challenges:**
  - **Data Volume and Velocity**: Real-time systems must handle high volumes of incoming data continuously, which can strain resources and infrastructure.
  - **Latency Sensitivity**: Achieving low latency in data processing requires optimized architectures and efficient data flow management.

- **Data Quality and Consistency**: Inconsistent or incomplete data can lead to inaccurate real-time insights, requiring careful handling to maintain quality.

Key AWS Tools for Real-Time Data Processing and Streaming Analytics

AWS provides several services designed for real-time data processing, each tailored to specific needs in data streaming, transformation, and analysis.

- **Amazon Kinesis:**
  - Amazon Kinesis offers a suite of services for real-time data streaming, including Kinesis Data Streams, Kinesis Data Firehose, and Kinesis Data Analytics.
  - Kinesis Data Streams enable data ingestion and processing at scale, ideal for scenarios requiring low-latency handling of large data volumes.
  - Kinesis Data Firehose allows for automatic loading of streaming data into AWS services, such as S3, Redshift, and Elasticsearch, simplifying data delivery for analytics.
  - Kinesis Data Analytics provides SQL-based analysis on streaming data, enabling transformations and aggregations in real-time.
  - **Use Case**: An IoT monitoring platform uses Kinesis Data Streams to collect sensor data from devices, which is then transformed and aggregated using Kinesis Data Analytics to monitor real time device health.
- **AWS Lambda:**
  - Lambda's serverless nature makes it ideal for processing event-driven streams of data. Lambda can trigger data processing tasks in response to events in data streams, enabling low-latency, on-demand processing.
  - **Use Case**: A retail application uses Lambda to process events from a Kinesis stream, triggering recommendations for users as they browse products in real-time.
- **Amazon Managed Streaming for Apache Kafka (MSK):**
  - MSK is a managed service for Apache Kafka, an open-source platform designed for building real-time data pipelines and streaming applications. MSK simplifies Kafka's deployment and scaling on AWS, making it easier to integrate real-time data feeds.
  - **Use Case**: A financial trading platform leverages MSK to stream data from multiple stock exchanges, enabling real-time analytics and decision-making for trades.

- **Amazon Elasticsearch Service (OpenSearch):**
    - OpenSearch (formerly Elasticsearch) is a managed service that supports near real-time indexing and searching of data. It is often used with other streaming services to provide fast search and analytics capabilities on incoming data.
    - **Use Case**: A customer support system uses OpenSearch to index support tickets and feedback in real-time, allowing teams to monitor and respond to high-priority issues promptly.

Implementing Real-Time Data Pipelines on AWS

Implementing Real-Time Data Pipelines on AWS empowers organizations to harness the power of real-time data processing, enabling actionable insights and faster decision-making through scalable, reliable, and cost-effective cloud-native solutions.

- **Ingesting Data with Streaming Services:**
    - Data ingestion is the first step in a real-time pipeline, where raw data is ingested continuously from sources such as mobile apps, IoT sensors, and social media feeds.
    - **Example**: A transportation app uses Kinesis Data Streams to capture GPS data from vehicles, providing up-to-the-second location data for live tracking.
- **Processing and Transforming Data:**
    - Once data is ingested, it is processed to extract insights, filter noise, and transform data into formats that support further analysis.
    - **Example**: Using Kinesis Data Analytics, the transportation app can aggregate and filter GPS data, calculating vehicle speeds and identifying traffic patterns in real-time.
- **Storing Processed Data for Analytics:**
    - Processed data can be stored in near real-time in Amazon S3, Redshift, or OpenSearch for further analysis and visualization.
    - **Example**: Processed GPS data is stored in S3, where it can be used to generate traffic heat maps and analyze historical traffic patterns.
- **Real-Time Analytics and Visualization:**
    - Real-time data is visualized through dashboards, reports, or alerts that provide instant insights to users and decision-makers.
    - **Example**: The transportation app uses QuickSight to create dashboards for monitoring live vehicle locations and alerting drivers to potential delays.

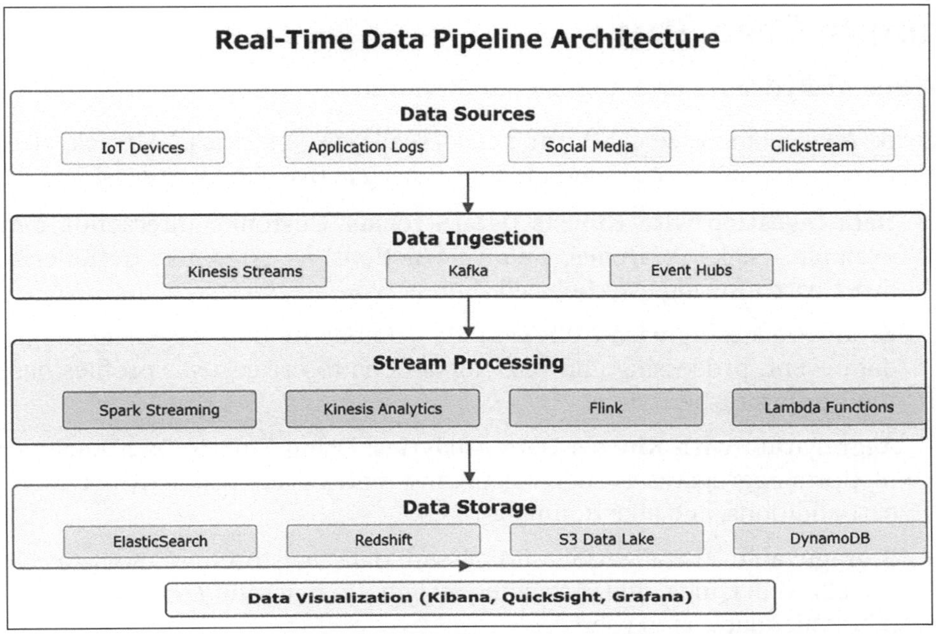

Figure 13.2: *Real-Time Data Pipeline Architecture*

Best Practices for Real-Time Data Processing

Here are the Best Practices for Real-Time Data Processing to ensure efficiency and scalability:

- **Optimize for Low Latency**: Minimize latency by using efficient data pipelines, such as keeping transformations lightweight and avoiding unnecessary stages.
- **Decouple Components for Scalability**: Decouple pipeline components using managed services, such as Kinesis or Kafka to scale individual stages independently and enhance flexibility.
- **Enable Fault Tolerance**: Use error handling and retries to manage transient failures in data streams, ensuring that minor issues do not interrupt the entire pipeline.
- **Monitor Streaming Performance**: Implement CloudWatch monitoring on key metrics (for example, ingestion rates and processing times) to detect and resolve bottlenecks in real-time.
- **Focus on Data Quality and Integrity**: Use techniques such as deduplication, validation, and enrichment to maintain data quality across real-time pipelines.

The following case study illustrates the implementation of real-time data processing to enhance an e-commerce platform's decision-making capabilities.

Example Case Study

Real-Time Analytics for an E-Commerce Platform

Scenario: An e-commerce platform needs real-time analytics to track customer behavior and personalize recommendations during active shopping sessions.

- **Data Ingestion with Kinesis Data Streams**: Customer interaction data (for example, clicks, searches, and cart actions) is streamed to Kinesis Data Streams, capturing user behavior in real time.
- **Event Processing with AWS Lambda**: Lambda functions get trigger for each data event, processing and filtering actions to create user profiles based on their browsing behavior.
- **Aggregation with Kinesis Data Analytics**: Using Kinesis Data Analytics, the platform aggregates events, calculating metrics such as active session time, cart additions, and abandonment rates.
- **Storage and Visualization**: Processed data is stored in Amazon S3 and visualized in QuickSight, providing insights to marketing teams and real-time recommendations to users.

This architecture allows the e-commerce platform to understand user behavior as it happens, making immediate adjustments to personalize the shopping experience and improve conversion rates.

Real-time data processing has become a powerful tool for gaining timely insights and responding to events as they happen. With AWS's suite of streaming and processing services, data engineers can build pipelines that support applications from customer analytics to IoT monitoring, empowering organizations to act in the moment and unlock new business value from their data.

Data Governance and Security in Modern Architectures

In today's data-driven landscape, maintaining robust data governance and security is essential for managing data responsibly, ensuring compliance, and protecting sensitive information. As distributed data architectures grow in complexity, governance frameworks help organizations establish control over data access, data quality, and data lineage. Simultaneously, security measures safeguard data from unauthorized access, ensuring privacy and compliance with regulations such as GDPR and CCPA.

Data governance and security are especially critical in cloud environments where data is accessed and processed across multiple services and regions. AWS provides tools that enable data engineers to establish governance, enforce data access policies, and secure sensitive information, creating a foundation of trust for data operations.

Key Components of Data Governance in Distributed Architectures

Here are the components of data governance in distributed architectures:

- **Data Access Control and Permissions**
  - Managing data access ensures that only authorized users and applications can access specific data resources, minimizing risk and ensuring compliance.
  - **Use Case**: A healthcare organization enforces strict access control on patient records, allowing only authorized healthcare professionals to view or modify records.
- **Data Quality Management**
  - Data quality governance involves defining standards to ensure data accuracy, consistency, and completeness across the data lifecycle.
  - **Use Case**: A financial institution defines data quality rules for transaction data, ensuring that incomplete or incorrect entries are flagged and corrected before analysis.
- **Data Lineage and Metadata Management**
  - Data lineage tracks the origin, transformations, and usage of data throughout the pipeline, ensuring transparency and aiding in auditing and compliance efforts.
  - **Use Case**: An e-commerce platform uses data lineage tracking to understand how data flows through different services, allowing for quick resolution of data inconsistencies.
- **Data Lifecycle Management**
  - Managing the data lifecycle includes defining retention, archiving, and deletion policies to control data over time, balancing accessibility and compliance.
  - **Use Case**: A marketing company defines lifecycle rules that archive inactive user data after two years, ensuring data is kept only as long as necessary.

Key AWS Tools for Data Governance and Security

AWS provides several services that empower data engineers to establish strong data governance and enforce security across their data architectures, including:

- **AWS Lake Formation:**
  - Lake Formation streamlines the process of building secure data lakes on S3, managing access control, permissions, and data catalogs centrally. It simplifies the creation of fine-grained data access policies.
  - **Use Case**: A large retail organization uses Lake Formation to create a secure, centralized data lake, applying access controls based on department (for example, marketing and finance) to restrict access to relevant data only.
- **AWS Identity and Access Management (IAM):**
  - IAM enables centralized control over access to AWS services and resources, allowing administrators to create and manage user roles, permissions, and policies.
  - **Use Case**: A technology company defines IAM roles for data engineers, data scientists, and analysts, ensuring each group has access only to the resources needed for their work.
- **AWS Glue Data Catalog:**
  - The Glue Data Catalog provides a metadata repository to manage data schema and lineage information, facilitating data discovery and supporting data governance.
  - **Use Case**: A media company uses the Glue Data Catalog to manage metadata for their data lake, enabling easy data discovery and tracking data transformations across various stages.
- **Amazon Macie:**
  - Macie is a managed service that uses ML to identify and secure sensitive data, such as Personally Identifiable Information (PII). It automatically scans S3 buckets, identifying risks and alerting teams to potential compliance issues.
  - **Use Case**: A legal firm uses Macie to identify and secure sensitive client information stored in S3, ensuring compliance with privacy regulations.
- **AWS CloudTrail:**
  - CloudTrail provides a comprehensive logging service that records AWS account activity, allowing organizations to audit access and usage patterns for compliance and security investigations.
  - **Use Case**: A government agency uses CloudTrail to log access to data resources, helping to track unauthorized access attempts and maintaining compliance with internal policies.

Steps for implementing a data governance framework on AWS:

1. **Define Data Governance Policies and Standards:**
    - Begin by defining clear policies and standards for data access, quality, and lifecycle management. These should be aligned with business objectives and regulatory requirements.
    - **Example**: A finance company establishes policies specifying who can access sensitive financial data, how long data should be retained, and minimum data quality standards for analysis.
2. **Set Up Access Control with IAM and Lake Formation:**
    - Use IAM for access control at the account level and configure Lake Formation to manage fine-grained access control on data lakes. This layered approach ensures robust access policies.
    - **Example**: In a health analytics platform, IAM manages overall AWS account access, while Lake Formation enforces restrictions on who can view patient data and at what level of detail.
3. **Establish Data Catalog and Metadata Management:**
    - Use the Glue Data Catalog to manage metadata and enable data discovery, maintaining a centralized view of data locations, schema, and transformations.
    - **Example**: A marketing firm catalogs customer data in Glue, tracking data sources, transformations, and schema changes to support transparent and reliable analytics.
4. **Monitor for Compliance and Data Security with Macie and CloudTrail:**
    - Regularly scan S3 for sensitive data with Macie, identifying risks and flagging sensitive information for further review. Use CloudTrail to monitor access and maintain audit logs.
    - **Example**: An HR department uses Macie to monitor S3 for accidental storage of employee PII, while CloudTrail logs any unauthorized access attempts for investigation.
5. **Implement Data Lifecycle and Retention Policies:**
    - Define and automate lifecycle policies to retain, archive, and delete data based on compliance and business needs, using S3 lifecycle rules to enforce these policies.
    - **Example**: A telecom company defines lifecycle policies for customer data, ensuring old records are archived or deleted after a specific period to comply with regulatory guidelines.

Best Practices for Data Governance and Security

Here are some of the best practices for Data Governance and Security:

- **Automate Compliance Checks and Alerts**: Use tools such as Amazon Macie and CloudTrail to automate compliance checks, setting up alerts for unauthorized access attempts or sensitive data exposure.
- **Apply the Principle of Least Privilege:** Ensure that each user and service has only the minimum level of access required, reducing the risk of data exposure.
- **Implement Data Encryption at Rest and In Transit:** Encrypt sensitive data using AWS KMS or S3 default encryption to protect it from unauthorized access during storage and transfer.
- **Regularly Audit and Review Access Logs:** Periodic auditing of access logs in CloudTrail and Lake Formation helps identify and address any unusual or unauthorized access.
- **Continuously Update and Evolve Governance Policies:** Regularly review data governance policies to adapt to changes in regulatory requirements, business goals, and emerging security threats.

Example Case Study

Data Governance for a Healthcare Analytics Platform

Scenario: A healthcare analytics platform manages patient data across multiple regions, requiring strict governance and security to comply with HIPAA regulations.

- **Data Access Control with IAM and Lake Formation:** IAM controls account-level access, while Lake Formation manages fine-grained access to patient records, ensuring only authorized healthcare professionals can access sensitive data.
- **Data Quality and Metadata Management with Glue Data Catalog:** Glue manages metadata and enforces data quality checks, ensuring consistent data formats across analysis workflows.
- **Sensitive Data Detection with Macie:** Amazon Macie scans S3 for PII, helping the platform identify and secure any sensitive data that may have been stored inadvertently.
- **Audit and Compliance Tracking with CloudTrail:** CloudTrail logs all data access events, providing a full audit trail for regulatory reporting and compliance monitoring.
- **Automated Data Retention Policies:** S3 lifecycle rules automatically archive or delete old patient data after a specified retention period, in accordance with HIPAA data retention standards.

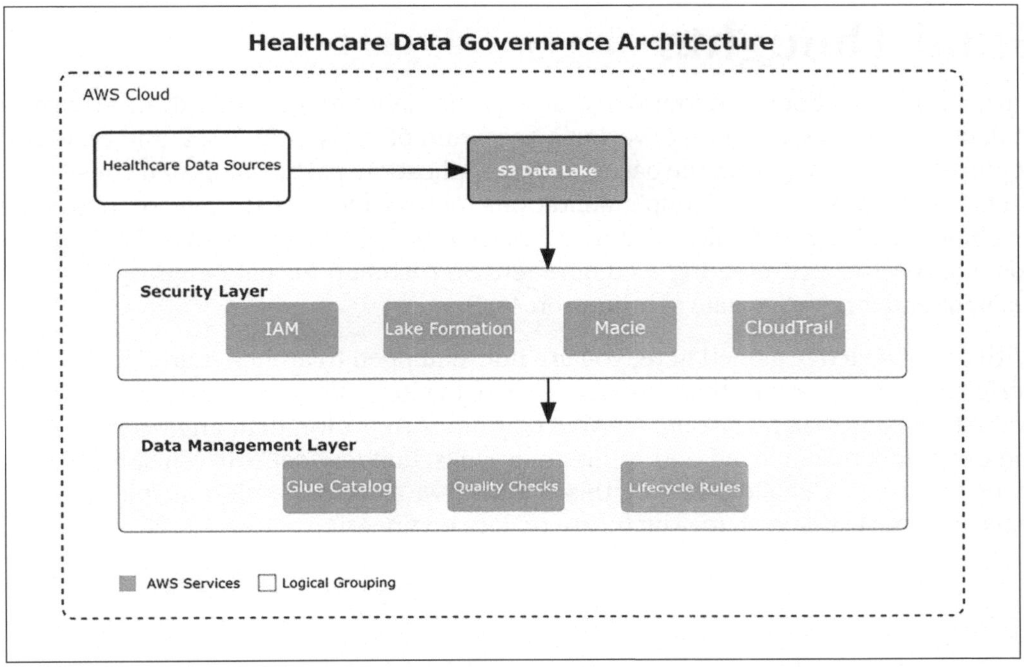

Figure 13.3: *Healthcare Data Governance Architecture*

This governance framework allows the healthcare platform to operate securely and comply with regulatory requirements, ensuring that patient data is handled responsibly and securely.

Conclusion

In this chapter on **Advanced Data Engineering on AWS**, we explored essential strategies for building resilient, efficient, and secure data architectures that leverage serverless computing, real-time streaming, and robust data governance. By implementing serverless workflows, data engineers can achieve scalability and cost efficiency, freeing them from the complexities of infrastructure management. We also covered real-time data streaming, highlighting how AWS tools enable applications to process and respond to data instantly. Finally, we examined best practices for data governance and security, ensuring data integrity, privacy, and regulatory compliance in distributed environments.

These advanced data engineering techniques allow teams to design architectures that not only perform reliably at scale but also adapt to changing business demands. Together, these methods and tools empower organizations to build forward-looking data infrastructures that support innovation and operational excellence.

Final Thoughts

Throughout this book, we journeyed across the foundational and advanced aspects of data engineering on AWS, covering a spectrum of tools, principles, and real-world applications. Starting from the basics of data replication, partitioning, and consistency, we moved to practical AWS implementations for scalable data storage, orchestration, machine learning, and finally, advanced data processing and governance. Each chapter has built on the last, creating a comprehensive roadmap for data engineers to build resilient and innovative data solutions on AWS.

With the knowledge gained here, you are now equipped to architect and deploy high-performing data systems that transform raw data into valuable insights, fueling growth and strategic decision-making. As AWS continues to evolve, data engineers will have the opportunity to expand and refine their skills, building data-driven solutions that meet tomorrow's challenges. Let this book serve as a foundation, inspiring you to explore, innovate, and shape the future of data engineering.

Index

A

B

C

D

R

S

T